Making
Crafts,
Making
Money™

Edited by Laura Scott

HOUSE of
WHITE
BIRCHES

PUBLISHERS
SINCE 1947

Making Crafts, Making Money™

Editor: Laura Scott
Associate Editor: Cathy Reef, Lisa Fosnaugh
Contributing Editor: Maria Nerius
Technical Editor: Läna Schurb
Copy Editors: Michelle Beck, Nicki Lehman
Publication Coordinator: June Sprunger

Photography: Tammy Christian, Jeff Chilcote, Christena Green,
Kelly Heydinger, Nancy Sharp, Justin Wiard
Photo Stylist: Tammy Nussbaum
Photography Assistant: Linda Quinlan

Art Director: Brad Snow
Publishing Services Manager: Brenda Gallmeyer
Graphic Arts Supervisor: Ronda Bechinski
Book Design: Jessi Butler
Graphic Artist/Cover Design: Amy S. Lin
Production Assistants: Janet Bowers, Marj Morgan
Traffic Coordinator: Sandra Beres
Technical Artists: Liz Morgan, Mitchell Moss,
Chad Summers

Chief Executive Officer: John Robinson
Publishing Director: David McKee
Book Marketing Director: Craig Scott
Editorial Director: Vivian Rothe
Publishing Services Director: Brenda R. Wendling

Printed in the United States of America
First Printing: 2003
Library of Congress Number: 2002107206
ISBN: 1-59217-003-X

Location shot on page 163 courtesy of The Gathering House, 105 W. Main St., Berne, Ind.

Welcome

Dear Crafter,

We crafters make our projects for a variety reasons. Some of us give our creations as gifts. Others use crafts for dressing up the home. Many of us make crafts to sell and earn extra spending money or even a full-fledged income.

An exciting moment for any crafter is when she (or he) is able to take her love for crafts and turn it into real money. Selling your crafts enables you to make money doing what you love, along with the convenience of setting your own hours and working from home. You feel a rush of joy and pride the first time—and every time thereafter—a stranger loves your crafts enough to buy them.

Making Crafts, Making Money is packed full of crafts that will appeal to craft enthusiasts of all kinds. Plus, these projects are economical enough to produce for profit. No matter what your niche is, we've got something for you in this book. To expand your craft market even more, we've included seasonal and holiday crafts for every month of the year.

As an extra bonus, throughout the book you'll find 100 valuable tips and words of wisdom from our contributing editor, Maria Nerius. Maria has spent more than 19 years fine-tuning her craft business.

On the following pages Maria shares the wisdom and nuts-and-bolts know-how she has acquired during her years of experience. Beginning with a small craft booth, Maria successfully developed her crafting business into a well-known enterprise in the Florida craft-show circuit. Her tips will help you embark on the adventure of turning what you love into your own small business, from getting started to pricing your crafts to what to take to the craft show.

Whether you decide to sell your crafts at a local bazaar or turn to the wholesale gift market, this book has advice for everyone. If you make the transformation from hobbyist to businessperson, you are sure to encounter many crafters just like yourself, expanding your network of crafting friends.

Warm regards,

Laura Scott

Contents

Chapter 1
Springtime Market

Filling your craft booth with colorful, lively items for sale can be a very profitable endeavor after the long winter months. Create sure-to-sell items from our spring collection, while educating yourself in the details of crafting for money.

Chapter 2
Summer Sales

Add summertime-themed crafts to your booth for a boost in sales! From bugs and flowers to seashells and Americana crafts, you'll find many projects in this chapter perfect for selling or sharing. Plus, learn how to price your items for sale, and how to purchase your crafting supplies for less!

Chapter 3
Fall Festival

Cool, crisp autumn days and fall crafts bring out some of the best buyers of the year! Draw more of those buyers into your booth with an assortment of friendly spooks and bountiful harvest crafts. More tips will help you find your selling niche.

Chapter 4
Winter Celebration

Stock up your holiday craft inventory with projects from this chapter's collection! With Christmas just around the corner, November and December are a crafting professional's busiest and most profitable months of the year. Learn how to make your festive booth stand above all others during the holiday rush!

Garden Stroll Sign

Displayed in your booth, this charming sign will "bee" hard for garden lovers to resist!

Design by Annie Lang

Materials

- 8¾" x 6" daisy header sign*
- Acrylic crafts paints*: antique gold, baby blue, calico red, Hauser dark green, lamp black, mistletoe, pineapple, tangelo orange, titanium white
- Paintbrushes: #4 flat shader, #0 liner, #2, #4, #5 and #8 pointed round brushes, #¼ angled shader
- 1" foam brush
- Glossy interior/exterior varnish
- Square cut from household sponge
- Extra-fine black permanent marker
- Sandpaper
- Tack cloth

Sign from Provo Craft; Americana acrylic paints from DecoArt.

Instructions

1. Trace pattern (page 8) onto tracing paper; flip over and retrace lines with pencil on wrong side. Flip pattern back to original side.

2. Sand sign; wipe off dust with tack cloth.

3. Using foam brush apply blue paint to coat back of sign; let dry. Sand lightly; remove dust. Apply second coat of paint; let dry.

4. Repeat step 3 on front and edges of plaque, substituting white paint for blue.

5. Slightly dampen sponge square with water. Dip into blue and tap up and down on palette a few times to work paint evenly into sponge. Using light, up-and-down tapping motion, pounce color here and there around edges of plaque front and side edges. Let dry.

6. Place traced pattern on center of painted sign; retrace over pattern lines to transfer pattern.

7. *Paint flowers:* Using #2 and #4 rounds, paint all flower centers pineapple; let dry. Use #2 round to apply a touch of gold shading to bottom edge of each flower center. Using #8 round, paint petals white. Using #2 round, paint leaves and stems mistletoe.

8. *Paint grass:* Using flat shader paint grassy area with mistletoe; let dry. Use angled shader to tap dark green shading onto grass under bee's feet and near base of flowers in grass.

9. *Paint butterflies:* Using #2 round, paint wings orange; let dry. Using liner, add touch of red near base of each wing. Using black, paint bodies with #2 round and antennae with #0 liner.

10. *Paint bee:* Using #8 round brush, paint face and top and bottom body stripes pineapple; let dry. Use shader to apply gold shading around edges of stripes. Using #8 round and black, paint arms, legs, hands and head; using shader and black, paint middle stripe. Using #8 round, paint bow tie red. Load #2 round with red; paint nose and cheeks; let dry. Using liner, add white highlights to nose, cheeks, each fold in tie, around foot outlines, finger outlines and down center of tummy.

11. *Lettering:* Paint with #5 round brush and black paint. Let dry.

12. *Outlining and details:* Add all outlines and details with extra-fine black marker or technical pen and black ink. Or, thin black paint to inky consistency with water and use #0 liner. Let dry.

13. Using foam brush, coat entire sign with varnish. ✀

Garden Stroll Sign

Garden Party Trio

Muted colors and beautiful roses make this project a gardener's most treasured decorative set. Sweet rosebuds and cheerful polka dots make this set extra special!

Designs by Cheryl Seslar

- Mylar or stencil plastic (see Project Note)
- Graphite or transfer paper
- Craft knife (see Project Note)
- Stencil sponges (see Project Note)
- Masking tape
- Acrylic craft paints*: AC flesh, Bambi brown, black, gypsy rose, leprechaun, light ivory, maple sugar tan, pine green, spice brown, trail tan
- Paintbrushes: ½" and 1" angular shaders, #4 and #12 shaders, #2 liner

Birdhouse

- Medium wooden cloud cabin birdhouse*
- Ultrafine-point black permanent pen
- Matte-finish spray sealer
- Brush-on exterior varnish (optional)

Candle

- 5" 2¾"-wide ivory or white pillar candle
- Candle-painting medium

Garden Gal

- 4" clay flowerpot
- 3" cube floral foam
- Dried Spanish moss
- Assorted silk roses and mums or flowers of your choice
- ¼"-thick MDF board or Baltic birch
- Scroll saw or band saw
- Medium sandpaper
- Tack cloth
- Tacky craft glue
- Ultrafine-point black permanent marker
- Matte-finish spray sealer
- Brush-on exterior varnish (optional)

Cabin from Walnut Hollow; Ceramcoat paints and candle-painting medium from Delta.

Project Note

As an option to stenciling the flowers and leaves, you may prefer to simply paint them, referring to pattern as you will find that the stenciling goes more quickly.

Making Stencils

Referring to instructions for "Using Transfer and Graphite Paper" in the General Instructions, transfer separate patterns for flower and leaf onto Mylar or stencil plastic; cut stencils with craft knife. Also cut a 1" circular stencil for Garden Gal's cheeks.

Birdhouse

1. Referring to directions for base-coating and shading under "Painting Techniques" (General Instructions, page 190), base-coat walls of bird-house with maple sugar; shade edges with spice brown. Base-coat roof and base with leprechaun; shade edges of roof with pine. Let dry.

2. Referring to directions for stenciling with sponge under "Painting Techniques" in General Instructions, stencil roses onto birdhouse using stencil sponges and rose paint; let dry. Stencil leaves with leprechaun; let dry.

3. Using liner brush and ivory paint throughout, add squiggly detail lines to flowers. Paint vertical lines around edges of base. Dot ivory spots on roof.

4. Using black marker, add spirals to birdhouse walls as shown; let dry.

5. Mist birdhouse with two or three light coats of sealer, allowing it to dry between coats. If birdhouse will be used outdoors, finish with a coat of brush-on exterior varnish.

Candle

Note: *Before painting, mix candle-painting medium with paints as directed by manufacturer.*

1. Using masking tape, mask off 1" band around base of candle. Using stencil sponge, paint band and bottom of candle with leprechaun. Let dry before removing tape.

2. Referring to steps 2 and 3 for birdhouse, stencil leaves and flowers randomly around candle. Let dry. Using liner brush and ivory, add maple sugar dots to candle between flowers. Let dry completely.

3. Using #12 shader, coat painted candle with transparent candle-painting medium; let dry.

Garden Gal

1. Referring to directions for "Using Transfer & Graphite Paper" in General Instructions, transfer patterns for one head with hat crown, one hat brim, one flower cluster and two hands, reversing one, onto wood. Cut out with saw. Sand edges until smooth; wipe clean with tack cloth.

2. Referring to directions for base-coating and shading under "Painting Techniques", base-coat body of clay pot (including bottom) and all surfaces of hat brim with maple sugar; shade with spice brown. Let dry.

Garden Gal Hand
Cut 2, reversing 1
(including spike),
from wood

3. Base-coat hands and face with AC flesh; shade with trail tan. Base-coat hair with Bambi brown; shade with spice brown. Base-coat flowerpot rim and spikes on wooden pieces with leprechaun. Let dry.

4. Referring to directions for stenciling with sponge under "Painting Techniques" using rose paint throughout, stencil flowers randomly on flowerpot; use brush to paint flowers on cluster; let dry.

5. Using leprechaun, stencil leaves on pot; paint leaves on cluster. Shade leaves with pine green; let dry.

6. Using liner and ivory paint throughout, add squiggly lines to flowers and dots to flowerpot rim.

7. Blend a little ivory paint into gypsy rose to make a lighter shade; stencil cheeks with mixture; dot on tiny black eyes. Let dry.

8. Using marker, add spirals to flowerpot as shown; let dry.

9. Using tacky glue, glue hat brim and flower cluster in place.

10. Hot-glue foam inside pot; push hands and head into foam as shown. Hot-glue Spanish moss over floral foam.

11. Arrange flowers in pot to just cover bottom of hands and head.

12. Lightly spray entire piece with spray sealer. ✂

Take Your First Steps

In any order, there are six important tasks that will lead to success in selling your crafts. The hard part will be the work that goes into making them happen.

1. Understand that your hobby—crafting—is now going to be a business, not just fun.

2. Select a craft you enjoy and have a work area where you can create it.

3. Shop smart! Purchase your supplies at competitive prices and be able to store those supplies.

4. Price your finished craft with profit in mind.

5. Create an inventory, and have space to store that inventory.

6. Find a market—people—to buy your craft and be willing to actively sell your products. **$**

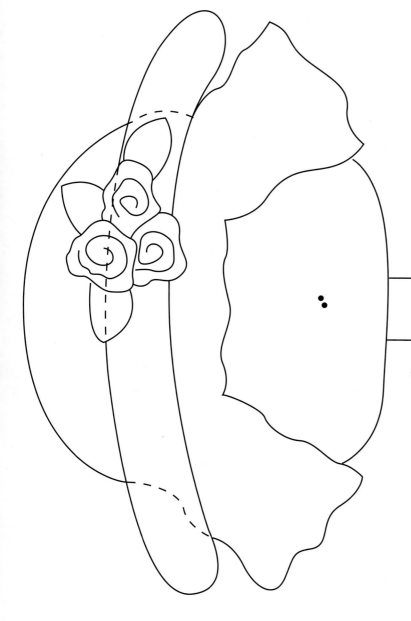

Garden Gal Head
Cut 1 head (including hat crown and spike), 1 hat brim and 1 flower cluster from wood

Flower & Leaf
Cut separate stencils

Butterfly Apron

Make various sizes and experiment with colors when making a selection of these colorfu[l] aprons to sell with your other wearable items. The great patterns and lively bugs will make this project a favorite moneymaking item.

Design by Mary Ayres

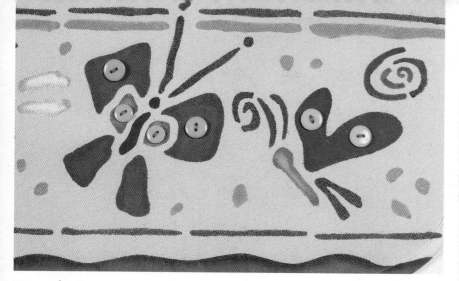

Materials
- Off-white apron
- Fun butterflies stencil*
- Fabric paints*: avocado green, baby pink, deep periwinkle blue, fuchsia, Hauser light green, true blue, white
- Metallic fabric paints*: imperial gold, plum, purple
- ⅜" and ½" stencil brushes for each color paint
- Masking tape
- Sewing needle
- Flat buttons: 4 (½") yellow, 4 (⁹⁄₁₆") blue, 4 (⁹⁄₁₆") pink
- Bright pink thread or embroidery floss

*Stencil #28797 from Plaid Simply Stencils; SoSoft fabric paints from DecoArt.

Instructions
1. Tape stencil across bottom of apron with uneven edge at bottom of stencil 1¼" above bottom edge; center of apron should be between large butterfly and dragonfly to its left.

2. Using light green and referring to directions for stenciling with brush under "Painting Techniques" in the General Instructions (page 190) throughout, stencil area under uneven edge. Stencil top and bottom line borders with plum; stencil second line border under top with gold.

3. *Stencil sideways butterfly on right:* Stencil top wings with fuchsia, body and head with pink, and remainder with purple.

4. *Stencil center butterfly:* Stencil top and bottom wings with periwinkle, inner section of top wings with gold, body and head with true blue, and antennae with purple.

5. *Stencil dragonfly on left:* Stencil wings with white, head and body with avocado and antennae with purple.

6. Stencil swirls with light green and spots with gold. Shade edges of each section except spots, border lines and purple sections with purple.

7. Clean stencil; turn over. Using same colors as in steps 2, 3 and 6, stencil small sideways butterfly, swirl, spots and border lines in unpainted area remaining on left side.

8. Clean stencil; tape to top of apron, centering large butterfly and positioning top uneven edge of stencil 1¼" from edge of apron.

9. Stencil neck strap and area above uneven edge with light green.

10. Stencil large butterfly and top line borders above butterfly using same colors as in steps 2 and 4.

11. Tape line border under butterfly, centering all four sections in space; stencil as in step 2.

12. Using light green and gold as in step 6, stencil swirl on each side of butterfly and random spots between borders.

13. Heat-set paints following manufacturer's instructions.

14. Using pink thread throughout, sew a blue button in center of each top blue wing; sew yellow button in center of each gold inner section on blue wings; sew two pink buttons in center of each fuchsia wing. ✂

Hobby or Business?

If crafting is simply your hobby, you can sell your crafts, but you don't have to make a profit. Many crafters who make more crafts than they could possibly use or give as gifts will sell their crafts at a church bazaar or garage sale once or twice a year.

The income from these sales is considered a way to pay for the hobby or make a hobby pay for itself. The main concern is not making a profit, but making sure that costs don't outweigh sales.

Your state may require you to collect sales tax on any item you sell to the public. Contact your state department of revenue to inquire about your responsibilities regarding state sales tax.

Tax Considerations
In most cases, to qualify as a business in the eyes of local and state government and the IRS, you must be in business to make a profit.

While this doesn't mean that you must show a profit every year, it does mean that you can't be giving your crafts away at prices that don't cover your expenses, including cost of goods, labor and overhead.

In most states you will have to collect state sales tax on any item sold to the public.

Most professional crafters organize their business as a sole proprietorship rather than a partnership or corporation, but the choice is yours. As a sole proprietor you'll have to deal with at least one additional form, Schedule C, when doing your taxes. On it you will need to declare your income and itemize your deductions. **$**

"I'd Rather Be Fishing"

Bring out the outdoors enthusiast in your customers with this rustic wall hanging. It makes a perfect gift for that special fisherman.

Design by Mary Ayres

Materials

- 3¼" x 10" wooden sign*
- 3 (3½" x 4") wooden trees*
- 4⅛" x 1⅝" wooden fish*
- 18" black 20-gauge wire
- Acrylic craft paints*: blue/grey mist, country red, dark chocolate, forest green, Hauser medium green, lamp black, sand, uniform blue, Williamsburg blue
- Paintbrushes: #5 and #8 natural bristle brushes, #3 round
- Black twin-tip permanent marker*
- Craft glue
- Craft drill with ³⁄₃₂" bit
- Scrap wood block
- Fine sandpaper

Sign and trees from Lara's Crafts; fish from Nicole Industries; Americana paints from DecoArt; ZIG Memory System writer from EK Success Ltd.

Instructions

1. Place two trees on scrap wood and drill hole in top of each. Lightly sand all wooden pieces.

2. Paint trees medium green; let dry. Using forest green and referring to directions for dry-brushing under "Painting Techniques" in the General Instructions (page 190), dry-brush edges and into surface of trees at indentations in branches.

3. Pencil a wavy line across bottom of sign about 1" up from bottom edge on left side and ⅜" up from edge on right side. For sky, paint sign blue/grey above line. Let dry; dry-brush bottom edge of sky with sand. For water, paint sign below line with Williamsburg blue. Let dry; dry-brush bottom edge of water with uniform blue.

4. Paint fish sand; let dry. Dry-brush top half of fish with the following colors, working from middle to top: blue/grey, medium green and forest green along top edge and top and back fins. Dry-brush bottom of fish with red; dry-brush edges of all fins with chocolate.

5. Using brush handle dipped in sand, paint eye and random dots through center of fish. Paint pupil in center

of eye black. Add a smaller dot of chocolate in center of each sand dot in center of fish. Using fine tip of marker, draw dotted line around edge of eye.

6. Plan placement of trees. Lightly pencil "I'd rather be fishing" on sky area between trees. Go over words with marker's bullet tip.

7. Glue one tree with hole to left of sign; glue remaining trees overlapping to right side of sign, making sure tree with hole is on outside. Glue fish to bottom of sign; let dry.

8. *Hanger:* Curl wire unevenly around pencil; slip pencil out without disturbing coils. Insert wire ends in holes in trees; wrap ends around wire to secure. Shape wire into hanger. ✂

Tool Smarts

Physical limitations should not limit your crafting ability. Many tools are ergonomically designed to cause less stress and fatigue. Look for spring-loaded tools with padded grips. Buy tools that fit comfortably in your hand.

There are three basic sizes—small, medium and large—for grips and handles. Match your hand size to the grip on a tool. If possible, "test-drive" the tool before purchasing. **$**

Crafter's Success Story
Vicki Schreiner

After I got married and started having my children, I began going to craft shows to get ideas for gifts. The shows fascinated me!

Mom and Dad caught my craft-show fever. They started going to any shows that happened to be in our area. Dad even talked a lot about how fun it would be to have a booth of his own someday.

I ended up making the decision for him. One day, out of the blue, I quit my job (which had been dragging me down) and called him up. "Dad," I said, "we're going into business!"

We developed a line of handcrafted woodburned gifts. Dad cut and assembled the wood; I did the designing and woodburning; Mom stained and varnished the finished projects; and my sister was our bookkeeper.

We lived close to Branson, Mo., a major tourist and craft area, so we decided to try our hand at wholesaling first. We made prototypes of each item, loaded the truck, and went door to door to individual craft shops to take orders. It worked!

In order to reach retail consumers as well, we entered a well-established local craft show that had been growing steadily for years.

Now, as a professional designer in the craft industry, I smile when I look back on the 10 years I spent in business with Mom and Dad. The first couple of years we did a lot of "learning as you go," which a friend of mine refers to as "craft college."

Along the way, I had the unique opportunity to gain a wealth of knowledge, information, experience and the self-confidence I needed to get where I am today.

Although I recommend that you plan ahead a little more than I did, it's important to take that leap of faith and do the things you really want to do. You'll never know if they'll work if you don't try! ✂

Spring Beauty Angel

Bring the season to life with this decorative doll. You can use different plaids and embellishments to vary the selection at your booth.

Design by Chris Malone

Materials

- Coordinating homespun plaid fabrics: ⅓ yard for body, ¼ yard for skirt
- 3½" x 12" strip muslin
- 4½" square natural osnaburg fabric
- Matching sewing threads and hand-sewing needle
- Sewing machine (optional)
- 1 cup plastic stuffing pellets
- Polyester fiberfill
- Embroidery floss: brown, red, green
- Pink cosmetic blusher
- Cotton-tip swab
- Flat buttons: 2 (⅜") mottled cream-and-brown, ⅞" green, 3 (⅝"–⅞") rust
- 24" jute twine
- 2 (4½"-long) bundles fine twigs
- 8" ³⁄₁₆"- to ¼"-diameter twig
- 14" 18-gauge black wire
- Dried Spanish moss
- Dried berries and flowers with leaves
- 4" piece 1"-wide ivory Cluny lace
- 6" grapevine bow
- Miniature bird
- Permanent adhesive*
- Seam sealant
- Wire snips
- Iron

Fabri-Tac adhesive from Beacon.

Instructions

1. Cut 10½" x 12" piece body fabric; sew muslin to one 12" edge. Press seam toward body. Fold fabric in half, right sides facing and matching seams. Using photocopier with enlarging capabilities, enlarge angel body pattern 133 percent. Place pattern on fabric, matching neckline to seam line. Trace around with pencil. Sew on traced lines, leaving opening where indicated on pattern. Cut out ⅛" outside seam; clip curves.

2. *Box bottom so angel will stand:* Match bottom seam with adjacent side seam; flatten to form point. Pin seams together and sew through both layers 1" from point and perpendicular to seams. Repeat on other side. Trim seam allowance to ¼"; turn body right side out through opening.

3. Stuff head firmly with fiberfill. Pour pellets into bottom of body; stuff remainder of body with fiberfill. Fold in seam allowance around opening and slipstitch closed.

4. *Face:* Positioning beginning and ending knots at top of head where they will be concealed by hair, straight-stitch eyebrows and a single ⅝" stitch down center for nose using 2 strands brown floss. Add small straight stitch for mouth using **2** strands red floss. Using thread, sew small mottled buttons side by side for eyes. Apply blush to cheeks with cotton-tip swab.

5. *Skirt:* Cut 6½" x 22" strip from skirt fabric. Sew short ends together to form tube; press and sew ¼" hem along bottom edge. Press under 1" hem at top. Sew gathering stitches around top ¾" from fold. Slip skirt on angel; pull threads to gather skirt to fit snugly. Knot and clip thread ends.

6. *Apron:* Apply seam sealant to edges of osnaburg; let dry. Using matching thread, sew rust buttons to front with middle button in center of square.

Using running stitch and 2 strands green floss, stitch stems and leaves on each button "flower," ending stems ¼" from bottom edge of apron. Sew gathering stitches ½" below top edge; pull thread to gather apron to 2½" across top. Apply glue to back of apron along gathers; press to front of skirt. Wrap jute around angel's waist; tie bow in front.

7. *Arms:* Trace two sleeves onto wrong side of fabric A; fold fabric in half, right sides facing, and sew on traced lines, leaving bottoms of sleeves open. Cut out ⅛" from stitching; clip curves and turn sleeves right side out. Fold and press 1" hem at bottom of sleeves. Sew gathering stitches ¾" from fold; do not knot or clip thread.

8. *Hands:* Slip one twig bundle in one sleeve, leaving 1" showing for hand. Add fiberfill to shape sleeve. Pull ends of gathering thread tightly around twigs; knot and clip thread ends. Repeat for second sleeve. Glue backs of sleeves to fronts of shoulders.

9. *Hair:* Glue Spanish moss to top of head. Glue flowers and berries over moss.

10. *Rake:* Wrap one end of 18-gauge wire several times around one end of 8" twig. Shape wire into five irregular prongs, then wrap remaining wire end around twig several times; clip off excess. Glue rake to front of one arm.

11. Glue lace around neck, overlapping ends in back. Sew or glue green button at center front neckline. Glue grapevine bow to back of angel for wings; glue bird to wings. ✄

Health, Wealth & Crafting

Who would believe there are occupational hazards in crafting? Just like the weekend athlete who aches in places she didn't know she could ache, you too can suffer if you're not careful.

Take a good look at your work area and the materials you use. Keep your work area clean and uncluttered. Organization can save you time and money and prevent accidents.

Proper Lighting

Poor lighting leads to mistakes and eyestrain. Provide enough light to see during the day and evening hours. Fluorescent lighting is available in a wide spectrum and can be mixed and matched in fixtures.

Take a Break

Many professional crafters and hobbyists sit for long periods. Check the height of your chair and desk or table. Your feet should not dangle or curl back under your chair but remain flat on the floor.

Be careful not to hunch or slump over your work. If you are feeling back or neck discomfort, ask your doctor for suggestions. Taking hourly breaks to stand and stretch can help relieve stress in your back and neck.

Hands-on Help

Arthritis and carpal tunnel syndrome can make crafting painful for professionals and hobbyists alike. Try the therapeutic gloves that have been designed to support and massage your hands as you work.

These lightweight Lycra gloves permit unrestricted movement. They are an excellent idea for all crafters who work for more than two or three hours at a time. **$**

Spring Beauty Angel Body
Enlarge pattern 133%

Leave open

Spring Beauty Angel Sleeve

Button & Basket Pillow

This delicate piece lets you show off your creativity by using a mix of materials. Customers will love the dainty ribbon embellishment.

Design by Mary Ayres

Materials

- 8" square doily with crocheted edging*
- Assorted 5/16"–3/4" flat 2-hole buttons in nine pastel colors
- 1 yard 1/4"-wide light pink satin ribbon
- Small safety pin
- 4½" square white felt
- Pastel yellow embroidery floss
- French wire basket stamp*
- Permanent brown wood-and-fabric ink*
- Polyester fiberfill
- White sewing thread
- Hand-sewing needle
- Small safety pin

*Wimpole Street Creations doily; All Night Media stamp from Plaid; InkXpressions ink from Creative Beginnings.

Instructions

1. Apply ink to basket stamp; stamp onto center of doily.

2. Using 6 strands floss, sew buttons to open area of basket under handle, knotting ends on front of buttons. Trim floss ends to 3/8".

3. Align edges of felt square and fabric panel on back of doily. Using needle and thread, whipstitch together along three edges, forming a pocket.

4. Stuff pocket evenly with fiberfill; whipstitch opening closed.

5. Attach small safety pin to one end of ribbon. Weave pinned end in and out through openings in doily edging, beginning and ending at center top of pillow above basket with ribbon ends even in front. Tie ribbon in bow; trim ends even. ✂

Set Out to Succeed

The first year is the most difficult for new businesses. Those that succeed work toward carefully thought-out short- and long-term goals and have a realistic cash budget.

Step 1: Planning

The No. 1 mistake is lack of cash flow, which means the business didn't consider the importance of careful planning. You need to take that first step and keep the mind-set that what you are crafting is now part of your business. **$**

Antique Hatbox

Make a selection of these classy containers in different colors. Customers will love the beautiful flower pattern adorning the front!

Design by June Fiechter

Materials

- Sandpaper
- 13" round luggage*
- Roses stamping blocks decorating kit*
- Acrylic craft paints*: bayberry, lemonade, portrait, pure black, wicker white
- Brown antiquing medium*
- Flat paintbrush
- Sponging mitt*
- White dimensional fabric paint*
- Satin-finish varnish

Large luggage #28-4135-000 from D&CC; Roses Stamping Blocks Decorator Kit #53405, FolkArt acrylic paints, Down Home Brown Antiquing Medium, sponging mitt and white Dimensional Fabric Paint from Plaid.

Instructions

1. Paint box and lid wicker white; let dry.

2. Draw 8" circle in center of lid. Using sponging mitt, apply bayberry over circle and lemonade paint inside circle; let dry.

3. With flat brush apply portrait paint to remaining surfaces of box; let dry.

4. Use sponging mitt to apply liberal coat of antiquing medium over portrait paint only. Let dry.

5. Following manufacturer's instructions on decorating kit package, stamp roses over line around center of lid and paint. **Note:** *Stamp each rose and leaf with wicker white first to keep base color from showing through.* Let dry.

6. Working only around roses, shade background with black. Let dry.

7. Outline and embellish design with dimensional paint; let dry.

8. To create aged appearance, lightly sand painted box using gentle circular motions. Wipe off dust.

9. Seal hatbox with varnish. ✂

Know Your Customer

Understanding your customers' motivations will help you serve them better. There are three basic types of retail customers.

Type 1: The Craft Aficionado

This person enjoys purchasing handmade items for herself or to give as gifts. She appreciates the time and effort that goes into making something by hand. Often this customer is talented in a different type of craft than the one you make.

This customer also likes to buy unique items. Mass-produced home decor pieces and gifts don't stimulate her, so she turns to craft shows or craft malls. This type of customer is a gift from the heavens.

Type 2: "Sell Me"

This customer doesn't think she has the talent or time to make handcrafted items. She's savvy, and she has the money to purchase what she wants, but she doesn't want to waste a second of her valuable time. She often seems to be in a hurry or not paying attention.

Don't be fooled! All you need to do is point out the value of your item, the quality of your workmanship and your craft's unique qualities. This customer wants to be "sold" on the item because it makes her feel that she is getting something valuable for her money.

Type 3: "Customer C"

This individual is a wannabe professional crafter. I call her "Customer C" for "cranky" and "crass."

She'll often pick apart your items to see how they were made. She wants to sketch or take pictures of your work. She might even loudly proclaim that she's buying an item to use as a pattern so she can tell the first-graders in her Sunday-school class how to make such a simple craft.

In other words, this customer is a challenge to your patience, wits and humor. She is every hobbyist's and professional crafter's worst nightmare.

But keep your head; it's your call. You can draw the picture for her—or you can politely ask her to leave. **$**

Finding Your Marketplace

With so many marketing options available, the professional crafter may find it difficult to choose just one avenue of sales.

The good news is you don't have to pick just one! Most successful professionals take advantage of several—sometimes all—available options that fit their craft and their business needs. Here are some options to consider:

- Arts-and-crafts shows
- Craft malls
- Community bazaars
- Arts-and-crafts co-ops
- The Internet
- Wholesale gift markets
- Teaching or demonstrating
- Home shows
- Selling direct to retailers
- Word of mouth
- Consignment shops
- Flea markets and swap meets

Floral Wall Cone

Make this delicate and classic project in several colors using a variety of flowers. It makes a great decorative piece for the living room!

Design by Mary Ayres

Materials

- 2-ounce bar tan modeling compound
- Dried flowers
- 10" jute twine
- Flower rubber stamp*
- White acrylic craft paint
- #8 natural bristle paintbrush
- Rolling pin
- Waxed paper
- Cookie sheet
- ⅛" wooden dowel
- Small piece wire screen
- Toothed clay tool or small-tooth comb
- Craft knife
- Tacky craft glue

Silhouette Florals stamp from Posh Impressions.

Instructions

1. Knead modeling compound; roll out on waxed paper until it is slightly larger than oval pattern. Cut oval from modeling compound with craft knife.

2. Press rubber stamp into clay; repeat to cover bottom two-thirds of oval, positioning impressions fairly close together and in all directions. Press toothed clay tool away from edges to give compound a jagged edge.

3. Turn oval over. Add texture to top third of modeling compound by imprinting it with screen.

4. Roll bottom right side of oval over to center; repeat with left side, overlapping edges. To make holes for hanger, push dowel through modeling compound where indicated by dots on pattern.

5. Place cone on cookie sheet; make sure it is symmetrical. Bake in pre-heated 275-degree oven for 10 minutes. Let cool.

6. Dilute 1 capful white paint with 1 capful water in disposable container. Paint cooled cone with diluted mixture and quickly wipe off excess paint with damp paper towel, leaving paint remaining in crevices. Repeat painting if too much paint is wiped off.

7. Dab ends of jute with glue; twist into points. Thread jute through holes in cone from back to front; knot ends in front and trim off excess. Insert dried flowers in cone; hang. ✂

Top

Floral Wall Cone

Celebrate Regional Flair

No matter what marketplace you select, remember to take advantage of regional factors to sell more crafts.

For example, if you are selling in an area that has lots of tourist traffic, you might attract the visitors as potential customers by creating souvenirs and gift items that highlight your area.

In New England you might see lobster and lobster-buoy motifs. In New Mexico you will definitely find a southwestern color scheme and Native American influences. In Florida, a tourist might want a keepsake that reflects her time in the sun and sand.

Show off your regional specialties in your crafts! **$**

Crafter's Success Story
Missy Becker

For a year, two friends with whom I did a lot of craft shows tried to get me to join a co-operative craft store. I thought they were crazy. How in the world would I be able the pay the rent and the commissions, which at the time were $35 per month and 8 percent of sales?

Finally, however, I gave in. I decided that I would start in September and leave after Christmas. So over the summer, I tried to stock up. I headed up to the store with a whopping $500 worth of merchandise—a lot, considering that my median price was $5.

Because this was a co-operative store, I was required to put in one shift a week. The first time I worked, about a week later, I was shown how to check my sales. In the very first week I had sold $250 worth of merchandise, and by the second week, my original stock had been depleted!

For the next three months I worked until all hours of the night. And my work paid off. By the end of the Christmas season, from the store where I was afraid that I wouldn't sell enough to pay the rent, I brought home a check for more than $3,000!

Needless to say, I decided to stay with the store year-round. My only regret is that I didn't start sooner! I really should have trusted my friends. ✂

Ivory Roses Barrette

Wear this esquisite barrette as you work at your booth to display its feminine beauty to customers. Try different colors and flowers for this versatile accessory.

Design by Nazanin S. Fard

Materials

- 4"-long pure silk barrette blank
- 7 cream mini swirl polyester roses
- 6 stems pearl sprays
- 10" piece ⅝"-wide lace trimming with pearls*
- Fabric glue

Wright's lace trim.

Instructions

1. Glue lace trim around edge of barrette.

2. Glue six roses in circle in center of barrette; glue seventh rose in center.

3. Trim sprays of pearls to desired lengths and glue in place, tucking ends under roses. ✂

Finding Shows

Research retail and consumer shows by networking with fellow professionals, calling your local chamber of commerce or using periodicals called "show guides"; the leading national show guide is *Sunshine Artist Magazine.*

You can find many regional show guides by searching the Directory of Periodicals at your local library.

Sunshine Artist Magazine (www.sunshineartist.com) and The American Craft Malls are just two companies that list hundreds of U.S. craft shows on their Web sites. And more Web-site show guides are popping up. Just enter "craft shows" or "craft show list" into your search engine.

Wholesale shows can be found through calendars and advertisements in industry trade journals like *Craftrends, Country Business* and *Gift and Stationery News.* $

Decoupaged Switch Plates

Flower motifs are always popular, so make several varieties of this decorative switch-plate cover.

Designs by Samantha McNesby

Materials

- 3½" x 5½" oversize white plastic switch plate
- Paper napkins with rose or violets motifs*
- Clear patio paint* or satin-finish acrylic sealer
- ½" flat paintbrush
- Gold chisel-point paint pen *or* metallic gold paint and small paintbrush

N19 Full Bloom Rose and N41 Violets Napkin Décor napkins, and Patio Paint Clear Coat #DCP-24, all from DecoArt.

Roses Switch Plate

1. Unfold roses napkin; lay on flat surface. Choose area of napkin with pleasing design and lay switch plate on top of it; trace around switch plate with pencil.

2. Cut out traced portion of napkin, cutting about ¼" outside traced lines. Carefully peel off single top printed ply; it should separate easily.

3. Coat front of switch plate with clear patio paint. Working quickly before paint dries, lay napkin right side up over switch plate. Add more paint to brush and brush all over surface to smooth napkin in place, taking care not to tear it. Smooth napkin edges over edges of switch plate with brush. Some ripples and wrinkles are to be expected; they add to the finished effect.

4. Before switch plate dries, use pencil point to poke holes for switch and screws.

5. Lay switch plate flat to dry. **Note:** *If a lot of paint has gathered on edges, place switch plate on top of a small cup or mug to dry, allowing edges of switch plate to hang over sides of cup. Let dry.*

6. Using paint pen, add thin line of paint around edges of switch plate. Let dry 24 hours before using.

Violets Switch Plate

Follow instructions for roses switch plate, substituting violets napkin. ✂

Show & Booth Fees

Show fees and amenities vary greatly, but you usually get what you pay for. Fees can be as low as $10 for a tabletop and chair for a one-day event, or up to $500–$1,000 for a 10-foot-square booth at a weekend or three-day show.

The industry standard is that your sales at a given show should equal 10 times the fee you pay for a show to which you must travel, or at least five times the fee for a local show that involves no travel expense.

Fees also vary within craft malls, consignment shops and co-ops. Make sure you understand what you are getting for your fees. **$**

Victorian Crackers

Capture the true beauty of this elegant project by displaying them in a wooden or wicker basket. You can add your own embellishments to make each one unique.

Design by Samantha McNesby

Materials

Each Cracker

- Cardboard roll from bathroom tissue
- 10" x 24" sheet tissue or crepe paper
- Coordinating scrapbook paper for "wrap"
- ½ yard ¼"-wide satin ribbon
- Assorted small embellishments: buttons, stickers, charms, etc.
- Assorted treasures and trinkets to fill cracker: wrapped candies, charms, jewelry, hair accessories, small toys, etc.
- Glue stick or tape
- Hot-glue gun and glue sticks *or* thick white craft glue

Instructions

1. Lay tissue paper on work surface. Center cardboard tube on one short (10") end; secure with glue stick. Carefully roll up tube in tissue; secure with glue stick.

2. Cut 9" piece from ribbon; gather and tie one end of tissue with ribbon.

3. Fill tube with treasures and trinkets. Close open end with remaining ribbon as in step 2.

4. Make "jacket" for cracker by cutting one or more scrapbooking papers to fit around tube; secure with glue stick. Decorate tube with desired embellishments, securing larger items with hot glue. ✂

Decoupaged Soaps

Inexpensive soaps dressed up with images from paper napkins make beautiful gifts and super bazaar offerings!

Designs by Samantha McNesby

Materials

- 3 bars white soap
- Paper napkins with violets, tea roses and urn motifs*
- Acrylic craft paints*: metallic gold, white wash, red
- Candle- and soap-painting medium*
- Satin-finish acrylic sealer
- ½" flat paintbrush
- Small, sharp scissors
- Small amount block paraffin (optional)
- Coffee can or double-boiler (optional)
- Disposable or foam brush (optional)

Napkin Décor napkins N41, N18 and N44; Candle and Soap Medium and Americana acrylic paints, all from DecoArt.

Project Note

Add candle- and soap-painting medium to paints before painting soaps.

Violets Soap

1. Combine equal parts gold and white paints; paint smooth surface of soap with one coat of mixture; let dry.

2. Paint stripes of undiluted gold paint on sides of soap.

3. Cut motifs from violets napkin; arrange cutouts on top of soap as desired. Remove cutouts.

4. Coat top and sides of soap with acrylic sealer. While still wet, lay

cutouts on top of soap. Carefully coat cutouts with more acrylic sealer; let dry. Add one more coat sealer to top of soap; let dry.

Note: *Soaps completed to this point are for decorative use only. For more permanent, usable soaps, continue with step 5.*

5. Carefully melt paraffin according to manufacturer's directions in old coffee can or other container. Apply melted paraffin to decoupaged surface of soap with disposable brush. Let cool; wait 24 hours before using soap. Image will last the life of the soap.

Tea Roses Soap

Repeat steps for violets soap, omitting gold and white paints and substituting tea roses napkin. Paint red stripes on sides.

Urn Soap

Repeat steps for violets soap, substituting urn-motif napkin. ✂

Word-of-Mouth Sales

Don't underestimate the power of word-of-mouth sales. If you have a unique craft that fills a need, your customers will brag to family and friends about the item they purchased from you. All those people then represent potential sales.

Make it easier for those potential customers to find you. Attach a label, including at least your name and phone number, to your crafts. You should also have business cards, and if you are trying to sell strictly by word of mouth, it's a good idea to have a brochure or price list to hand out.

Consider rewarding customers who promote your crafts to others. This is easy to do with a simple card that gives loyal customers a percentage off their next purchase after two to five referrals. **$**

Floral Bath Set

Make this three-piece set in several colors and you're sure to increase sales. These pieces will add a decorative touch to any bathroom!

Designs by Marilyn Gossett

Materials

Each Project

- Acrylic craft paints*: coastline blue, light foliage green, napthol red light, white
- Matte-finish varnish
- Paintbrushes: ¾" wash brush, #12 shader
- Wood glue
- Sandpaper
- Tack cloth

Washcloth/Napkin Holder

- Wooden shapes*: 2 (4½" x 4½" x ⅛"-thick) hearts, 2⅝" x 5⅜" x ⅛"-thick rectangle, 4 (¾" x ¾" x ⅛"-thick) hearts, 2 (⅞") bowls, 4 (½") blocks

Trinket Box

- Wooden shapes*: 2 (¾") bowls, 4 (¾" x ⅛"-thick) hearts
- Small wooden trinket box or treasure chest

Cotton Swab/Toothpick Holder

- Wooden shapes*: 1¹⁵⁄₁₆" x 1¾" flowerpot, 2 (¾" x ⅛"-thick) hearts, ¾" round head plug, 1" x ³⁄₁₆"-thick scalloped heart

Wood products from Lara's Crafts; Ceramcoat acrylic paints from Delta.

Instructions

1. Sand all wooden pieces; wipe clean with tack cloth.

2. Paint all wooden bowls and head plug red; paint all smooth-edge hearts green. Let dry, then proceed as directed for individual pieces.

Washcloth/Napkin Holder

1. Lay 2⅝" x 5⅜" rectangle on work surface, long edges running horizontally. Lightly mark a point in center of rectangle and ¼" up from bottom edge; lightly mark a matching point ¼" below top edge.

2. With right side of heart facing out, glue point of one large heart to one of the positions marked in step 1. Secure by stacking two blocks behind heart and gluing them to heart, to base and to each other. Repeat on other side; let dry thoroughly.

3. Paint entire holder blue inside and out; let dry.

4. Glue red bowl flat side down and two green hearts to center of one large heart to make flower; repeat on other side.

5. Thin white paint with water; "wash" washcloth/napkin holder and flowers with mixture. Let dry.

6. Using brush handle dipped in undiluted white, place single highlight dot off center on each red flower; add border of dots around edges of hearts. Let dry.

Trinket Box

1. Paint trinket box blue inside and out; let dry.

2. Glue red bowl flat side down and two green hearts to upper left corner of lid to make flower; repeat on front of box below latch.

3. Thin white paint with water; "wash" box and flowers with mixture. Let dry.

4. Using brush handle dipped in undiluted white, place single highlight dot off center on each red flower; without redipping handle between dots, place a cluster of three highlight dots on front of box above right-hand leaf. Let dry.

Cotton Swab/Toothpick Holder

1. Glue scalloped heart to bottom of flowerpot; let dry thoroughly.

2. Paint flowerpot blue inside and out; let dry.

3. Glue head plug, flat side down, and two green hearts to rim of pot to make flower.

4. Thin white paint with water; "wash" flowerpot and flower with mixture. Let dry.

5. Using brush handle dipped in undiluted white, place single highlight dot off center on red flower; add cluster of three dots to flowerpot below one leaf. Let dry. ✂

The Right Craft for the Right Marketplace

If an item is not self-explanatory, or if it needs to be demonstrated, don't put it in a craft mall or consignment shop; take it to a craft show.

I don't care how good your label or signage is; mall customers don't have the time to figure out what your product can do. And if you can't display it for sale, the craft will not sell. **$**

This display features crafts in a variety of media—including ceramic pieces, decorative boxes and teddy bears. The coordinated use of white throughout ties it all together and makes it appealing to the eye.

Heading to the Mall?

Craft malls began to open in the late 1980s and provided a solid footing for professional crafters who wanted to sell their products.

In many ways, the craft mall is like a year-round craft show under one roof. Crafters lease space in the store for displaying their items. You can lease a single shelf, a 10-foot-square area or almost any size area in between.

You are responsible for setting up your display and restocking it. The craft mall usually has a uniform method for affixing prices—tags, SKU or handwritten price stickers—but you decide the actual price of each of your items.

Read the Fine Print

While the mall owner/manager may charge you only a lease fee for the space, most also take a percentage of the retail price for each item sold.

For example, you might sign a contract for leasing a space for six months at $50 per month with an additional 5 percent of all sales paid to the craft mall. Leases also vary; month-to-month, six-month and year leases might all be available.

The lease is a legal document, so read the contract carefully and ask about anything you do not understand.

Assess Your Competition

Some craft malls jury prospective exhibitors, but most do not. Anyone who wants to lease space is welcome.

It's also important to note if the craft mall sells commercial or imported items. Many craft malls supplement their income by selling mass-produced objects at lower prices than craftspeople can afford to charge for similar products made by hand. **$**

Molded Rosy Toppers

Pair these beautiful projects with coordinating candles for your display. This is a project that allows you to add personal creative touches.

Designs by Lorine Mason

Materials

Votive Toppers
- Air-drying modeling compound*: white and green *plus* red, yellow or blue
- Mini glass votive holder
- 2½"-diameter x ¼"-thick wooden disk
- Votive candle
- Polymer floral/leaf clay cutters
- Coordinating pink, yellow or blue acrylic paint

Trinket Boxes
- Air-drying modeling compound*: white, red, orange, yellow
- Small heart-shaped papier-mâché box with lid
- Acrylic craft paints: white, red, orange, yellow
- Decorative paper edgers
- Craft glue

Each Project
- Paintbrush
- Satin-finish water-base varnish
- Toothpick
- Rolling pin
- Hot-glue gun

Crayola Model Magic modeling compound from Binney & Smith.

Project Note

Keep modeling compound wrapped in plastic to keep it from drying out.

Preparing Modeling Compound

1. *Color variations:* Start with 1" ball of modeling compound; add a small amount of white. Knead until thoroughly mixed. Add additional white to achieve a variety of hues.
Note: For coral clay, start with red and add yellow and white.
2. *Marbleizing modeling compound:* Start with equal amounts compound in colors of your choice, formed in step 1. Roll each color into a long rope. Lay ropes side by side and twist together. Fold in half and roll. Continue rolling, twisting and folding in half until compound is marbleized. Experiment with different amounts of color to create a variety of marbleized effects.

Petals & Leaves

1. *Rose petals:* Pinch ¼" ball compound into rounded teardrop shape between thumb and index finger. Take the time to thin the edges. Make at least four petals for smallest flower, up to nine for larger roses.
2. *Roses:* Tightly roll a single petal shape for rose center. Add three more petals, slightly overlapping each, working around center. Flare petal edges outward slightly. As each row of petals is added, move down the rolled center to achieve a more balanced look. Continue adding petals until rose is desired size. Pinch off any excess clay from bottom.
3. *Rosebuds:* Form from two or three tightly rolled petals, with only the last petal's top edge flared slightly outward.
4. Using clay cutter, cut leaves and calyxes from flattened green compound. Imprint veins with toothpick. Attach calyxes to bottoms of completed roses. Let dry completely.

Votive Topper

1. Roll ⅛"-thick layer of compound using color to match/coordinate with roses. Using open end of votive holder as pattern, trace onto compound and cut out; let dry.
2. Press ½" ball of matching compound on hard surface to flatten bottom; pinch top into a ½"-tall cone. Let dry.
3. Paint wooden disc in coordinating color; let dry. Repeat if necessary. Apply a single coat of water-base varnish.
4. Hot-glue compound circle in center of bottom of painted disk. Hot-glue cone shape to center of other side. Hot-glue roses to cone in a pleasing arrangement, adding green leaves as desired.

Trinket Box

1. Paint box and lid white, inside and out; let dry. Repeat if necessary; let dry. Using tip of brush handle dipped in paints, dot colors on lid and box to match roses; let dry. Seal with one coat varnish; let dry.
2. Roll yellow modeling compound ⅛" thick. Measure width of lid's edge. Using paper edgers, cut a strip of modeling compound this wide and long enough to fit around lid, allowing for overlap. Let strip dry for a few minutes, then glue to edge of lid with craft glue. Give strip a lacy look by indenting it with toothpick or head of pin in desired pattern.
3. Hot-glue roses and buds to lid as desired. ✂

Is Consigning for You?

Consignment shops, like some craft malls, charge crafters a percentage of the receipts for any items sold. Most craft professionals do not prefer to offer their work through consignment shops because there are too many negatives.

The consignment shop is not responsible for any items under its roof. If your products are lost, stolen or damaged, the shop is not legally obligated to compensate you.

For the most part, your crafts are free inventory for the consignment shop. You have no control over how the item is promoted or displayed, and in many cases you don't even get the final word in pricing—other than to remove your products from the shop.

However, if you have a lot of inventory but little space for storing it, a consignment shop might be ideal.

Consignment shops do not jury prospective merchandise per se; the owner or manager will either accept your items or turn them down. $

Avoid displays that look picked over. This one surely doesn't! It gives the customer lots of choices, encouraging her to feel like she gets the treat of picking out the very best product!

Bright Blooming Pincushion

Put customers in the buying mood with a window box full of these hardworking blooms! Their bright, cheerful colors shout, "Celebrate spring!"

Design by Chris Malone

Materials

- 2½"-diameter x 9" wooden candlestick*
- Acrylic crafts paints*: bright green, cadmium yellow, peony pink, titanium white
- ¼" and ½" flat paintbrushes
- Spray matte finish
- Bright print fabrics: 6" x 12" pink, 5" x 6" green, 3" square yellow
- ⅛ yard craft batting
- Needle and matching sewing threads
- Sewing machine (optional)
- Small piece polyester fiberfill
- Small piece cardboard
- Fabric Glue

Candlestick from Lara's Crafts; Americana acrylic paints from DecoArt.

Candlestick

1. Referring to instructions for base-coating under Painting Techniques in General Instructions (page 190), base-coat entire candlestick with white; let dry.

2. Referring to photo, note positions of seven "bands" or sections of candlestick. Counting from top to bottom, paint second and sixth bands with another coat white.

3. Add white to a little green and a little pink to make lighter shades. Paint remaining bands: *Top (first) band:* light green; *third:* bright green; when dry, dot on light green with tip of paintbrush handle; *fourth:* yellow; *fifth:* pink; when dry, dot on smaller light pink dots with tip of paintbrush handle; *seventh:* light green; when dry, add bright green vertical stripes with ¼" brush.

4. Paint bottom of candlestick light green; let dry.

5. Spray with matte finish; let dry.

Pincushion

1. *Petals:* Trace six petals onto wrong side of one half of pink fabric. Fold fabric in half, right sides facing and traced lines on top; lay doubled fabric on batting. By hand or machine, sew around petals through all three layers, leaving straight ends unsewn. Cut out close to seam; clip curves and turn petals right side out. Sew gathering stitch through bottom of each petal, connecting all six petals in a circle. Pull thread to gather; knot and clip thread end.

2. *Flower center:* Cut one 1⅜" circle from cardboard and two small matching circles from batting; stack batting circles and glue to cardboard. Cut one large circle from yellow fabric. Sew gathering stitches around circle ⅛" from edge; place ball of fiberfill in center on wrong side and cover with cardboard, batting side down. Pull thread to gather around cardboard; knot and clip thread ends. Glue in center of flower, covering ends of petals.

3. *Leaves:* Referring to technique for petals in step 1, make three leaves using green fabric.

4. Glue leaves evenly around top rim of candlestick. Glue flower on top of leaves. ✂

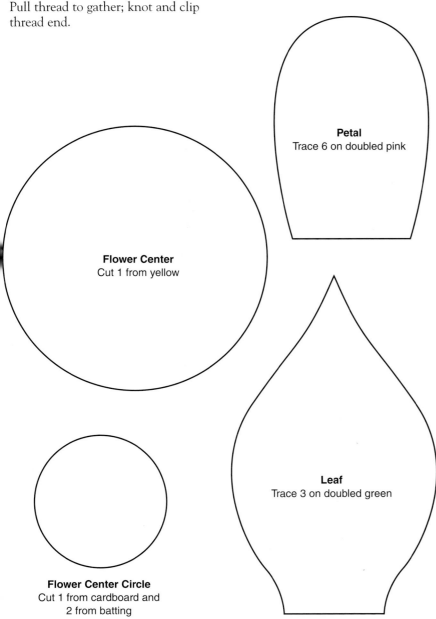

Petal
Trace 6 on doubled pink

Flower Center
Cut 1 from yellow

Flower Center Circle
Cut 1 from cardboard and
2 from batting

Leaf
Trace 3 on doubled green

Cooperation Is the Key

While a craft co-op can look like a craft mall or consignment shop, it is different in that every member has a voice in how the co-op is run.

Co-ops are almost always juried by a panel of co-op members. Acceptance is usually based on two criteria. First, your crafts should not directly compete with any current member's.

The second criterion is usually workmanship; most co-ops want variety and well-made, hand-crafted items. Most co-ops will not allow any buy/sells or commercially mass-produced items.

Your Obligations

Co-op members usually pay a monthly fee for space, plus a percentage that goes back into the co-op for overhead.

You may also be asked to work a few days each month, stocking, cleaning and waiting on customers, as a condition of membership.

Individual members may be financially responsible for business within the co-op, so read all contracts carefully. **$**

Take the time to create the best displays for your crafts. These handmade candles are shown off best on wooden pegs.

Felt Easter Ornaments

Make basketfuls of these adorable ornaments for your stand. They're sure to sell quickly, and they make perfect Easter basket gifts.

Designs by Chris Malone

Materials

Both Ornaments

- Felt*: apple green, light yellow, mango tango, misty blue, pink mist, white
- Cotton embroidery floss to coordinate with felt colors: black, blue, emerald green, orange, pink, deep yellow
- 6" piece pink pearl cotton
- Embroidery needle
- 4 (3mm) black beads
- 6mm black half-round bead
- ⅜"-wide gingham check ribbon: 14" each pink-and-white and blue-and-white
- Polyester fiberfill
- Craft glue

Rainbow Felt Classic from Kunin.

Chick

1. Referring to patterns, cut pieces from felt: two eggs from blue; large flower from pink; small flower from

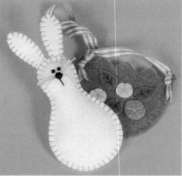

white; two chicks and small flower from yellow; beak from mango; three leaves from green.

2. Arrange flowers and leaves on one egg as shown; tack in place with pin or dot of glue. Using 2 strands floss throughout, attach each flower with dark yellow, making five straight stitches out from flower center and adding French knot in center. Attach each leaf with two fly stitches of emerald green.

3. Pin eggs together, wrong sides facing; join by sewing blanket stitch around curved edges with blue floss.

4. Knot each end of blue checked ribbon; tack or glue knots to front of egg pocket.

5. Using black floss, sew beads to one chick for eyes; fold beak and glue to face.

6. Pin chick front and back together, wrong sides facing. Join by blanket-stitching around edges with orange, stuffing lightly with fiberfill before closing. Tuck chick into egg.

Bunny

1. Referring to patterns, cut pieces from felt: two eggs from pink; large flower from blue; small flower from yellow; two bunnies, four ears and small flower from white; three leaves from green.

2. Repeat steps 2–4 as for chick, substituting pink floss for blanket stitch and pink checked ribbon.

3. Using black floss, sew bead eyes to one bunny; add ½" straight stitch down center of face. Cut three 2" pieces pink pearl cotton; tack centers to face for whiskers; glue on black half-bead for nose.

4. Using pink floss throughout,

Wholesale Markets

Some professional crafters eventually turn to the wholesale marketplace to sell their designs. In this case, you sell directly to a retailer who then sells the items to the public.

You can do this by hiring a sales rep, by being your own sales rep, or by selling at wholesale gift marts.

Most professional crafters will attend a gift mart with prototypes. If advance sales of these prototypes

are good, then the professional crafter will produce the item in quantity.

There are gift marts in most large cities like New York, Chicago, Atlanta, Dallas and San Francisco. You will set up much as you would for a craft show, but you will price your items for the wholesale market.

Can You Deliver?

One key to your success in this marketplace is your ability to deliver the

orders placed by your wholesale customers within a reasonable time frame. You might get an order for 5,000 pieces—but can you produce them within three weeks?

At this point you are really becoming a small manufacturer. You need to consider how you will handle wholesale orders, including all the tasks involved in shipping your products. **$**

blanket-stitch ears together in pairs. Pin bunny front and back together, wrong sides facing. Join by blanket-stitching all around bunny, catching ends of ears in head and stuffing lightly with fiberfill before closing. Tuck bunny into egg. ✂

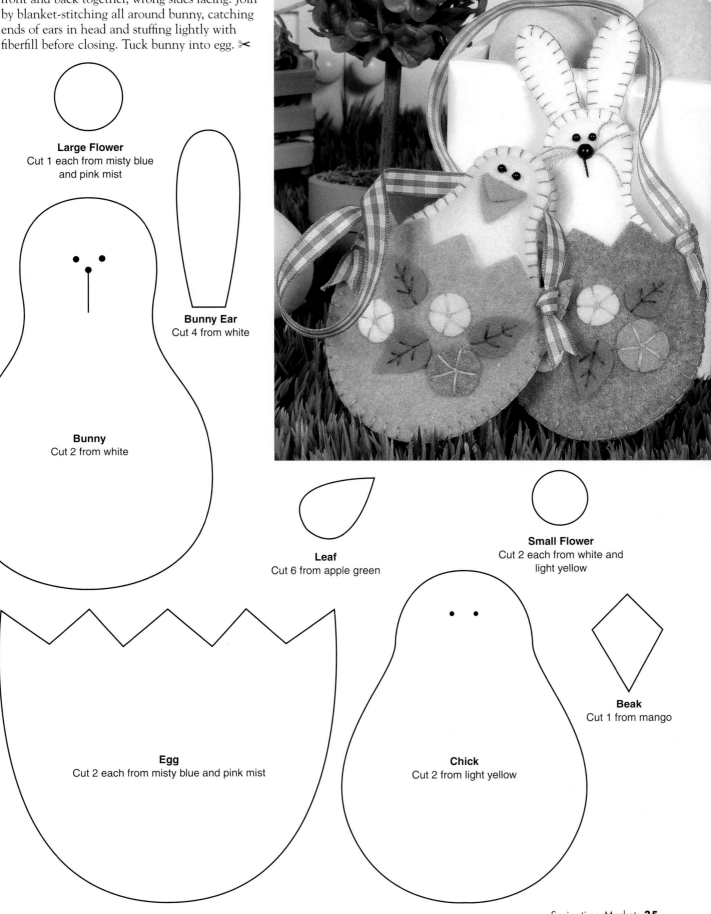

Large Flower
Cut 1 each from misty blue
and pink mist

Bunny Ear
Cut 4 from white

Bunny
Cut 2 from white

Leaf
Cut 6 from apple green

Small Flower
Cut 2 each from white and
light yellow

Beak
Cut 1 from mango

Egg
Cut 2 each from misty blue and pink mist

Chick
Cut 2 from light yellow

Kids' Fun Box

Try displaying this brilliantly painted box filled with toys or any of your crafts for kids. Make several using different color combinations and designs.

Design by Mary Ayres

Materials

- Large (6½" x 14½" x 6½") wooden box*
- 4 (2¼") wooden blocks with bases*
- 10 (1" x 2") wooden triangles*
- 5" x 7¾" piece ¼"-thick cork *or* 2 pieces 5" x 7¾" ⅛"-thick cork glued together
- 10 flat yellow ½" buttons
- Spiral stencil*

- Acrylic craft paints*: bright orange, calypso blue, Hauser light green, lavender
- Paintbrushes: ¼" stencil brush, large round bristle brush
- Craft glue
- Black permanent bullet-tip marker
- Fine sandpaper
- Tack cloth

Box and blocks from Plaid Essentials; Woodsies triangles from Forster; Simply Stencils spiral stencil #28146 from Plaid; Americana paints from DecoArt.

Instructions

1. Lightly sand wooden pieces; wipe off dust with tack cloth.

2. Paint inside of box lavender; paint outside and edge around opening blue. Paint blocks with bases (for box's feet) light green; paint triangles orange. Let dry.

3. Using lavender and referring to directions for stenciling with brush under "Painting Techniques" (General Instructions, page 190), stencil spirals and dots, evenly spaced and pointing in all directions, to cover front of cork. Stencil spiral and four dots symmetrically in each corner of box sides and front.

4. Using black marker, draw dotted line around each spiral and dot on box. Using side of bullet tip to make larger dots, draw dotted line around edge of cork and each triangle.

5. Center and glue corkboard to box front. Glue triangle to each corner of corkboard, to bottom of one side of two feet and bottom of two adjoining sides of remaining two feet. Glue button in center of each triangle; let dry.

6. Glue bases of wooden block feet to bottom corners of box so that triangles show on front and sides; let dry. ✂

Types of Shows

Art Show

This is strictly for art-type items such as paintings, pottery, jewelry, sculpture and mixed media. Usually juried, it may be held indoors or outdoors.

Most art shows have an award system; often cash prizes are awarded. They may be annual events, with good advertising and public relations, and may be supported by the local artistic community.

Arts & Crafts Show

This show allows for a mixture of arts and crafts. Often there are two distinct areas within the show, one for art vendors and one for craft vendors.

They are usually juried for workmanship and to limit vendors in various categories (i.e., a maximum of 12 decorative painters, four doll- makers and

25 wood turners) to give the show more variety.

Craft Show

Usually you will find little art at this type of show. Although it may be juried for workmanship, there is no vendor limit within a category.

Bazaar

This is a wonderful hodge-podge where anything goes. Rarely juried and often small in size, this is the type of show we think of around the winter holidays. Bazaars are often promoted by churches and local service organizations.

Promoter's Show

This show is run by a promoter who makes his living by organizing and promoting these shows. Often a promoter has a circuit— perhaps a series of shows in several cities within a state or region.

A list of responsibilities is usually given to each vendor; i.e., to insure uniform appearance, everyone must have blue fitted table coverings.

Most promoters have advertising budgets and work hard to promote upcoming shows.

Home Show

Think Tupperware™!

You send out invitations, then organize and set up your own craft show in your home or a friend's home.

This is a great once-a-year event if you do several craft shows in your local area. Create a mailing list from those who buy from you, and feel free to invite several other crafters to participate—preferably in different media—so you can share the expenses. $

Sunny Smiles Cabinet

Painted wood projects like this charming [...]
let your crafting skills shine!

Design by Annie Lang

Materials

- 17" x 17" x 4½" wooden letter caddy with drawers*
- Wooden cutouts*: 3 (2⅛") sunflower shapes, 4 (1⅛") tulip shapes
- Acrylic craft paints*: baby blue, buttermilk, cadmium yellow, cranberry wine, Hauser dark green, lamp black, tangelo orange, true blue
- Satin-finish acrylic paints*: dark ecru, sage green
- Bright blue metal paint*
- Paintbrushes: #10 flat shader, #0/2 and #1 liners, #4 and #10 pointed round brushes
- 1" foam brush
- Glossy spray sealer/finisher
- Sandpaper
- Tack cloth
- Wood glue

Caddy from Provo Craft; Woodlet wooden shapes from Craft Catalog; Americana acrylic and satin paints and No-Prep Metal Paint, all from DecoArt.

Instructions

1. Trace pattern section onto tracing paper; flip and retrace with pencil on wrong side. Flip pattern back to original side.

2. Sand all wooden pieces; wipe off dust with tack cloth.

3. Remove drawer knobs. Using #10 round brush, paint center of each knob bright blue metal paint; let dry. Apply a second coat; set aside to dry.

4. Referring to instructions for base-coating in "Painting Techniques" (General Instructions, page 190), use foam brush to base-coat entire cabinet with ecru satin paint; let dry. Sand lightly, remove dust with tack cloth, and apply a second coat; let dry.

5. Use foam brush and sage to paint drawer interiors and center front panel just above drawers; let dry.

6. Using #4 round brush, "squiggle" a sage border around each drawer front and across top of cabinet ¼" from top edge; paint knobs on pegs at bottom of cabinet.

7. Using #4 round brush, "squiggle" a true blue border around center panel

black. Using #1 liner, paint eyes and smiles black. Using #0/2 liner and black, paint dashed face lines and edge outlines.

10. Transfer tulip stems and leaves to sage panel as needed, positioning them so that suns will be centered above drawers.

11. Glue suns and tulips to sage green panel on cabinet as shown.

12. Using #4 round brush and dark green, paint stems and leaves. Using tip of #4 round, add sets of small true blue dots above each short tulip and in bottom corners of center panel.

13. Spray center panel with several coats of sealer/finisher, letting it dry between coats. Reattach drawer knobs. ✂

Craft Show Checklist

Here's a list of items you'll need for any type of show in which you will be setting up a display away from your home or workplace. It was compiled by seasoned professional crafters who want to share what they've learned—often the hard way!

1. An inventory of craft items in easy-to-handle containers. If at all possible, preprice all items and have several copies of a complete price list.

2. A secure cash box and plenty of small bills and change. Be prepared for customers to use $20s and $50s. The cash box should also contain a receipt book, tax table, blank pricing labels or stickers, calculator and several pens. Many states require you to display a copy of your state tax certificate where you are selling your crafts, so keep the copy in your cash box.

Do not keep large amounts of money in the cash box, however. Have a plan and place the cash in your car trunk or other secure place. You are a sitting target if you flash large amounts of money in your cash box. You never know who is watching, so err on the safe side.

3. All display items. Make a list of all items needed within your display like tables, chairs, table coverings, shelves, a canopy and all its components, toolbox (for making repairs or putting together display items). Check items off the list as you pack your car or truck for the show.

4. Appropriate clothing. If it's a sunny day, bring a hat or sunscreen. If the event is air-conditioned, bring a light coat or sweater.

Bring an appropriate attitude, too. Be friendly and smile.

The most important thing you can do before any show is to get a good night's sleep. Don't wait until 24 hours before the event to get organized. Think ahead!

5. Bring refreshments if it is allowed. Some shows ban all food and drinks except those sold at the show, but it's a good idea to have a container of water and something to nibble on during the day if you are working alone.

What Not to Bring

Don't bring young children who need constant supervision, pets, a book or anything else that will distract you from interacting with potential buyers. **$**

Sunny Suggestion Box

Place this project with similarly themed projects, such as gifts for teachers. This whimsical box, featuring happy daisies, would make a wonderful addition to your home. It's also a terrific gift item!

Design by Annie Lang

Materials

- 4" x 8" x 15" wooden tabletop mailbox*
- Acrylic craft paints*: bright green, Hauser dark green, Indian turquoise, lamp black, leaf green, pineapple, primary yellow, pumpkin, titanium white
- 1" foam brush
- Small square cut from household sponge
- Paintbrushes: #⅜ angle shader, #2, #5 and #10 pointed rounds, #0 and #2 liners
- Red pastel chalk
- Craft drill with ¼" bit
- Sandpaper
- Tack cloth
- Stylus
- Matte-finish spray acrylic sealer
- 3" square self-stick notepad
- Double-sided tape (optional)

Mailbox from Cabin Crafters; Americana acrylic paints from DecoArt.

Suggestion Box Back

Attach notepad here

Suggestion Box Door

Join a Web Auction

Web auctions have been very successful marketplaces for high-end craft professionals who sell anything from jewelry to porcelain dolls to quilts. A service fee is usually part of the deal if the item is sold.

You have considerable control over the end price, but you are responsible for all shipping and handling costs.

Pros & Cons

Most auction sites have some built-in protection for sellers. The bottom line for you, however, is covering all your expenses. And be aware: Some fraud does occur.

Since there is no long-term commitment, you can experiment with different items to see what sells best for you and get almost instant feedback. **$**

Preparation

1. Trace pattern sections onto tracing paper; flip over and retrace lines on wrong side with pencil.

2. Drill small hole into but not through base in one corner; hole should be large enough to hold pencil snugly.

3. Sand all wood pieces; wipe off dust with tack cloth.

Base-coating

1. Referring to instructions for base-coating under "Painting Techniques" in General Instructions (page 190), use foam brush to base-coat entire base with Indian turquoise; let dry. Sand lightly; remove dust with tack cloth.

2. Slightly dampen sponge square and dip into a little bright green; tap sponge up and down on palette a few times to evenly distribute paint. Gently tap color around center hole of base using up-and-down motion.

3. Base-coat top half of post with turquoise and bottom half with bright green. Using method described in step 5, sponge turquoise over post where green and turquoise meet. Colors should appear to blend gradually.

4. Using foam brush and yellow, paint interior of mailbox including inside of door; let dry. Sand lightly; remove dust with tack cloth. Apply a second coat; let dry.

5. Using foam brush, apply turquoise to underside of mailbox. Measure up 3½" from bottom of mailbox; lightly mark this point all around mailbox and paint area below line with turquoise. Base-coat top (curve) of mailbox with yellow; base-coat unpainted band around middle of mailbox with bright green.

6. Using method described in step 5, sponge bright green along lines where turquoise and green meet, and again where green and yellow meet, gently graduating and blending colors as for post. Let dry.

Transferring Patterns

1. Center patterns on sides, back and door. Using stylus, trace over main lines only to transfer them to mailbox.

2. *Door:* Using #2 round, paint small leaves leaf green; let dry. Add dark green shading to base of each leaf and bright green highlighting to each

Suggestion Box Side

tip; let dry. Using #2 liner, paint lettering black.

3. *Flower stems and leaves:* Using round brushes, base-coat with leaf green. Load long-bristled side of angular shader with dark green and apply as shading to one side of each leaf and stem. Clean brush, then load long-bristled side with bright green and apply as highlighting to opposite side of each leaf and stem.

4. *Flower petals:* Using round brushes, apply two coats white to all petals; let dry. Load one side of angular shader with thinned turquoise; apply color to base of petals next to flower centers. Using #2 liner, pull some of this shading onto petals near each fold line.

5. *Flower faces:* Using #10 round, base-coat each flower center with white; let dry. Apply two coats pineapple over base-coated areas; let dry. Using angular shader, float pumpkin shading around edges of faces; let dry.

Transfer pattern details to faces as needed. Paint noses pumpkin with #2 round brush. Apply a touch of blush to each cheek by rubbing them with a bit of red pastel chalk. Fill mouths with black using #2 round brush and leaving tongues yellow. Use #0 liner and black to add eyes, smiles, outlining and details. Let dry completely.

Finishing

1. Spray all sections with two or three coats sealer, letting it dry between coats.

2. Attach notepad to door, using double-sided tape if desired.

3. Insert turquoise end of post in bottom of mailbox; insert remaining end in base.

4. Place sharpened pencil in hole in corner of base. ✂

Original or Imitation?

Every designer, professional crafter and hobbyist must be very careful not to infringe on the copyrights of another individual or publisher.

For years, we've heard the rumor that if you change 10 percent of a design, or three parts of a design, you may claim it as your own. However, as is the case with most rumors, there is no legal foundation for this notion.

What Is Original?

An original design is one you create on your own merits or using your own skills. Motifs and techniques are not copyrighted, so anyone can use them.

Many talented people have created soft-sculpture dolls; however, no one may copy the Cabbage Patch Kids. You are allowed to use a licensed pattern to make a Cabbage Patch Kid for personal use or to give as a gift. But you may not sell that doll, or profit from it in any way.

Perhaps you aren't yet confident in your ability, or comfortable with a particular technique; you might work from published patterns to build your skills. But you may not sell that work for profit unless you have written permission from the designer or publisher.

Limited Use

Some publishers allow restricted use of their designs and patterns by the professional crafter. But this doesn't include commercial use—only a limited production of handmade items.

A wonderful example of this rule of thumb is the use of rubber stamps in craft designs. If you were to use a hand-stamped image on a greeting card from the rubber stamp manufacturer, you are allowed to sell the finished product in a limited number (which varies from manufacturer to manufacturer). Most rubber stamp manufacturers allow an average of 30 exact images to be used for resale.

There are some exceptions. Stay away from licensed designs like Disney or Marvel Comics. It's also a good idea to ask the rubber stamp manufacturer for permission to use the stamped image.

Know the Law

Copies of U.S. copyright laws are available from the Library of Congress, your local library and on the Internet. It's a good idea to be familiar with the copyright laws, both as a hobbyist and as a professional.

There may come a time when you will wish to file a copyright for a design or group of designs. That's one of the reasons I'm so adamant that professionals know the law.

Litigated disputes over copyrights and infringements are becoming commonplace. The only way to protect your interests and have a hope of winning is to be well-documented and prepared. **$**

Smiling Stars Ornaments

These adorable stars are a perfect gift for a child or teenager! Make up at least a dozen or so of these as they're sure to sell quickly!

Design by Delores F. Ruzicka

Materials

- Tacky craft glue
- Cornstarch
- 2 plastic foam stars*
- Acrylic craft paints*: coral rose, golden straw, titanium white, yellow light
- Paintbrushes: #2, ¾" wash brush
- Matte-finish spray sealer
- Black fine-point permanent pen
- 2" 20-gauge wire
- Disposable bowl

Plastifoam stars from Syndicate Sales; Americana paints from DecoArt.

Instructions

1. In bowl combine 1 cup glue and 1 cup cornstarch; stir until flaky. Knead mixture with hands until it is the consistency of clay, gradually adding more glue or cornstarch as needed.

2. Mold a ball of clay about the size of a large walnut; flatten it with your hands until it is about ⅛" thick, then mold it to the foam star (it will adhere). Continue until entire star is covered. Smooth clay with your fingers. **Note:** *Any unused clay should be stored at room temperature in an airtight, self-sealing bag; it air-dries very hard.*

3. *Hanger:* Poke end of wire through point of star; shape wire into hanging loop. Let star dry overnight (drying time may vary depending on humidity). Turn star over; let other side dry.

4. Coat star with yellow paint using wash brush; let dry and add a second coat, if necessary; let dry. Shade edges with golden straw; let dry.

5. Lightly pencil facial features on star if necessary. Using #2 brush, paint eyes white and heart-shaped cheeks coral rose; add coral rose mouth. Let dry.

6. Using black marker, outline eyes and add pupils and eyelashes; add nose; let dry.

7. Add tiny white highlight dots to eyes and cheeks; let dry.

8. Spray star with sealer; let dry. ✂

Magical Webbed Accessories

Make this beautiful, decorative set with simple webbing. You're sure to impress your customers with this eye-catching collection.

Designs by Joan Fee

Materials

- Gold chiffon webbing spray*
- Blue pillar candle
- Gold candle plate
- Blue vase
- Blue mercury glass ornament
- Strands of gold and blue beads

Krylon Webbing Spray

Instructions

1. Vigorously shake can of webbing spray for two minutes *after* mixing balls begin to rattle.

2. *Apply webbing spray to candle, plate, vase and ornament:* Hold can 18" above object or surface to be sprayed, pointing spray nozzle valve above and to one side of it. Start spray off to left and stop off to right, sweeping across surface fairly quickly. Try to spray webbing into the air and allow it to fall onto surface.

3. Turn object slightly; spray again. Repeat until desired look is achieved. Set objects aside to dry.

4. Immediately clean spray valve on can by turning can upside down and spraying until no webbing escapes. Let dry.

5. Tie a strand of gold beads around neck of vase. Place candle in holder; arrange strand of blue beads around base. ✂

Set Up Shop on the World Wide Web

It's easier than ever to create your own Web site. Try one of the user-friendly software programs available at computer stores; there are even simple-to-understand tutorials on the Web.

You'll have to register a Web address and create your Web pages from there. There are many resources, from books to other Web sites, that can help you with the details. If you prefer a simple Web site, you can be up and running for under $500.

Hire a Pro

Or, you might prefer to hire a Web master—a professional designer of Web sites and Web pages—to create your site.

Research different craft Web sites that appeal to you; somewhere within the sites, a Web master may be listed. Usually for a set fee, the Web master can handle everything from digital photography to setting up secure forms for online orders.

Cost can vary greatly. In most cases, you will be charged a flat fee for a specific service, such as applying for the Web address, or designing a set number of pages with a set number of graphics. You'll be billed separately for additional services. **$**

Is the Internet Right for You?

As with any other marketplace, you need to check out a few things when selling from the Web.

Visibilty

How many potential buyers are finding your site or pages?

You can have a "counter" placed on your site's home page to record how many people drop in. Your Web master can offer other options for keeping track of your site traffic.

And if you are part of a larger site, the owner should be able to tell you how many "hits" a page has had; that is, how many times a person has at least stopped at the page.

Online Ordering

Is your typical customer secure and confident enough to order online—or do you want to include a phone number or fax number for receiving orders?

Taking Care of Business

Are you prepared for the tasks of invoicing, packing, shipping and collecting payment from any sales from the Web site? This takes some serious organization; you may have to collect state sales tax even if the buyer is from outside your state.

Advertising vs. Sales

Do you intend to use your Web site or pages as promotional/advertising tools rather than for online sales?

Teachers, demonstrators and craft designers often use a Web site to promote their talents and availability. It's a good way to tell the world you are available.

Why limit yourself by selling only finished products when you might enjoy teaching or designing for publication? **$**

Joyful Picnic Table Centerpiece

Take a turn from the traditional with this classy picnic centerpiece. Onlookers will be drawn to your booth by its creativity and vibrant color!

Design by June Fiechter

Materials

- 10" square wooden frame with 3" square opening*
- 4 wooden pillar legs*
- 3" square jar candle
- Wood glue
- 1 sheet dark purple threaded art paper*
- Alphabet letters*
- Acrylic craft paints: baby blue, green
- Matte-finish decoupage finish*
- 2-step eggshell crackle medium*
- Satin-finish exterior sealer
- Glazing medium*
- Sandpaper
- Cotton-tip swab

Frame #3587 from Walnut Hollow; pillar legs #75038 from Plaid; Threaded Dark Tone Purple Paper from Embossing Arts; Whimsical Alphabet #MW-Sheet from K & Co.; Mod Podge decoupage finish, Eggshell Crackle Medium and Glazing Medium, all from Plaid.

Instructions

1. Glue legs to corners of back of frame; let dry.

2. Paint all wooden surfaces baby blue; let dry.

3. Measure and mark four 1¼" x 6" rectangles on purple paper. Using cotton-tip swab moistened with water, carefully rub over drawn lines. Then, carefully tear out rectangles along moistened lines.

4. Using decoupage finish, attach paper rectangles to top of frame as shown, about ½"–¾" from edge, brushing paper from center out to create fringe.

5. Position letters to spell "Joy," "Hope," "Rest" and "Love" on top of rectangles; attach with decoupage finish, then coat entire top surface with decoupage finish.

6. Following manufacturer's instructions, paint top of frame with crackle medium.

7. Mix equal parts glazing medium and green paint to make stain; rub stain over crackles, working on a small area at a time and rubbing off excess with paper towel as you work. Continue staining over sides and down legs. Let dry.

8. Sand edges and legs of frame, sanding down to bare wood in some spots.

9. Paint project with several coats of exterior sealer, letting sealer dry between coats.

10. Insert candle in opening. ✁

Business Credentials

There are a few items of paperwork that you should have to support your work in any marketplace. The proper credentials help establish you as a legitimate business in the eyes of customers, suppliers and the business community.

- *Business licenses*

State, city and/or county licenses, where applicable.

- *Résumé*

This should include your listing name, contact address, contact numbers like phone, fax, e-mail; photo of yourself and of your work; a listing of shows and other markets in which you've participated; and your company's mission statement. The résumé is your advertisement, your foot in the door that introduces you to potential buyers.

- *Portfolio*

This is a "picture book" of your accomplishments, awards and items for sale. The photos need not be professionally done, but make sure they are sharply focused, with good contrast and accurate color, and that they show your product(s) from different angles. Include measurements if photos do not show proportions.

- *Business cards*

Make your card unique. It must include your business name as well as your own, your contact address and phone number. If you have an e-mail or Web site, always include it on your business card and all other business materials.

- *Letterhead*

This usually is designed to match the business card. It is a must for all business and professional correspondence.

- *Business checking account*

No business should be without one. It is also highly recommended to have a business savings account. Consult your accountant, lawyer, bank or savings institution on all small-business matters. Do not use your personal savings or checking account. Never mix personal and business funds, and never borrow from your business accounts for personal reasons unless it is a true emergency.

- *Copy of resale or tax collection certificate*

Keep a copy on hand at all times when selling or making a sales presentation if your state collects sales tax.

- *Copy of a supplier invoice and a customer invoice*

This is a basic requirement of most trade shows. You'll need them to fill out credit information for your suppliers of raw materials. **$**

Martini Set

Bring the party to your booth with this bright and creative set! It makes a perfect wedding gift or a great addition to any kitchen.

Design by Samantha McNesby

Materials

- Set of 4 martini glasses
- 4 (4") white ceramic tiles
- Air-dry glass paints*: beyond turquoise, celestial, fuchsia, marshmallow, tangerine
- Metallic gold air-dry paint pen*
- Air-dry clear glossy sealer
- Paintbrushes: ¼" and ½" flats
- 1" masking tape
- 9" x 12" sheet blue felt (optional)
- Thick white craft glue (optional)

*PermEnamel air-drying paints, Accent Liner pen from Delta.

Glasses

1. Clean glasses thoroughly to remove fingerprints, dust, etc. Let dry.

2. *Base-coat:* Mask off top and bottom of stem; paint all remaining areas tangerine, leaving an even ⅝"-wide unpainted band around rim of glass. Let dry; repeat with second coat. Let dry. Remove tape; paint masked-off areas on stem marshmallow.

3. Repeat with remaining glasses, painting one fuchsia, one turquoise, and the fourth blue. Let dry completely.

4. *Squares:* Using ¼" brush, add marshmallow squares around top and base of each glass. Squares need not be perfect but should be evenly spaced. Let dry.

5. *"Beaded" trim:* Use gold pen to add dimensional paint "beads" to glasses just above squares on base and below squares at top of glass: Touch tip of pen to glass and squeeze with gentle pressure; release pressure and lift pen, leaving "bead" of paint. Let dry overnight.

6. Using ½" brush, apply sealer to all painted surfaces; let dry. Let glasses cure for 10 days before washing.

Coasters

1. Clean tiles thoroughly to remove fingerprints, dust, etc. Let dry.

2. Crumple several paper towels. Using ½" brush, paint top and sides of one tile tangerine; quickly pat with crumpled paper towel to remove some of the paint. Continue patting tile, replacing towel as needed, until desired effect is achieved.

3. Repeat with remaining tiles, painting one fuchsia, one turquoise and one blue. Let dry completely.

4. *Squares:* Using ¼" brush, add marshmallow squares around perimeter of tile, continuing stripes down sides. These need not be perfect, but should be evenly spaced. Let dry.

5. *"Beaded" trim:* Referring to step 5 for glasses, add row of dimensional paint "beads" to tiles just inside squares.

6. Using ½" brush, apply sealer to all painted surfaces; let dry. Let cure for 10 days before washing.

7. *Optional:* Cut four 4¾" squares from felt; glue one to bottom of each coaster. Let dry. ✂

Sign on the Dotted Line, Please

Whether it's a craft show or craft mall, most marketplaces require some form of contract. But before you enter into any kind of a legal agreement, take the time to visit any craft mall, consignment shop, co-op (considered storefronts) or craft show as a customer first. This will give you insight into how your potential customers are treated.

At the end of your visit, if you like what you see, inquire about additional details. Consider the following questions before you sign on the dotted line. (And yes, a craft show application is a legal document!)

For Both Storefronts & Shows

1. How long has the storefront or show been active? The longer the better!

2. How much promotion and advertising is done? The more the better!

3. Is it in a good location with lots of traffic and easily visible from the street?

4. Are there other vendors that will be direct competition for you?

Additional Considerations for Storefronts

1. Do you receive your checks for items sold weekly, monthly or quarterly? Is the storefront's statement easy to understand, and do they practice inventory control?

2. Can you network with the other vendors? Some storefronts hold monthly meetings for their vendors.

3. Are you given options for the length of the lease? Can you avoid long-term commitments until you get a feel for how your work is selling?

4. Does the storefront have special events or promotions, like a spring open house or private Christmas show for loyal customers? **$**

Fruit Coasters

These will sell no matter what the season, and they are within almost everyone's price range.

Designs by June Fiechter

Materials

- 4 round plastic coasters with cork centers
- Acrylic mosaic pieces*: cobalt, jade, light rose, light tiger coral, rose, tiger coral, violet
- Silicon glue
- Ivory grout
- Wicker white acrylic craft paint
- Flat paintbrush
- Plastic paints*: fudge brown, metallic gold
- Matte-finish decoupage finish*
- Brown felt
- Tacky craft glue

Clearly Mosaics marbleized acrylic pieces from The Beadery; Paint for Plastic and Mod Podge decoupage finish from Plaid.

Instructions

1. Paint cork surface wicker white; let dry.

2. Referring to patterns, arrange mosaic pieces in coasters. On samples, lemon is light coral; pear is coral with single light coral highlight; grapes are mixture of rose, light rose and violet hexagonal tiles; and strawberry is rose with a couple of light rose tiles for highlights; all leaves are jade and backgrounds are cobalt. Secure pieces with silicone; let dry.

3. Referring to package directions, apply grout over mosaics; let dry.

4. Prepare rims of coaster as directed by instructions on bottles of plastic paints. Paint coaster rims brown, then dab on gold; let dry as directed.

5. Apply at least one coat of decoupage finish to coaster rims; let dry.

6. Cut felt circles to fit bottoms of coasters; glue in place. ✂

Patterns continued on page 71

Ladybug Welcome

Welcome customers to your stand with this charming ladybug sign. They'll be sure to want to take one home!

Design by Paula Bales for Dow Chemical

Materials

- 4 (2½"–3") plastic foam eggs*
- 4⅞" x 11⅞" x ¹³⁄₁₆" plastic foam slab*
- 18" green plastic foam swag*
- Serrated knife
- Tacky craft glue
- Acrylic craft paints*: cadmium yellow, kelly green, lamp black, Santa red, titanium white
- 22-gauge licorice wire
- Wire cutters
- Rubber cement
- Paintbrushes: #4 shader, #8, #1 liner
- 11" x 4" plaid paper
- 9½" x 3" yellow paper

STYROFOAM® brand plastic foam is a product of Dow Chemical; Americana acrylic paints from DecoArt.

Instructions

1. Cut jagged edge in top of swag for grass; paint swag green; let dry. Outline grass with black; using end of paintbrush handle dipped in paint, dot on white flowers with yellow centers.

2. *Ladybugs:* Cut eggs in half. Using handle of paintbrush, press indentation to delineate head and body, and another down middle of back to delineate wings.

3. Paint bodies red; paint heads black with white eyes. Let dry, then dot black dots on bodies and white eyes.

4. *Antennae:* Cut seven 4" pieces wire; bend each in half and curl ends. Poke and glue an antenna into indentation between head and body on each ladybug.

5. Paint foam slab white; let dry. Glue plaid and yellow papers in center. Paint "Welcome" in black; highlight with red.

6. Glue ladybugs to grass and sign.

7. Cut two 10" pieces wire; poke and twist through sign and swag to connect them. ✂

Formal Business Pricing Formula

The standard business pricing formula is Cost of Goods (COG) + Labor + Overhead = Selling Price.

The COG should include the cost of every supply used to create the item. Many professional crafters just estimate the COG, but you should take the time to break down every supply used, including that drop of glue or scrap of ribbon.

Consider the following sample formula for beaded bracelets.

Cost of Goods Per Bracelet

10" elastic string	$ .35
80 beads	$1.50
Clasp	$ .37
Dab of glue	$ .03
Total Cost of Goods	$2.25

Bug Patio Ware

Colorful flowers and bugs will make this set a top seller. Market items as sets or as individual pieces depending on the demand.

Design by Barbara Matthiessen

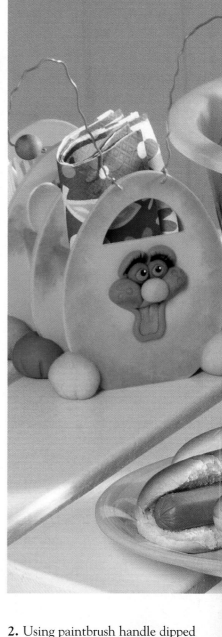

Materials

- Acrylic or plastic bowl, pitcher, tumblers, salt and pepper shakers
- Plastic paints*: black, bright red, bright yellow, fuchsia, green, green apple, lime, turquoise, white
- Primer for plastic paints*
- Sealer for plastic paints*
- Bug and flower stencils*
- White vinegar
- Painter's tape
- Assorted stencil and liner brushes
- 1" foam brush

Paint for Plastic paints, primer and sealer, and Simply Stencils Garden Critters #28136 and From the Garden #28220 stencils all from Plaid.

Preparation

1. Wash all plastic/acrylic pieces with soap and water; dry, then wipe with white vinegar to remove all residues, traces of detergent and oils, etc. Let dry.

2. Referring to manufacturer's instructions, apply primer to plastic ware; let dry as directed.

Stenciling & Painting Guidelines

1. Tape stencils in place; if stenciling over a painted surface, check to make sure tape will not lift off paint when you remove stencil.

2. Using a separate brush for each color, dab on colors with an up-and-down motion; let dry. Samples were painted as follows:

Ladybugs: red body, black head and antennae.

Bees: white wings, yellow body, black head.

Butterflies: yellow wings, black body.

Dragonflies: white wings, turquoise body.

Flowers: fuchsia petals, lime leaves.

3. Add second and third coats if necessary for complete coverage; let dry.

4. Coat with sealer at this point, or add details with small and/or liner brush(es) and let dry completely. Samples were detailed as follows:

Ladybugs: Using black, paint stripe down center of back; dot on spots with paintbrush handle dipped in paint.

Bees: Add black stripes and antennae.

Butterflies: Add black details, outlining corners of wings, small lines radiating from body onto wings, antennae and dots on wings.

Dragonflies: Add turquoise line along underside of each wing; using black, dot on eyes and add antennae.

Flowers: Stroke white and fuchsia out from center; dot center with yellow.

Pitcher

1. Using round brush and/or liner, stroke first darkest green, then lighter greens up from base for grass, allowing paints to blend and overlap by turning your brush as you stroke on the paints. Let dry.

2. Stencil and detail bugs on sides of pitcher. Let dry.

3. Apply sealer to painted surfaces, following manufacturer's instructions. Let cure as directed.

4. Wash by hand as needed.

Salt & Pepper Shakers

1. Stencil and detail ladybugs on one shaker and bees on another.

2. Using paintbrush handle dipped in paint, dot clusters of two red dots and one black between ladybugs, and clusters of two white dots and one yellow between bees; let dry. Add "flight paths" of dotted or dashed black lines behind bugs, if desired. Let dry.

3. Apply sealer to painted surfaces, following manufacturer's instructions. Let cure as directed.

4. Wash by hand as needed.

Tumblers

1. Paint 3" x 2½" leaves on tumblers with green apple; outline and add veins with green. Let dry.

2. Stencil and detail ladybugs and butterflies on tumblers; let dry.

3. Apply sealer to painted surfaces, following manufacturer's instructions. Let cure as directed.

4. Wash by hand as needed.

Bowl

1. Stencil and detail four fuchsia flowers, including small flowers and lime leaves, evenly spaced around bowl. Shade leaves with green apple. Let dry.

2. Stencil and detail four pairs of butterflies and four dragonflies, evenly spaced, around bowl. Let dry.

3. Apply sealer to painted surfaces, following manufacturer's instructions. Let cure as directed.

4. Wash by hand as needed. ✂

Discount Supplies

The following companies have set up quantities and minimums with the heavy user or professional crafter in mind:

CreateForLess
P.O. Box 2230
Beaverton, OR 97075
(866) 333-4463
www.createforless.com

Marasco's Craft King
12750 W. Capital Dr.
Brooksfield, WI 53005
(262) 781-9660
www.craftking.com

National Artcraft
7996 Darrow Rd.
Twinsburg, OH 44087
(888) 937-2723
www.nationalartcraft.com

Zim's
4370 S. 300 W.
Salt Lake City, UT 84107
(801) 268-2505
www.zimscrafts.com

Happy Helper Picnic Worm

Delight kids and adults alike with this whimsical worm for picnicking, or use it as a fun home accent.

Design by June Fiechter

Materials

- Soft polymer clay*: golden yellow, green dayglow, orange, turquoise, violet
- 18-gauge neon blue plastic-coated wire*
- 3 wooden egg-shaped pocket containers*
- False eyelashes
- Wood glue
- Tacky craft glue
- Acrylic craft paints*: bright green, lamp black, titanium white, yellow green
- Satin-finish varnish
- Needle-nose pliers
- Fine-grit sandpaper
- Waxed paper
- Baking sheet
- Oven
- Toothpick
- Craft drill with small bit
- Paintbrush
- Powdered cosmetic blusher
- Sandpaper

*Fimo Soft polymer clay and Fun Wire, both from Amaco; Egg Pocketful containers from Provo Craft; Americana acrylic paints from DecoArt.

Instructions

1. *Body:* Glue pocket containers together with wood glue; let dry. Sand rough edges; wipe off dust.

2. Paint containers yellow green; let dry. Shade outer edges with bright green.

3. *Feet:* Cut off three-quarters of yellow clay chunk; cut this piece in half and roll each half into a ball. Press onto base of egg to create indentation; use a toothpick to create toes.

4. Repeat step 3 with turquoise, orange and violet clays.

5. Carefully place feet on baking sheet lined with waxed paper.

6. From remaining violet clay, roll two ¾" balls for antennae and two round, flat ⁵⁄₁₆" eyeballs. Using toothpick, pierce ¾" balls to make "beads"; lay all pieces on waxed paper on baking sheet.

7. *Referring to pattern throughout, form face on waxed-paper–lined baking sheet:* Roll two ½" balls green clay; press smaller violet eyeballs on top. Roll ¾" ball yellow clay for nose. Roll two 1" balls green clay for cheeks. Shape and position them so that they appear to be raised in a smile.

8. Roll 3" log of green clay about ⅛" in diameter for lower lip. For tongue, break off a small chunk of orange; shape and press into space between cheeks and lower lip. Add groove down tongue with toothpick.

9. Roll six tiny balls of orange clay for freckles; press onto cheeks. Roll two narrow logs of green clay 1" long for eyebrows; arch them and position above eyes.

10. Referring to manufacturer's instructions, bake clay face, feet and beads for antennae and let cool.

11. Using tacky glue throughout, glue feet and face to body.

12. Cut two 8" pieces wire; bend to crimp every ½", then straighten out slightly. Drill two tiny holes at top of front (face) egg, run ends of wire antennae through holes and twist to secure. Thread violet beads (step 6) onto ends of antennae and crimp wire to hold them in place.

13. Cut one strand of eyelashes in half; glue one piece over each eye. Apply blusher to cheeks and nose with fingertip.

14. Apply a dot of black paint to each eyeball and let dry; apply tinier highlight dot of white; let dry.

15. Coat project with varnish; let dry. ✂

Don't Labor Over Labor Fees!

You can decide your labor fee in one of two ways. The first is to pay for labor by the hour. Try to be realistic here; we all would love to earn $25 or even $100 dollars per hour, but that is not the going rate of most manufacturers.

You can always give yourself a raise as your business grows, but try to start out around minimum wage, or what your local economic community is averaging.

You can also calculate labor "piecemeal," or by the piece. For this method, simply calculate labor costs using a set rate per piece you create. **$**

Happy Helper Picnic Worm

Fancy Gourd Birdhouses

Add variations in color and accents to these delightful birdhouses to entice your customers. Items like these are a great way to enter a specialty crafting area.

Designs by June Fiechter

Strawberry Birdhouse

Materials

- 7" dried birdhouse gourd* with 1¼" hole drilled in side near top
- Heavy-test fishing line for hanger
- Craft drill and small bit
- True red acrylic paint
- Metallic acrylic paints*: royal ruby, crystal green, glorious gold
- Sealer
- Satin-finish varnish
- ¼" paintbrush
- Soft cloth
- Gold wire: 24" 16-gauge, 2" 22-gauge
- Needle-nose pliers
- Green polymer clay
- 3½" plastic leaf
- Cornstarch
- Natural raffia
- Craft glue
- Woodburning tool with stencil-cutting tip*
- Waxed paper
- 3 small oven-safe bowls
- Wooden spoon
- Sharp knife
- Baking sheet
- Oven

Gourd from Gourd Central; Dazzling Metallics paints from DecoArt; Walnut Hollow woodburning tool.

Preparation

1. Coat gourd with sealer; let dry.

2. Drill two small holes 2" apart in top of birdhouse (bottom of gourd). Run ends of fishing line for hanger down through holes and out through larger hole in front; knot. Pull hanging loop up at top.

3. Wrap 22-gauge wire around strands of hanger near surface of gourd.

Leaves

1. Place bowls upside down on baking sheet.

2. Lay plastic leaf on waxed paper, bottom facing up. Sprinkle leaf with cornstarch; dust off excess.

3. Cover leaf with thin, even layer of clay. Turn over; trim excess compound with knife; gently peel away leaf. Drape molded leaf over bowl. Repeat to make a total of three leaves.

4. Bake leaves according to manufacturer's instructions; let cool before removing from bowls.

Painting

1. Paint gourd with red acrylic paint; let dry.

2. Using woodburning tool fitted with stencil-cutting tip, burn small, teardrop-shaped "seeds" over surface of gourd.

3. Using a soft cloth, apply ruby metallic paint over painted surface, avoiding seeds; let dry.

4. Apply green metallic paint to leaves; remove excess with soft cloth; let dry.

5. Using soft cloth, apply gold highlights to leaves and strawberry; let dry.

Assembly

1. Glue leaves around top of birdhouse. **Note:** *Do not cover holes drilled for hanger.*

2. Varnish birdhouse and leaves; let dry.

3. Cut 16-gauge wire in half; coil each piece around wooden spoon handle; slide off and expand coils. Glue one end of each tendril into one of the holes drilled for attaching hanger; arrange as desired.

4. Tie raffia into bow and glue to top of birdhouse to hide space between leaves.

Floral & Fruit Gourd Birdhouse

Materials

- Mexican bottle gourd*
- 20" twine string
- Craft drill with 1¼" and ¼" bits
- Natural raffia
- Wood stain*
- 4 orange-slice halves
- 4 yellow silk flowers
- Tiny white filler flowers
- 4 small pinecones
- Hot-glue gun
- Keyhole saw (optional)
- Sandpaper
- Fruit preservation and glazing kit*
- Clear coating*

Gourd from The Gourd Factory; Aleene's wood stain #AW105 from Duncan; Fruit Preservation & Glazing Kit from Syndicate Sales; UV-Resistant Clear Coating #1035 from Krylon.

Instructions

1. "Dry" and preserve the orange slices following manufacturer's instructions from preservation and glazing kit.

2. Saw or drill 1¼" hole near top of bottom half in gourd; sand edges smooth.

3. Stain gourd following stain manufacturer's instructions.

4. Drill two ¼" holes near top of gourd about 1¼" from stem on opposite sides; thread twine through holes and knot ends to make hanging loop.

5. Wrap several strands of raffia around neck of gourd; knot at front (over opening) and leave ends protruding.

6. Hot-glue flowers, orange slices and pinecones around gourd over raffia. Arrange, shred, fray and trim ends of raffia as desired.

7. Spray entire project with clear coating. ✂

Summer Garden Birdhouse & Wall Urn

Show your artistic side with creative painted projects. Customers will love the care and personal touches you put into them!

Designs by Vicki Schreiner

Ladybug Terra-Cotta Birdhouse

Materials

- Large (5½" x 7½") round terra-cotta birdhouse*
- Acrylic craft paints*: brown velvet, butter yellow, dark foliage green, eucalyptus, tompte red, white
- Satin finish exterior-interior varnish
- Clear glaze base*
- Paintbrushes: #3 round, #4 and ½" flats, #1 liner
- Black fine-line pen
- Removable tape
- Graphite transfer paper
- Toothpick
- Ballpoint pen
- Fine-grit sandpaper

Birdhouse #20-5263 from Provo Craft; Ceramcoat paints and Ceramcoat Clear Glaze Base from Delta.

Surface Preparation

Referring to directions for "Using Transfer & Graphite Paper" (General Instructions, page 190), transfer patterns 1–7 randomly over surface of birdhouse, tracing over designs with ballpoint pen and using removable tape to hold patterns in place. Do not transfer stippling dots; these are for your reference in shading. Mistakes can be removed by gently rubbing with fine-grit sandpaper.

Painting

1. Using #3 round or #4 flat brush as needed, base-coat areas as follows: leaves: *eucalyptus;* flower petals: *white;* flower centers: *yellow;* ladybug bodies: *red.*

2. *Shading:* Mix equal parts glaze base with dark green and brown paints, then add a little more glaze base. Using #4 flat brush, shade leaves with dark green mixture, and petals and flower centers with brown. Let dry, then repeat applications to darken as necessary.

3. Using ½" flat brush, apply one coat varnish to entire birdhouse; let dry.

4. Using fine tip of black pen, outline all designs and add dots to ladybugs;

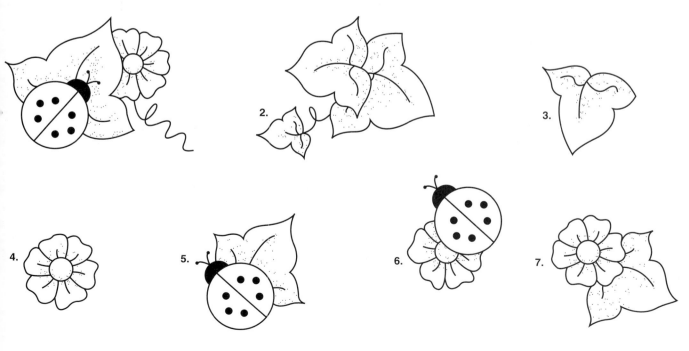

Ladybug Terra-Cotta Birdhouse

fill in ladybugs' heads and randomly add tiny stippling dots around each flower center.

5. Mix equal parts glaze base and brown paint. Using #4 flat brush, shade area below each design to create a shadow. **Note:** *This step must be done at this point and not at the same time as other shading described in step 2. The bare clay would absorb the moisture too quickly to achieve a soft, shadowing effect.*

6. Using #1 liner, apply small white comma stroke to right side of each flower center. (See "Painting Techniques".)

7. Using toothpick dipped in white, add tiny dot to each black dot on ladybugs. Let dry.

8. Using ½" flat brush, apply one coat varnish to entire birdhouse.

Dragonfly Wall Urn

Materials

- Small (4¾" x 5¼") terra-cotta urn*
- Acrylic craft paints*: Bridgeport grey, brown velvet, bungalow blue, butter yellow, dark foliage green, eucalyptus, opaque blue, white
- Satin finish exterior-interior varnish
- Clear glaze base*
- Paintbrushes: #3 round, #4 and ½" flats, #1 liner
- Black fine-line pen

- Removable tape
- Graphite transfer paper
- Toothpick
- Ballpoint pen
- Fine-grit sandpaper

Herb urn #20-5297 from Provo Craft; Ceramcoat paints and Ceramcoat Clear Glaze Base from Delta.

Project Note

In addition to the patterns given here, leaf and flower patterns 2, 3, 4

Recommended Reading

Art Marketing 101: A Handbook for the Fine Artist by Constance Smith (ArtNetwork)

The Artist in Business from Arts Extension Service/Continuing Education (University of Massachusetts/Amherst)

The Business of Crafts from The Crafts Center (Watson-Guptill Publications)

The Designer's Common Sense Business Book by Barbara Ganim (North Light Books)

Marketing Your Arts & Crafts by Janice West (The Summit Group)

Profitable Crafts Marketing: A Complete Guide to Successful Selling by Brian T. Jefferson (Timber Press)

Promoting & Marketing Your Crafts by Edwin M. Field and Selma G. Field (Macmillan Publishing Company)

Working From Home by Paul and Sarah Edwards (Putnam) **$**

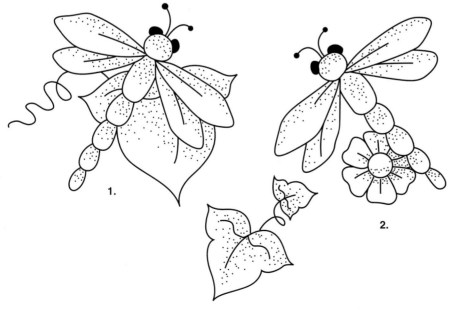

and 7 from the Ladybug Terra-Cotta Birdhouse (page 61) are also used.

Surface Preparation

Refer to Surface Preparation instructions for "Ladybug Terra-Cotta Birdhouse."

Painting

1. Using #3 round or #4 flat brush as needed, base-coat areas as follows: leaves: eucalyptus; flower petals and dragonfly wings: white; flower centers: yellow; dragonfly bodies: bungalow blue.

2. *Shading:* Mix equal parts glaze base with dark green, brown, grey and opaque blue paints, then add a little more glaze base. Using #4 flat brush, shade leaves with dark green mixture, petals and flower centers with brown, dragonfly bodies with grey and wings with blue. Let dry, then repeat applications to darken as necessary.

3. Using ½" flat brush, apply one coat varnish to entire urn; let dry.

4. Using fine tip of black pen, outline all designs; fill in dragonflies' eyes and randomly add tiny stippling dots around each flower center.

5. Mix equal parts glaze base and brown paint. Using #4 flat brush, shade area below each design to create a shadow. **Note:** *This step must be done at this point and not at the same time as other shading described in step 2. The bare clay would absorb the moisture too quickly to achieve a soft, shadowing effect.*

6. Using #1 liner, apply small white comma stroke to right side of each flower center. (See "Painting Techniques.")

7. Using ½" flat brush, apply one coat varnish to entire birdhouse. ✂

Best Price?

A great deal of research has gone into the subject of prices. Most research indicates that prices ending in a five or nine—$2.75, $3.99, etc.—work! Consider this when pricing your work. A craft might sell faster at $9.95 than $10. It may seem silly, but it's true! **$**

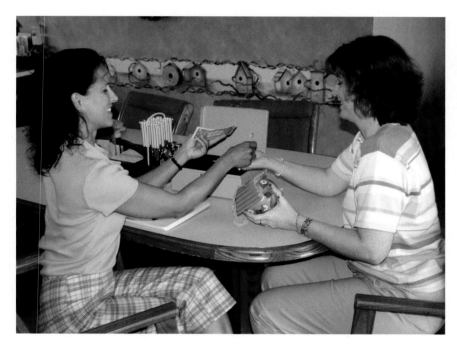

Crafter's Success Story
Annie Lang

Seven years after exhibiting at my first craft show, I launched my home-based business, Annie Things Possible. I operated the retail end of my business from a local co-op gift store where I was eventually joined by 27 other crafters offering a wide variety of handcrafted specialty items and services to local customers and visiting tourists.

Participating in a co-op offered numerous advantages. Each business had control over pricing, and entering businesses were juried to prevent conflict-of-interest issues. It was an affordable way to operate a small business without overhead and the expense of running an individual storefront.

We were able to purchase wholesale supplies collectively, which made it easier to meet minimum order requirements. We shared new craft techniques and information about trends. We voted on issues of mutual concern, shared costly advertising expenses and worked the counter on a rotating basis.

Most co-op members, including myself, continued to participate in local craft fairs, bringing in new customers and craft business through word-of-mouth. ✂

Silk Vegetable Basket & Wreath

These delightful pieces capture the essence of a country garden and are great conversation pieces. Use painted or natural baskets to give customers a choice.

Designs by Elaine Pecora

Garden Grapevine Wreath

Materials

- 18" grapevine wreath
- Terra-cotta half-flowerpot
- 6 feet silk ivy garland
- 2 stems silk herbs
- 3 stems berry vine
- 2 lightweight garden hand tools
- 1 pair garden gloves
- Assorted seed packets
- Assorted miniature silk vegetables
- Large and miniature imitation tomatoes
- Spider-plant ribbon*
- 18-gauge wire
- Wire cutters
- Hot-glue gun

Ribbon from Regency.

Instructions

1. Draw outline of wreath on a sheet of newspaper; draw or scribble ivy garland on paper wreath. Arrange garden tools, vegetables, etc., on paper wreath, referring to photo for placement, or arranging items as desired.

2. Wire ivy to wreath, trimming off any excess. Save it to use later.

3. Attach half-flowerpot and hand tools.

4. Arrange berry vine as in photo.

5. Fill flowerpot with silk herb stems. Cut other herbs in pieces and place around wreath.

6. Glue seed packets and vegetables to ivy leaves and around hand tools. Create "levels" to make your arrangement more interesting.

7. Fashion ribbon into a bow; attach to wreath.

8. Fill any empty spots with silk greens or miniature vegetables.

9. Attach wire hanging loop to back of wreath.

Silk Vegetable Basket

Materials

- 12" wicker basket
- Clear spray-on acrylic coating*
- White spray paint*
- 3 (1" x 12") plastic foam disks*
- Long T-pins or corsage pins
- Tacky craft glue
- Assorted artificial garden vegetables (see Project Notes)
- 3 stems silk dusty miller
- Hot-glue gun (optional)
- Lazy susan (optional)

Acrylic Crystal Clear and paint from Krylon; foam disks from Syndicate Sale.

Project Notes

When selecting vegetables—silk, plastic or homemade—include two or three larger items to create a focal point. Use multiples of some vegetables to create a "fresh from the garden" look. Sample project used an eggplant, three mushrooms, two potatoes, two artichokes, two tomatoes, two bulbs garlic, a radish, carrot, lemon and pepper.

Working on a lazy susan will help you view your arrangement from all sides as you work. A hot-glue gun works very well, but take care that no glue will show on finished project.

Instructions

1. Spray-paint basket white; let dry, then add a coat of spray acrylic coating; let dry.

2. Layer and secure two foam disks in basket. Save the third to cut into wedges to create height for smaller vegetables.

Continued on page 67

Figuring Your Overhead

Overhead is usually calculated as a percentage of your cost of goods (COG) and labor.

Overhead percentage is a way to include in your selling price the cost of doing business that is not directly involved with COG or labor, such as utilities, phone, rent, travel expenses, show fees and other expenses you incur simply by being in business.

Keep It Under Control

All small businesses must keep tight control of overhead costs or they'll soon be out of business. You can't make a profit if you let overhead expenses get out of control.

Experts vary on what percentage overhead should be, but realistically, you can't allow overhead to total more than 25 percent of your price, and that's the high end; a better goal is 10–15 percent.

Sample Calculations

Let's say we're figuring the overhead and the final selling price for a rag doll.

Our overhead percentage is 10 percent (we run a tight ship!).

First, add COG ($5) and labor ($6): $5 + $6 = $11

To calculate the overhead figure, multiple that total by the overhead percentage: $11 × .10 = $1.10

To calculate your final selling price, remember the basic formula: COG + Labor + Overhead = Selling Price $5 + $6 + $1.10 = $12.10

Whimsical Wheelbarrow

Use this project to store some of your smaller related items to double your display and profit-making space!

Design by Annie Lang

Materials

- 23" x 9" x 9½" wooden wheelbarrow
- Sandpaper
- Tack cloth
- Acrylic craft paints*: antique mum, daisy cream, patio brick, sprout green, sunflower yellow, tiger lily orange
- Acrylic clear coat*
- 1" foam brush
- Paintbrushes: #8 flat shader, #1 liner, #2 and #10 pointed rounds
- Square cut from household sponge
- Transfer or graphite paper

Americana acrylic paints and clear coat from DecoArt.

Instructions

1. Sand wheelbarrow; remove dust with tack cloth.

2. Using foam brush and green, base-coat handles, bottom exterior, legs, wheel and interior of wheelbarrow; let dry. Sand lightly; wipe with tack cloth. Apply a second coat; let dry and sand.

3. Using foam brush and cream, base-coat unpainted surfaces of wheelbarrow including top edges; let dry. Sand lightly; wipe with tack cloth. Apply a second coat; let dry and sand.

4. Dampen sponge square slightly; dip into antique mum and pounce sponge up and down a few times to work paint into sponge. Pounce color

up and down over cream sides; let dry. Sand lightly and wipe with tack cloth.

5. Use photocopier to enlarge pattern 133 percent before transferring. Referring to instructions for "Using Transfer & Graphite Paper" (General Instructions, page 190), transfer pattern to side of wheelbarrow, continuing pattern as shown to fill side. Repeat on other side. Apply matching pattern to front end, and add border of squiggly lines and flowers across narrow back of wheelbarrow.

6. *Paint squares:* Using shader, paint every other square brick; let dry. Using liner, add narrow orange lines; let dry.

7. *Flowers:* Using #10 round, paint heart centers orange and petals yellow; let dry. Using #2 round, outline hearts with brick and petals with green; add green dots between flowers; let dry. Using liner, add cream highlights to hearts and petals. Let dry.

8. Squiggly lines: Using #2 round, squiggle brick lines above and below flowers; let dry. Add a green squiggly line to separate checks from flowered sections; let dry.

9. Coat wheelbarrow with clear coat; let dry. ✂

Whimsical Wheelbarrow
Enlarge 133% before transferring

Silk Vegetable Basket & Wreath
Continued from page 65

3. Place largest vegetables in center to create focal point; temporarily pin through vegetables into foam. When pleased with arrangement, remove pins, glue and repin.

4. Continue to add vegetables around focal point, pinning and gluing. Group similar vegetables together. Glue small pieces of foam in basket to raise smaller items as needed.

5. Cut each dusty miller stem into three pieces. When all vegetables are arranged and secured, fill open spaces with dusty miller sprigs. ✂

Web Sites of Interest

Crafter's Success Story
Gail Green

've been a professional crafter for 19 years now—and all because my preschooler fell in love with a mistake.

That "mistake" was my first attempt at designing a stuffed fabric "boot buddy" (picture a cat's head, with two long legs that were stuffed into a pair of boots to keep them standing upright). I figured out what was wrong with the first one and corrected the pattern. I gave the first one to my son (he thought it was a stuffed animal) and he took it to preschool.

When I picked him up at preschool that day, his teacher met me, wide-eyed. What, she wanted to know, had he been carrying around all day? When I told her it was a "boot buddy" mistake and that I had fixed it, she asked if I could make one for her. I did. Then two other teachers saw the corrected version, and each ordered one, too.

I invested the money from those first sales in more materials and started manufacturing in quantity. I created Boot Buddies with different heads and in different colors, and sold them at two local retail boutiques and craft shows.

Then I developed more designs—draft stoppers, appliquéd bibs, stuffed toys—and filled custom orders in custom colors, too. Eventually I was juried into the larger seasonal and holiday boutiques in the Chicago suburbs.

Although I designed primarily fabric items, I also ventured into florals, rubber stamping, decorative painting and other crafts. What had originally started as a hobby had grown into a year-round business!

Becoming a professional crafter not only offered me the opportunity to help out financially while working from home, but it also helped me grow creatively and learn how to run a business. I learned how to keep accurate records (including inventory, sales tax information and bookkeeping), find suppliers, spot trends and stay current with colors and styles.

I also gained a great deal of confidence dealing with other professionals. I attended trade shows and networked; I read trade magazines and spent a great deal of time doing "creative research" everywhere I went—including vacations, which drove my family crazy!

Although I no longer mass-produce my designs for stores, boutiques or craft shows, I owe all my success and current status to what I learned from being a professional crafter. The crafting industry is one of the warmest, most caring industries in the world. It's a place where you can develop lifelong friendships, grow creatively and realize your dreams!

I have three important pieces of advice to offer to someone just starting out:

1. Dream big. Even if you are starting as a hobbyist, think of yourself and your efforts as a business and present yourself professionally. Take the time to run your hobby as a business. Keep accurate books and records.

2. Attend trade shows. Find suppliers who are willing to work with you and sell you materials at wholesale prices. When I started, few suppliers considered professional crafters as credible wholesale buyers. Today, there are few that do not.

3. Keep up with trends, as well as color palettes and styles. Don't let your designs become old, or your colors grow outdated. Keep a step ahead of the retail market and offer your customers the most up-to-date, unique products you can create!

I knew craft producers who built such a loyal customer base that when those customers moved away, they actually flew into towns just to attend specific boutiques where those designers were offering their products!

Most of all, though, have fun! I cannot think of a more rewarding, enjoyable job! ✂

Gardening Storage Shelf

Show your crafting versatility with this hand-painted shelf. The delightful bee adds charm and originality to this project.

Design by June Fiechter

Materials

- 6⅛" x 2⅞" rectangle of ³⁄₁₆"-thick wood
- 4 (1¼") wooden ball knobs
- 2 small (6⅛" x 6¾" x 5⁵⁄₁₂") wooden rectangular boxes*
- 2½" x 1¼" bee plaster mold*
- Quick-setting plaster*
- Paintbrushes
- Acrylic craft paints*: Hauser green light, pure black, slate blue, yellow ochre
- Matte-finish plaster glaze*
- Wood glue
- Sandpaper

Boxes #75042, Butterfly & Bee Faster Plaster Mold #67361, Faster Plaster, Folk Art paints and Plaster Glaze #67924, all from Plaid.

Instructions

1. Glue boxes together along 6⅛" x 5½" sides; let dry.

2. Paint all surfaces of boxes and wooden rectangle green; let dry.

3. Glue wooden rectangle to front of shelf as shown (bottom of rectangle is even with bottom of "shelf" where boxes are glued together); let dry, then sand all edges of wood.

4. Following manufacturer's instructions, mix plaster and pour into bee mold; let dry. Pop out.

5. Paint body stripes black and yellow; paint wings with a wash made from equal parts slate blue and water. Let dry, then coat with plaster glaze; let dry.

6. Glue bee to front of wooden rectangle. Paint bee's antennae on shelf front with black.

7. Paint wooden ball knobs yellow; let dry. Sand lightly and glue at bottom of shelf for feet. ✂

Butterfly Garden Stake

Seasonal items like this are great warm weather projects. Contrasting colors and bright copper make this a wanted addition to any garden.

Design by June Fiechter

Materials

- Pointed wooden 4" x 14½" picket*
- Pure black acrylic craft paint
- Glossy enamel paints*: turquoise, bright green
- #10 flat nylon paintbrush
- Satin-finish exterior sealer
- 2 ebony 8mm cube beads*
- Wire: black 18-gauge, silver 22-gauge
- Black soft polymer clay
- 3½" x 5" aluminum sculptor's mesh*
- Metallic embossing sheets with embossing tool*: medium copper, medium aluminum
- Craft drill with small bit
- Metal cutter or tin snips
- Fine-grit sandpaper
- Tacky craft glue

*Picket triangle #75036, Gloss Enamel paints and Satin Outdoor Sealer, all from Plaid; beads from The Beadery, Sculptors Mesh and ArtEmboss Pure Metal Sheets, from AMACO.

Instructions

1. Position mesh at top of picket; mark where two holes can be drilled in each corner in order to wire mesh to picket. Remove mesh; drill holes

2. Transfer pattern and cut along outer outline for copper butterfly; cut along inner outline for aluminum butterfly. Using embossing tool provided with metal and working on wrong side of aluminum butterfly, emboss shape with designs.

3. Paint right side of aluminum butterfly first with bright green and then with turquoise, letting paints dry between applications. Paint picket black; let dry.

4. Sand painted butterfly lightly to remove paint from raised lines in embossed designs. Glue aluminum butterfly in center of copper one.

5. Paint picket with several coats sealer, letting it dry between coats.

6. Referring to pattern, drill four holes in center of butterfly.

7. *Body:* Roll ⅝" ball soft black clay for head and ½" x 2½" tapered piece for body. Using toothpick, press holes in head for antennae. Make two indentations in top of body where beads will be positioned. Press head onto larger end of body and bake as directed by manufacturer. Let cool completely.

8. Curl one end of two 1" pieces black wire around paintbrush handle for antennae; glue straight ends in holes in head.

9. Cut two 3" pieces black wire; run each through a black cube bead and wire clay body onto butterfly wings and butterfly onto wire mesh, settling beads in indentations created in step 7 and running wire ends through holes and twisting them together on wrong side of mesh. Clip off excess wire.

10. Using silver wire, attach mesh to picket through holes in corners; twist wire ends together on back.

11. Bend wings to give them addemdd dimension. ✂

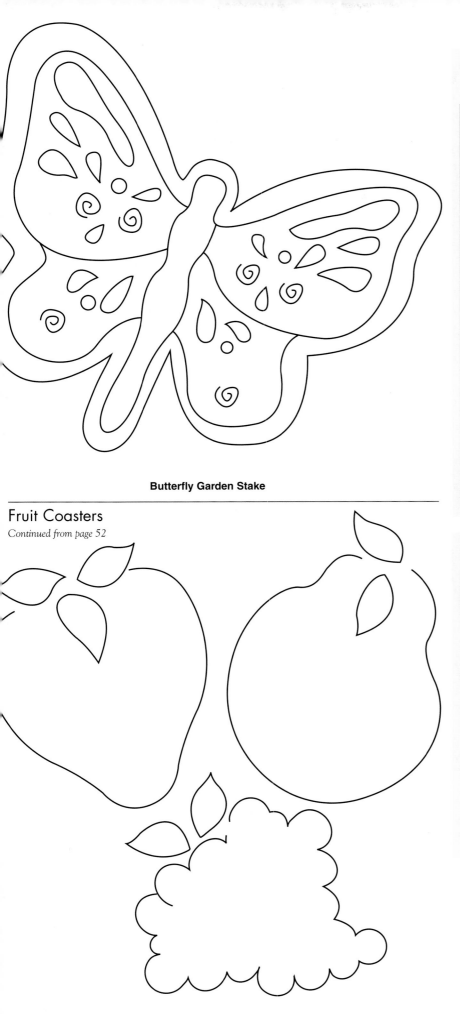

Butterfly Garden Stake

Fruit Coasters

Continued from page 52

Get Some Feedback

When you need feedback, advice or a fresh point of view, you can rely on your network of associates and peers to give you more than you ever needed.

However, sometimes it is better to get input from outside the craft industry. Here are just a few of the people who can give you a different viewpoint from a fresh perspective:

- Family
- Friends
- Neighbors
- Person waiting next to you at the doctor's or dentist's office
- Businessperson from another industry
- Community groups
- Children and teens

Other Pricing Considerations

Remember that you can always adjust your prices as you see fit. If your product sold out when priced at $9, you might want to raise the price. If your items *didn't* sell as well as expected, you may want to lower it.

Local economics play a role, too. The same item that sold well for $9 in a big-city craft show might not move so quickly at that price in a small town where there have been major layoffs. **$**

Cherry Watering Can

Draw gardening enthusiasts to your stand with this decorative watering can. It will look great filled with dried flowers or faux gardening tools.

Design by June Fiechter

Materials

- Papier-mâché watering can*
- Acrylic craft paints*: bright green, cadmium red, camel, lamp black, sapphire, titanium white
- Glossy-finish fine-line paint writer*
- Glossy black enamel paint
- Paintbrushes: #2 and #12 flats
- Graphite transfer paper

Watering can #28-4101-000 from D&CC; Americana acrylic paints, Ultra Gloss paint writer from DecoArt.

Instructions

1. Using #12 brush, paint watering can camel; let dry.

2. Referring to directions for "Using Transfer & Graphite Paper" (General Instructions, page 190), transfer pattern onto front of can.

3. Using #12 brush, paint background sapphire, cherries red and leaf green.

4. Using #2 brush, paint frame with black and white checks.

5. Outline design with paint writer and glossy black enamel paint.

6. Add highlights to leaf and cherries with camel; add larger highlights with white.

7. Dot black paint on end of spout to resemble holes. ✂

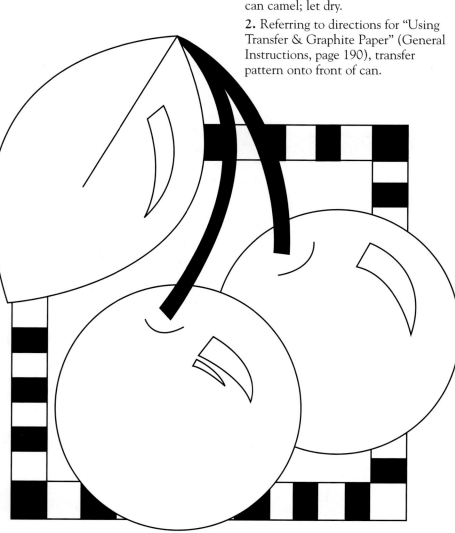

Cherry Watering Can

Basic Multiplying Pricing Formula

One of the most difficult aspects of selling crafts is pricing. It's difficult to put a price tag on anything creative, especially when you made it with your own two hands. But it is critically important to price your crafts with profit and business in mind.

There are many ways to come up with a selling price, and the formulas can be confusing. The simplest way is to simply multiply your costs—twice, three times, or perhaps five times the cost of the raw materials. If it costs you $1 in supplies to make an item, you will sell it for $2, $3 or $5.

The major drawback of this formula is that it often doesn't realistically cover your labor costs. But it *is* simple to calculate. **$**

Networking Works!

Networking with other professional crafters is an important part of your business life. Networking simply means keeping in touch with a circle of associates so that you are up to date with what is happening in your business world.

Keep in Touch

Hobby crafters and professional crafters need a multilevel business network. It's important that you stay in touch with manufacturers, distributors and retailers. This group will keep you informed about supplies, good buys and industry trends.

Give & Take With Your Peers

Another key group is your peers—but this can be a sensitive area. You don't want to breach etiquette by asking financial details of your peers, but communicating openly and honestly helps overcome obstacles and problems.

If one person complains about a poorly planned craft show, the promoter might brush off the comment. However, if 20 exhibitors come forward, the promoter is likely to listen rather than lose a high percentage of exhibitors! **$**

Fancy Flowers Candles Set

Make this set a seasonal item by using different flowers and color schemes to match the appropriate time of year.

Designs by Vicki Schreiner

Materials

- 6¾" and 9" hardwood candlesticks*
- 2 (5") ivory taper candles
- Acrylic craft paints*: brown velvet, bungalow blue, butter yellow, coastline blue, dark foliage green, eucalyptus, village green, white
- Candle- and soap-painting medium*
- Clear glaze base*
- Satin-finish interior varnish
- Permanent adhesive
- Paintbrushes: #3 round, #4 and ½" flats, #1 liner
- Paintbrush handle or stylus
- Toothpick
- Natural sea sponge
- 3-ply jute
- Graphite transfer paper
- Dull No. 2 pencil
- Paper towels

Candlesticks from Viking Woodcrafts; Ceramcoat paints, painting medium, glaze base from Delta.

Candle Preparation

1. Buff surface of candles with paper towel, avoiding touching sides of candle with your fingertips; hold candle near tip, at wick, or at bottom.

2. Wet sea sponge with water until soft. Wring out excess water into paper towel until sponge is only damp. Mix equal parts village green and candle-painting medium. Dab sponge into mixture, then blot once on palette to remove some paint. Turning wrist as you work, dab sponge onto surface around lower half of candle to create flecked appearance. Let dry completely.

3. Repeat step 2, substituting eucalyptus for village green; let dry.

4. Referring to directions for "Using Transfer & Graphite Paper" (General Instructions, page 190), transfer pattern for Flower Cluster to candle using dull pencil; hold pattern and graphite paper in place without using tape. Do not transfer stippling dots; these are for your reference in shading.

Painting Candles

Note: Mix equal parts candle-painting medium with paints for following steps.

1. Using #3 round or #4 flat brush as needed to fit area, base-coat areas: *leaves:* eucalyptus; *large flower petals:* yellow; *large flower centers:* brown; let dry.

2. Using #1 liner, line leaves and stems with dark foliage green; line large petals with brown; let dry.

3. Using #3 round brush, add brown shading streaks out from each flower center; shade leaves with dark foliage green. Let dry.

Small Flowers

Flower Cluster

1.   **2.**   **3.**   **4.**   **5.**

Steps for Small Flowers

4. Referring to Steps for Small Flowers diagram, use paintbrush handle or stylus to dot on petals of small flowers with bungalow blue; dot yellow center in each. Let dry.

5. Using toothpick, scatter tiny dots of white around center of each large flower; add tiny white dot to right side of each small flower center. Let dry.

6. Using ½" flat brush, apply two coats painting medium over each entire candle; let dry.

Painting Candlesticks

1. Using #3 round or #4 flat brush as needed to fit area, base-coat as follows: candle cup and bottom ring of base: *bungalow blue*; first ring under cup and second ring of base just above bottom ring: *butter yellow*; second ring under cup: *eucalyptus*; third ring from bottom of base: *white*; fourth ring from bottom: *coastline blue*; let dry. Large center section remains unpainted.

2. Referring to Small Flowers diagram and using paintbrush handle or stylus, randomly add small flowers and leaves around white ring at bottom: Dot on petals of some flowers with bungalow blue and some with yellow; dot yellow centers onto blue flowers and brown centers onto yellow flowers. Using toothpick, add tiny white dot to right side of each flower center. Using #3 round brush, randomly add small leaves with eucalyptus. Let dry.

3. Using #4 flat brush, add eucalyptus checks around yellow ring near bottom. Let dry.

Finishing Candlesticks

1. *"Antique" finish:* Mix three parts glaze base with one part brown paint. Using ½" flat brush, apply mixture to all painted areas and immediately wipe off with paper towel. Let dry.

2. Apply two coats satin varnish to all painted areas. Let dry.

3. *Jute trim:* Starting at top of large center unpainted section, apply adhesive to candlestick and wrap tightly with jute, gluing and wrapping until middle section is covered; trim off excess. ✀

Don't Take It Personally!

Many professional crafters who are disappointed with their sales worry that their workmanship or craft is just not appreciated or wanted by the buying public.

In fact, the problem might be that they are not using the best marketplace, or selling their work at a price that is comfortable for that area. So before you get downhearted about lackluster sales, take a good look at the economy of the geographical area. **$**

Fancy Gift Boxes

Display these colorful boxes on a bright and cheery background cloth to draw attention to each exquisite detail.

Designs by Sandra Graham Smith

Materials

- Card stock: 8½" x 11" sheet yellow, white or blue, plus scraps of blue, yellow, green, yellow and/or red
- Stylus
- Straightedge
- Tacky craft glue
- 6 flat white buttons (for flower box only)
- Black fine-tip permanent marker (for watermelon box only)

Instructions

1. Use photocopier to enlarge pattern for gift box 133 percent before transferring. Cut one gift box from white, yellow or blue card stock.

2. Using stylus and a straightedge, score pattern along dashed lines.

3. Fold pattern along scored lines; glue side tab inside box.

4. Fold up box bottom; tuck in ends.

5. Close top by bending bows and fitting slots together.

6. Finish as directed for individual designs.

Flower Box

1. Cut three flowers from yellow card stock and three from pink; fold each petal along center to give flowers dimension. Cut six leaves from green; curl slightly to give leaves dimension.

2. Alternating colors, glue two flowers to each side of blue gift box and one flower to each end; glue leaf under each flower.

3. Glue button in center of each flower.

Watermelon Box

1. Cut two outer watermelons from green card stock and two inner watermelons from red; glue together and glue watermelon to each side of yellow gift box.

2. Using black marker, draw seeds on watermelon and add ants up side and over top of box.

Stars Box

1. Cut two large stars, three medium and two small stars from red card stock; cut same stars from blue.

2. Alternating colors throughout, glue a medium star to each large star. Glue two large stars to each side of white gift box; glue remaining medium stars to ends. Glue small stars to top of box. ✂

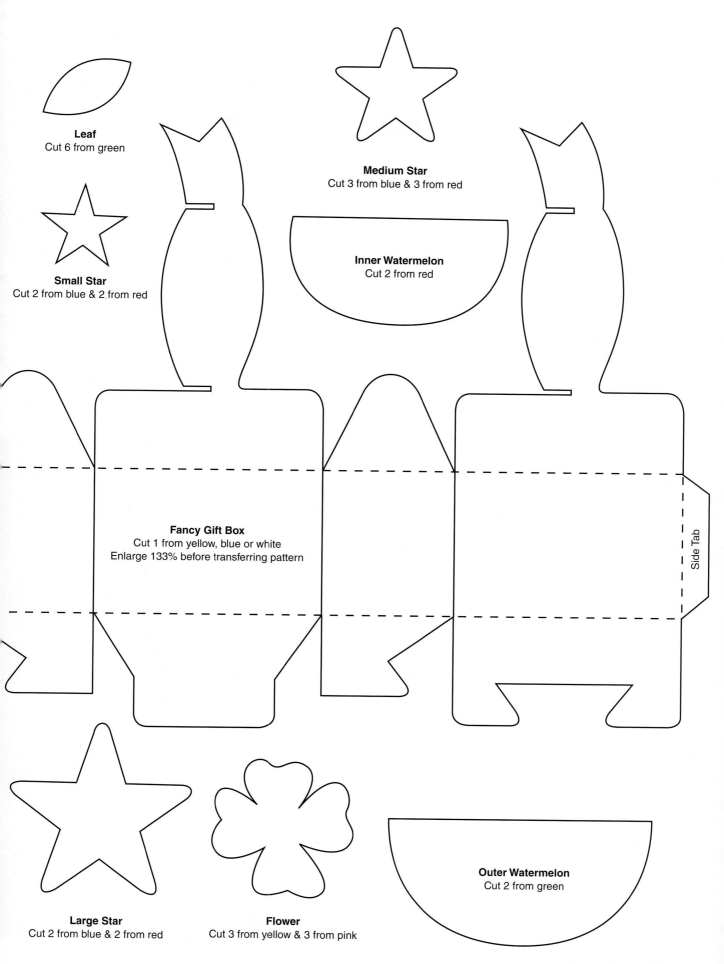

Leaf
Cut 6 from green

Medium Star
Cut 3 from blue & 3 from red

Small Star
Cut 2 from blue & 2 from red

Inner Watermelon
Cut 2 from red

Fancy Gift Box
Cut 1 from yellow, blue or white
Enlarge 133% before transferring pattern

Side Tab

Large Star
Cut 2 from blue & 2 from red

Flower
Cut 3 from yellow & 3 from pink

Outer Watermelon
Cut 2 from green

At the Ball Game

Delight will surround your booth as people see this darling pig. He's a perfect gift for the baseball fan in your life.

Design by Jackie Haskell

Materials

- Polymer clay*: beige, blue, ivory, red, tan, terra cotta
- 2 (3mm) black ball beads
- Pink powdered cosmetic blusher
- Cotton-tip swab
- Straightedge tool for cutting and making lines
- Round wooden toothpick
- Straight pin
- Paintbrush
- Clean white rag
- Ovenproof plate
- Oven

Sculpey III polymer clay from Polyform Products.

Instructions

1. *Body:* Soften and roll half of one section of beige clay into a ball; form into fat teardrop. Pinch two indentations in fat end where legs will be attached. While holding body upright, slightly flatten bottom by pressing it gently on table.

2. *Legs:* Roll marble-size ball of beige clay; cut in half. Use one half for each leg. Roll each into a ball, then into ¾" log. Form foot by pinching end up and rounding foot, making it flat on the bottom. Using straightedge, make a slit in end for hoof. Attach legs to body at indentations.

3. *Arms:* Cut one-quarter from a marble-size ball of beige clay for each arm. Form each into a ball, then form each ball into a ¾" cone. Slightly flatten and round fatter end of each, using straightedge to make slit for hooves. Attach smaller end of each arm to top of body.

4. *Head:* Cut one-quarter from a

section of beige clay; soften and roll into a ball. Push beads on their sides into head for eyes until none of hole can be seen. Blush cheeks with cotton swab and blusher.

5. *Nose:* Shape one-quarter of a pea-size ball of beige clay into an oval; attach to face. Indent nostrils with tip of paintbrush handle.

6. Attach head to top of body. For mouth, insert end of round toothpick

and pull down slightly to open. Use tip of toothpick to indent belly button.

7. *Cup:* Form pea-size ball of ivory clay into slight cone shape; set cup on each end and carefully press down on table to flatten; it should resemble cup without opening. Use end of paintbrush handle to make opening in larger end, making hole larger by rotating paintbrush. Attach cup to body; curve arm around it.

8. *Hot dog:* Roll pea-size ball of tan clay into ½" log for bun; flatten slightly and round ends. Using straightedge, cut bun open but not all the way through. For hot dog, thoroughly blend a pea-size ball of tan clay and another of terra cotta. Cut in half; cut one-eighth from one half (reserve remainder of this half) and roll into a ½" log; round ends. Place hot dog in bun. Roll tiny ball of red clay; roll into ½" rope and lay on top of hot dog for ketchup. Attach hot dog with bun to pig's other arm.

9. *Baseball glove:* Roll remainder of blended tan and terra cotta clay from step 8 into ball; flatten slightly into circle. Using straightedge, indent edge to define fingers of glove, making thumb larger than fingers.

10. *Baseball:* Roll half of a pea-size ball of ivory clay into a ball. Define lines of baseball with straightedge. Attach ball to glove and position glove with ball beside pig, attaching it to leg.

11. *Cap:* Roll half of a marble-size ball of blue clay into a ball; shape into cap by placing ball on thumb and rounding top. (Inside of cap is indented.) Roll pea-size ball of red clay and flatten into a half-circle for bill. Attach straight edge of bill to cap. Roll a tiny ball of red for button and attached to top of cap. Attach cap on top of pig's head, positioning it slightly off to one side. Use straightedge to indent five evenly spaced lines around cap, from center button down to edge.

12. *Ear:* Remove all traces of red clay from hands. Form half of a pea-size ball of beige clay into ½" flattened teardrop; attached rounded end to head and fold point forward.

13. *Tail:* Roll one-eighth of a pea-size ball of beige clay into a ½" rope. Attach one end to pig and curl twice, one curl on top of the other.

14. Bake pig on ovenproof plate in preheated 275-degree Fahrenheit oven for 10 minutes; let cool completely before handling. ✂

A Swingin' Summer

Remembering the joys of summer year-round is easy with this little clay bunny. She's sure to be a big hit.

Design by Jackie Haskell

Materials

- Polymer clay*: black, dusty rose, ivory brilliant, tan, turquoise
- 2 black seed beads
- Straightedge tool for cutting and making lines
- Straight pin
- Paintbrush
- Twine
- Ovenproof plate
- Oven

Sculpey III polymer clay from Polyform Products.

Instructions

1. *Tire:* Soften one section cut from block of black clay; roll into a ball, then roll ball into 4¼" log. Bring ends together; connect. Smooth seam with finger. Set tire upright; gently roll along table to flatten tire surface. Gently flatten both sides of tire by laying it flat on table and pressing down slightly. Use straightedge to mark treads on tire.

2. Cut 16" length twine; tie loop in one end and tie other end around tire, being careful not to tie it too tightly.

3. *Body:* Soften and roll one-quarter of one section of tan clay into a ball; form into fat teardrop. Pinch two indentations in fat end where legs will be attached.

4. *Arms:* Roll two pea-size balls tan clay; roll each into ¾" cone. Slightly flatten and round fatter end of each. Attach smaller end of each arm to top of body.

5. *Head:* Roll marble-size ball tan clay; cut off one-quarter and roll remaining into ball for head. Push beads on their sides into head for eyes until none of hole can be seen. Use straight pin to indent eyelashes and eyebrows.

6. *Muzzle and nose:* Cut one-quarter from a pea-size ball of ivory clay; cut that quarter in half and roll each into ball for muzzle. Attach to face side by side below eyes. Roll a very tiny ball of dusty rose for nose; press atop muzzle.

7. Attach head to top of body so face looks off to side.

8. *Legs:* Roll four pea-size balls tan

Continued on page 81

Seconds Count!

The average retail customer will spend one hour at an arts-and-crafts show. If the show in which you are participating has 100 exhibitors, you have approximately *6 seconds* of that potential buyer's time! Use it wisely by putting together an eye-catching display of your work.

The average retail customer spends less than 30 minutes shopping in a retail gift shop like a craft mall or craft co-op. You *still* only have about *6 seconds* to grab the buyer's attention! But this time, you aren't even there in person to help promote your craft! More than ever, you need a display that proves itself a top-notch sales tool. **$**

Ring Around the Posy Dress

Decorate a variety of sizes and colors of dresses adorned with darling ladybugs to sell with your other wearables.

Design by June Fiechter

Materials

- Blue knit dress*
- Paper ladybug napkins*
- Decoupage medium for fabric*
- Assorted fabric-painting brushes
- Fabric paints*: black, calico red, green apple, ivy green, white
- Air-soluble fabric-marking pen

Dress from Land's End; Ladybug Florals #57186 Mod Podge Napkins, Fabric Mod Podge medium and Brush-On Fabric Paints, all from Plaid.

Instructions

1. Wash and dry dress without fabric softener according to instructions on tag.

2. Cut one medium, five large and two small ladybugs and one small and seven medium leaves from napkin; peel off unprinted layers and discard.

3. Arrange leaves and ladybugs on front of dress as shown; trace around each with fabric-marking pen.

4. Following directions on container of decoupage medium, remove each leaf and ladybug one at a time and brush decoupage medium over traced areas on dress, covering an area a little larger all around than the cutout; replace ladybug or leaf. Brush more medium over each piece, ¹⁄₁₆" beyond edge of cutout. Let dry completely.

5. Paint over decoupaged ladybugs and leaves using matching colors. Paint stem of ladybug "flower" on bodice using green apple and ivy paints; let dry.

6. Using black paint, outline and

embellish designs, adding legs and antennae, dotted line from "late" ladybug, etc. Highlight with white paint. Let dry completely.

7. Refer to paint manufacturer's instructions for laundering and care. ✂

A Swingin' Summer

Continued from page 79

clay; roll two balls together into a larger ball for each leg. Shape each ball into ¾" log; turn up ¼" at end of each for foot. For footpads, roll two small balls rose clay; form into flat teardrop shapes and attach one to bottom of each foot, point toward heel. Define toes on all four paws with straightedge. Attach legs to body at indentations, positioning them in seated position. Sit bunny in tire; attach paws, legs and side of face to tire.

9. *Ears:* Cut pea-size ball of tan clay in half; use one piece for each ear. Roll each onto ½" cone, then flatten slightly. Indent line down center of each with straightedge. Attach ears to each other side by side, then attach to top center of head and curve ears forward slightly.

10. *Tail:* Attach pea-size ball of ivory clay to back of bunny.

11. *Bow:* Roll pea-size ball turquoise clay; cut off one-fourth and cut that piece in half; use one of those pieces for each side of bow. Roll each into ball and flatten into small triangle; indent with straightedge from one corner to center. Attach triangles to each other at points where lines begin; attach bow to head. Roll tiny ball of turquoise; attach in center of bow.

12. Bake bunny and tire (with twine attached) on ovenproof plate in preheated 275-degree Fahrenheit oven for 10 minutes; let cool completely before handling. Hang from shelf peg, on an indoor tree, or pin to curtain to hang in window. ✂

Check Out the Competition's Price

Most pricing formulas do not take into consideration what the competition is charging. It's important that you do some research to find out how your pricing compares with that of similar products.

While pricing by using a formula can seem very scientific, there is still some "art" that must be factored into the bottom line. Your formula supports your pricing by assuring that you are covering your cost of supplies, labor and overhead plus some additional profit. But you also should consider the going price for similar products.

Let's say you are selling 12-inch teddy bears, and your bottom-selling price (meaning we are making a profit from each sale) is $12.

A little research gives us the following information on the competition:

Catalog price.............$13.95 plus $5.95 shipping

Gift shop $14.95

Craft mall $12.50

Discount superstore.....$10

Internet Web site ....$12.50 plus $4.50 shipping & handling

Chances are you can average these ($14.87) and increase your selling price accordingly. It's an option you should consider. **$**

Jumping Rag Dolls

Jumping their way into your heart, these two country rag dolls will appeal to young and old alike!

Designs by Barbara Woolley

Materials

Both Dolls

- 2 sheets opaque oven-shrink plastic*
- Artist-quality colored pencils
- Black waterproof fine-point permanent marker
- ¼" round paper punch
- 2 (10") pieces red plastic-coated wire
- 2 (½") round white wooden beads
- ⅛"-wide red satin ribbon
- 8 (1") head pins
- Spray satin varnish
- Fine-grit sandpaper
- Nonstick or parchment-lined baking sheet
- White carpet or button thread
- Needle-nose pliers

Aleene's Shrink-It Opake.

Instructions

1. Using sandpaper, rough up one side of shrink plastic sheet, sanding in both directions.

2. Referring to patterns, trace two arms reversing one, two legs reversing one and one body/head on rough side of plastic using black marker.

3. Color pieces with colored pencils, then cut out with sharp scissors.

4. Using ¼" punch, punch holes in body/head, arms and legs where indicated.

5. Arrange plastic pieces face up on nonstick cookie sheet, or on regular cookie sheet lined with baking parchment or sprinkled with baby powder.

6. Bake in a preheated 275-degree Fahrenheit oven for three to five minutes, or until plastic pieces are approximately the thickness of a nickel. Immediately remove cookie

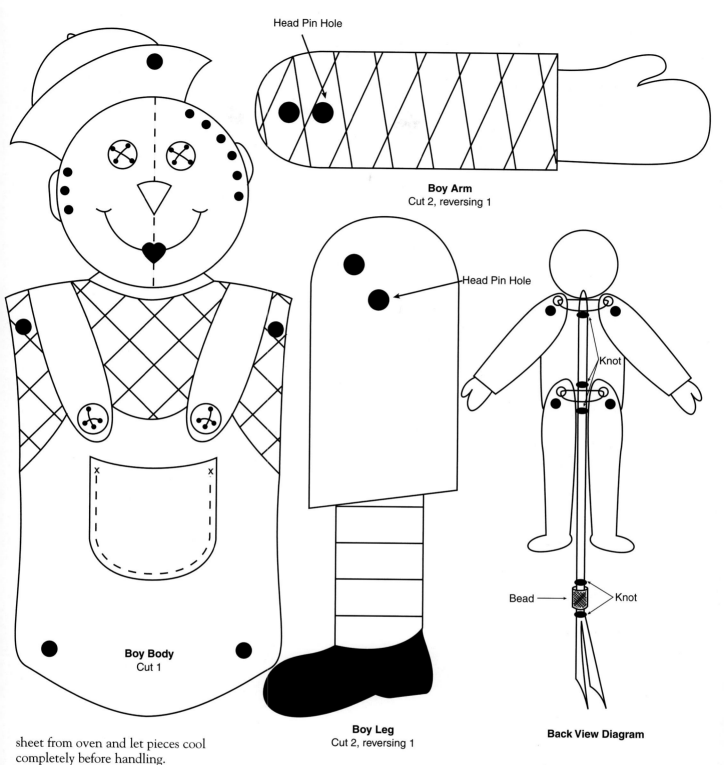

Head Pin Hole

Boy Arm
Cut 2, reversing 1

Head Pin Hole

Knot

Bead → Knot

Boy Body
Cut 1

Boy Leg
Cut 2, reversing 1

Back View Diagram

sheet from oven and let pieces cool completely before handling.

7. Spray doll parts with varnish; let dry.

8. *Hair:* Cut wire in 1" pieces; curl tightly around pencil. Attach curls to doll's head through punched holes in head.

9. Join arms to body using head pins inserted through shoulders and bottom armholes; loop ends on back to keep head pins in place and clip off

Take Stock & Restock

Keep building and replenishing inventory all year round. It will help take the edge off crunch times and give you some breathing room. Be positive and open-minded to opportunities and possibilities while working ahead, but don't ignore the fact that you may be reaching your maximum stress level. Adrenaline (and sheer panic) often fuel creativity; however, you should never force the issue and overwork yourself. **$**

excess. Attach legs with head pins inserted through lower body and bottom leg holes.

10. Referring to Back View Diagram throughout, tie arms together through top armholes, and legs together through top leg holes with carpet/button thread. Tie a 12" piece of ribbon to arm and leg threads and thread bead onto bottom of ribbon; knot to hold in place.

11. Tie red ribbon loop through hole in top of head. Holding doll by top loop, pull down gently on bead dangling from bottom to make doll "jump." ✂

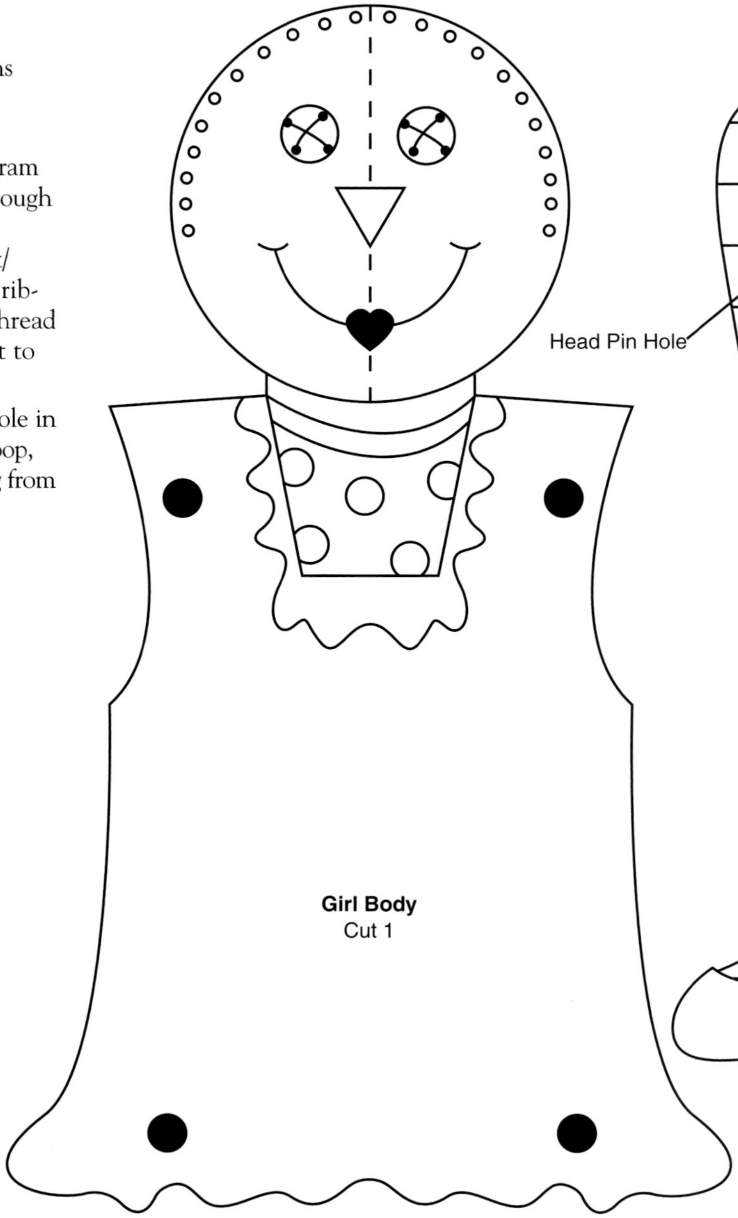

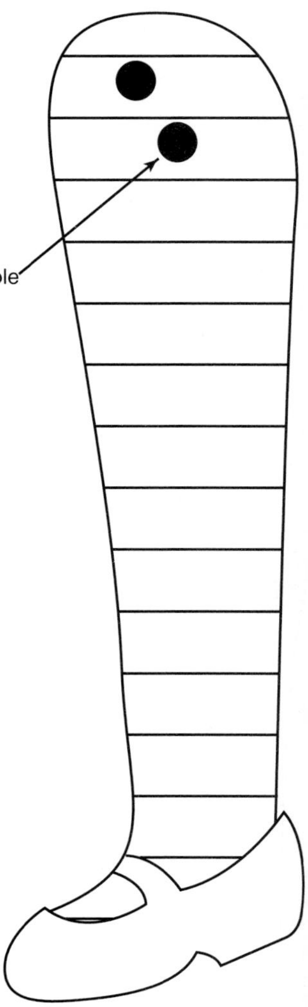

Head Pin Hole

Eye Pin Hole

Girl Body
Cut 1

Girl Leg
Cut 2, reversing

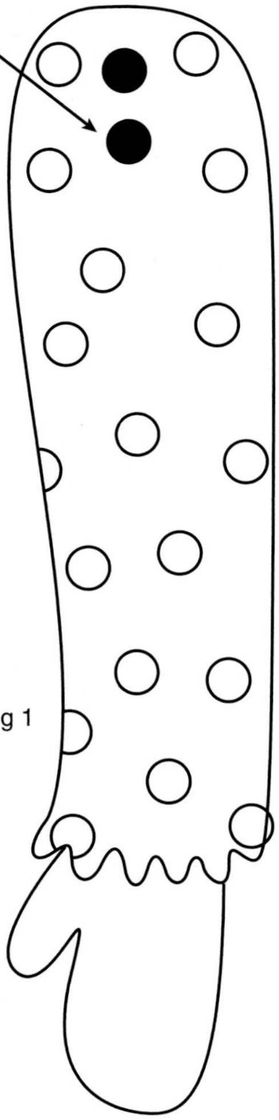

Girl Arm
Cut 2, reversing 1

Seasonal or Nonseasonal Displays?

It's easy to use a holiday or the season for your display theme. Christmas, for example, lends itself to filling your display with colorful lights, a cheerful evergreen garland, bright red bows, glistening snowflakes or a scarf-and-mitten set. Look through holiday and home-decor magazines and books to help inspire your imagination. **$**

Display Your Craft

If you prefer to a nonseasonal display, think about your craft and how to express it. A basket weaver might decorate a booth with reeds or a half-finished basket to show off her skills. A seamstress might use an antique sewing machine as a prop or scatter interesting buttons around the display. A woodworker might include a few pieces of exotic wood. Details like these make your display more interesting. **$**

Stenciled Gift Bags

Fill these bags with scented soaps or potpourri at your display to enhance the beautiful stencil work.

Designs by Mary Ayres

Materials

- Set of 3 (small, medium and large) pintucked gift bags*
- Stencils*: star, heart, seashell, squares border
- Acrylic fabric paints*: *glitters*— karat gold; *matte acrylics*—alizarin crimson, antique gold, plum; *metallics*—imperial gold, yellow; *shimmering pearls*—baby pink, light teal, lilac
- 9 (⅜") stencil brushes
- Masking tape
- Cardboard

Gift bags from Wimpole Street Creations; Simply Stencils from Plaid; SoSoft acrylic fabric paints from DecoArt.

Stenciling & Shading

Hold stencil in place with masking tape.

Dip dry stencil brush in paint; wipe on paper towel to remove excess paint and prevent seepage under stencil. Apply paint to cutout areas, brushing with circular motion and holding brush perpendicular to surface.

For shading, brush should be nearly dry; apply color only around edges of section.

Instructions

1. Cut a piece of cardboard slightly smaller than bag; place inside bag to keep paint from seeping through.

2. Center border squares—eight for small bag, 11 for medium bag, and 13 for large bag—¼" above top line of pintucking. Stencil squares first with imperial gold and then with karat gold. Stencil a second row of squares centered ¼" below bottom line of pintucking.

3. Center main motif on bag just above top row of squares, stenciling

and shading as follows:

Small bag—Stencil heart with pink; shade edges with crimson.

Medium bag—Stencil middle and end sections of shell with lilac and

remaining sections with light teal; shade edges of all sections with plum.

Large bag—Stencil star with yellow; shade edges with antique gold. ✄

Seashell Candle

Stock items such as this and watch your sales skyrocket! This delightful candle is great for any room, and it makes a great gift for many occasions.

Design by Deborah Brooks

Materials

- Candlewick with metal anchor
- Candle wax
- Assorted clean, dry seashells, small starfish, etc.: 5 or 6 tiny (less than ½"), 5 or 6 small (½"–1"), 2–4 medium (1½"), 3 large (3"), plus one larger shell to hold candle and wick
- Industrial-strength glue*
- Sand
- Aluminum dish

E6000 glue from Eclectic.

Instructions

1. Nestle shell that will hold candle in sand in aluminum dish to hold it level and steady as you work.

2. Melt wax according to manufacturer's instructions; dab a small amount on bottom of wick and press into bottom of shell. Pour in melted wax to fill to within ¼" from top; let wax cool and harden.

3. Arrange three large shells flat sides down to form base. Glue shell with candle to base. Use cups and other small, heavy objects to support shells until glue dries.

4. Fill gaps with medium shells, gluing them in place and supporting them as needed until glue dries. Base should be sturdier at this point.

5. Glue on small and tiny shells, filling gaps and creating the appearance of a natural "pile" of shells. Let dry completely.

Note: *Never leave burning candle unattended, and do not burn close to flammable objects. Candle can be refilled with wax and new wick as needed.* ✂

Creative Trends

One trend that has exhibited real staying power is the trend toward buying seasonal rather than holiday motifs. For example, you might end up selling more items with colorful leaves and pumpkins (motifs of the fall season) than witches and goblins (Halloween motifs) or turkeys and pilgrims (Thanksgiving). General spring motifs may sell better than those focused on Easter. **$**

Using themes is a great way to have a powerful display. These crafts have a delightful mix of Americana.

Seaside Fishbowl

Fill one of these fishbowls with colorful rocks and water—or even a fish—for an eye-catching display. Seeing how the project can be used will encourage customers to buy.

Design by Deborah Brooks

Materials

- 2 (4") terra-cotta flowerpots
- 6½" terra-cotta saucer
- Glass fishbowl with 4⅜"-diameter mouth
- Assorted seashells
- Acrylic craft paints*: lamp black, Payne's grey, slate grey, titanium white, Victorian blue
- Paintbrushes: flat brush, stippler
- Gloss-finish varnish
- Industrial-strength glue*

Americana acrylic paints from DecoArt; E6000 glue from Eclectic.

Instructions

1. *Base:* Glue pots together, bottom to bottom; let dry.

2. Glue saucer upside-down on top of one of the pots; let dry.

3. Paint pots and saucer black; let dry. Swirl together puddles of blue, slate grey, Payne's grey and white without blending them completely. Load stippler with all colors and stipple entire base with swirled colors, blending until you achieve the desired effect; let dry.

4. Coat with varnish; let dry.

5. Cement fishbowl to base, applying several dollops of glue to edge of top of base and placing fishbowl on it. Let dry completely.

6. Glue seashells to front of base as desired; let dry. ✂

Lighthouse Peg Board

Bring this seascape to life by hanging ocean-theme ornaments in your booth. Or, display this detailed piece hung with a swag of fishnet.

Design by June Fiechter

Materials

- Wooden semicircular peg board*
- Wooden lighthouse half*
- Sculpting/molding compound*
- Neutral beige acrylic sand-finish paint*
- Acrylic craft paints*: baby blue, burnt umber, lamp black, raw sienna, taffy cream, true blue, true red, ultra blue deep, white wash
- Venetian gold metallic acrylic paint*
- Satin-finish clear varnish
- Fine-grit sandpaper
- Natural sea sponge
- Paintbrushes: #8 and #2 flat paintbrushes
- ¾"-wide cellophane tape
- Wood glue
- Toothbrush

*Circle plaque peg board #W91648 from Design Works; Darice lighthouse #9160-76; Sculptamold sculpting/molding compound #41821C from AMACO; Sandstones Textural Acrylic, Americana acrylic paints, Dazzling Metallics acrylic paint and Dura Clear varnish, all from DecoArt; Crafter's Pick Sand-n-Stain wood glue from API.

Instructions

1. Draw horizon line across bottom of peg board 4½" above edge; add sand line 1¾" above edge.

2. Paint pegs and water ultra blue; let dry. Position pegs on board and draw around each to know where not to paint sand.

3. Paint sky baby blue; let dry.

4. Lightly sponge true blue and white over sky to create clouds; let dry.

5. Using chisel edge of #8 brush, brush waves onto water with true blue and white; let dry.

6. Paint lighthouse white; let dry. Paint top band gold; let dry.

7. Wrap tape around lighthouse to create diagonal stripes; press tightly to seal edges. Using #2 brush, paint roof and stripes red; let dry Remove tape.

8. Paint windows, door and band under gold band with black; let dry. Add true blue doorknob; let dry.

9. Glue lighthouse to peg board at left of center.

10. Apply sculpting/molding compound under lighthouse to create rocky beach; let dry completely.

11. Paint several light coats of sand-finish paint over dry sculpting/molding compound (heavy applications will produce cracks). Continue to paint all along bottom 1¾" for sand.

12. Using white and taffy cream and #2 brush, paint sun in upper right area.

13. Mix equal parts varnish and raw sienna; apply to outer edges of board—not to sand—with paper towel. Rub off excess and reapply as needed to create an aged look. Let dry.

14. Spatter painted surface with undiluted burnt umber using toothbrush. Let dry.

15. Brush one coat of varnish over all painted areas—not sand.

16. Attach pegs to board. Paint sand around bases of pegs; let dry. ✂

Welcome to the Family!

While you might sometimes feel isolated in your occupation as a crafter, you really are not alone. There are thousands of creative people just like you trying to succeed.

When 12 craft professionals—including craft teachers, designers and demonstrators—were asked to list the pros and cons of being in the business of selling their crafts, they offered the following points.

The Positives
- Being your own boss
- Expressing your creativity
- Setting goals
- Making money
- Hobby pays for itself
- Creating and coordinating displays
- Sharing your love of crafting
- Opportunity for travel
- Staying on top of current trends
- Meeting new people, including other crafters
- Enjoying the outdoors
- Setting your own hours
- Don't need a baby sitter
- The whole family can get involved
- Buying better tools

The Negatives
- Pricing your crafts
- Overhead costs
- Labor
- Being a salesperson
- Setting up and breaking down a booth
- Damage to crafts from public and weather
- Unhappy customers

- Theft/shoplifting
- Organizing everything
- People copying your original work
- Juried shows
- Keeping paperwork and bookkeeping up to date
- Initial payout for shows, displays and tools
- Working with the public
- Scheduling work and family **$**

Patriotic Candleholder

Light up your home or craft booth by burning a candle in this charming patriotic decoration.

Design by Mary Ayers

Materials

- Recycled pint jar (mayonnaise jar was used for sample)
- Glass votive candleholder with lip
- Red votive candle
- 4 (2½" x 4") "long" wooden stars*
- 36" jute twine
- 4 (5") pieces 20-gauge gold wire
- Swirl-shaped paint-stamping sponges*
- 2 glaze applicators* *or* 2 (2") squares household sponges
- Enamel paints*: true gold, Williamsburg blue
- Acrylic craft paints*: antique white, country red, Mississippi mud
- #5 and #8 natural bristle paintbrushes
- Extra-fine-tip opaque gold writer*
- Craft drill with ⅜" bit
- Scrap block wood
- Vinegar
- Fine-grit sandpaper
- Needle-nose pliers

*Lara's Crafts stars; Fun to Paint swirls sponge #50125 and Stamp Décor glaze applicators from Plaid; Ultra Gloss Air-Dry enamel paints and Americana acrylic paints from DecoArt; ZIG Memory System Writer from EK Success Ltd.

Stamping With Sponge

Pour paint onto paper plate. Dip one side of applicator (or household sponge) in paint; dab onto sponge stamp, making sure entire design has paint on it. Press sponge firmly onto surface, then lift straight up so paint doesn't smear. Wash applicator and sponge as soon as you finish stamping; pour unused paint back into jar.

Instructions

1. Wash jar with soap and water; remove adhesive. Wipe jar with paper towel moistened with vinegar and take care not to touch outside of jar with your hands while you work. Let dry.

2. Using a dabbing motion, paint entire jar with several coats of blue, letting paint dry between coats, until paint is opaque.

3. Using small swirl stamp and gold paint, stamp swirls evenly spaced around jar.

4. Wrap jute around top of jar three times; knot ends together. Trim ends to 1"; fray ends.

5. Placing stars on scrap wood first (to keep them from splitting), drill hole through each side point in each star; sand lightly. Paint stars white; let dry.

6. Referring to directions for drybrushing in "Painting Techniques" (General Instructions, page 190), drybrush star edges with Mississippi mud. Stamp a large red swirl in center of each star; let dry.

7. Using gold writer, draw "running stitch" around edge of each star; let dry.

8. Join stars in a circle so that they stand on their bottom points by inserting wire ends through holes from back to front and twisting ends together. Place jar inside stars and twist wire ends more tightly until stars fit jar snugly. Curl wire ends around pencil.

9. Insert glass votive in mouth of painted jar and place candle in votive. ✂

But the Weatherman Said Sunny Skies!

When exhibiting outdoors, always plan for weather. Most companies that sell canopies sell sides that fit them. They might be worth the investment if you plan to do several outdoor shows a year.

Otherwise, bring along some plastic to protect your display in case of rain or high winds. Many crafters also make weights for canopy legs to steady them in windy weather. $

Americana Wind Chime

Make a patriotic-theme area to display this project and watch your sales soar. This is a great project for the Fourth.

Design by Bev Shenefield

Materials

- Black metal triangular wind chime with heart on chain*
- Chalk pencil
- Fine-point black permanent marker
- Fine-line gold pen*
- Household vinegar
- Metal paints*: red, bright blue, white
- Paintbrushes: #8 flat, #20/0 liner

Wind chime available at JoAnn's stores; Marvy gold pen from Uchida; No-Prime metal paints from Delta.

Instructions

1. Clean wind chime thoroughly; wipe sides with vinegar; let dry. Add pattern of stars and stripes with chalk pencil.

2. Using flat brush and painting all sides identically, paint top third of triangular area blue; let dry. Paint lower two-thirds in alternating stripes of red and white; paint both sides of heart red; let dry.

3. Paint white stars on blue areas; let dry.

4. Outline stars with gold pen; separate stripes and blue area with squiggly lines and crosshatches using black marker.

5. Using liner and white paint, write "LET LIBERTY RING" on both sides of heart; let dry. ✄

Check Out Your Checkout

At craft shows, make sure you have a checkout area that gives you plenty of room to move. You'll need to tally and bag customers' purchases, and often return change to the customer. Give yourself some breathing room. **$**

Faux Metal Sunshine

Add sparkle to your booth by making this gorgeous
wall hanging in different metallic shades
such as mauve or deep blue.

Design by June Fiechter

Materials

- 15" square wood up to ½" thick
- Band saw or jigsaw
- Transfer or graphite paper
- Sculpting/molding compound*
- Face mold*
- Acrylic crafts paints*: aqua, azure blue, licorice, pure black, real brown
- Paintbrushes: large scruffy brush, 1" brush
- Tacky craft glue
- Toothed hanger
- Sandpaper
- Gilding kit*
- Clear coating*

Sculptamold molding compound #41821-C from AMACO; Face Form molds #52009 from Roylco Ltd.; FolkArt paints from Plaid; Gallery Glass gilding set from Plaid; UV-Resistant Clear Coating #1305 from Krylon.

Instructions

1. Use photocopier to enlarge pattern 200 percent. Referring to "Using Graphite & Transfer Paper," transfer pattern to wood and cut out with saw. Sand edges until smooth. Nail hanger on back at center top.

2. Mix molding compound according to package directions; pour into mold. Let dry for several days; unmold.

3. Glue face in center of wooden sun.

4. Mix additional molding compound and use it to fill in seam between face and wood; smooth and let dry. Sand lightly to smooth.

5. Using 1" brush paint entire project brown; let dry.

6. Using scruffy brush loaded lightly with licorice, go over project, leaving many brown areas showing through. Let dry.

7. Go over project with brush and mixture of equal parts blue and aqua, leaving many areas of underlying colors showing through. Let dry.

8. Rub black paint into indented areas (eyes, nostrils, lips); let dry.

9. Following manufacturer's instructions, use your finger to rub gilding creams sparingly over raised surfaces; let dry.

10. Spray with clear coating. ✂

Faux Metal Sunshine
Enlarge 200% before
transferring pattern

Shop Smart

It's important to buy your supplies with a pricing formula in mind. If you purchase your supplies wholesale from a distributor or manufacturer, you will have to purchase in minimum quantities (usually by the dozen or gross), and often there will be a minimum purchase required that could range from $50–$2,500.

Most start-up craft businesses try to purchase supplies on sale from retailers, or order supplies from discount craft suppliers. The lower your cost of goods, the more profit you will make.

Calculate Replacement Cost

However, when calculating your price, you should use the *replacement cost* of your supplies.

If you purchased your clasps on sale for 25 cents, you should still calculate your price using the regular, non-sale cost of the clasp—say, 35 cents.

You can't guarantee that you'll always be able to purchase the clasp on sale. If your pricing is based on the sale price, you stand to lose 10 cents per bracelet. That may not seem like much—but it is if you sell 300 bracelets! $

And the Survey Says ...

Always evaluate any show you do soon after it concludes. Some items to note include: total sales, total inventory count before and after, weather, traffic in the booth and ease of setting up. It is equally important to write a brief evaluation of each show; it will come in handy when you are scheduling future engagements. $

Enchanting Glass & Copper Ivy Bowls

Individualize each bowl with different embellishments to add to this project's unique style and customer appeal.

Designs by Lorine Mason

Materials

- Clear glass ivy bowl
- Stained glass colors*: yellow, red or blue
- #8 copper piping*
- Copper wire*
- Glass beads
- Decorative glass marbles
- Silicon glue
- Needle-nose pliers
- Votive, tea light or plant

*Krylon Stained Glass Color; copper piping and wire available in plumbing department of hardware and home improvement stores.

Instructions

1. *Bend copper piping around bowl in a decorative fashion using one of the following methods:*

- Create a curved design using pliers to decorate front of bowl; then bend piping around neck of bowl and straight up to create hanger. Form hanging loop by winding piping into a decorative coil.

- Bend piping into a 1" circle and continue loosely wrapping pipe around itself to create coiled base for bowl. Wrap piping across front of bowl and around neck. For hanger, leave 12" straight section before bending end into decorative coiled hanging loop.

2. Gently unbend piping just enough to remove bowl.

3. Following paint manufacturer's instructions, spray bowl with desired stained glass color; let dry.

4. Gently reinsert painted bowl in copper framework. Secure piping around bowl by wrapping wire around piping at joining points.

5. *Add decorative accents as desired:*

- Wrap 24" piece wire around piping at neck of bowl, threading beads onto wire as you wrap. Trim wire end; tuck under piping.

- Insert 6" piece wire around piping at neck of bowl. Thread bead onto both ends of wire and unwrap wire ends, creating spirals or separating wire threads to create a wire "tassel."

- Insert 12" piece wire through top hanging loop. Thread both ends through single bead. Form 2" coil with each wire end and thread a bead onto each end. Unwrap wire and create spiral coils with individual wire threads.

- Glue marbles along edge of bowl.

6. Insert candle or plant. ✂

Pumpkin Candles

Bring out the beauty of these candles by having one set aside to keep lit throughout the day at your booth.

Design by June Fiechter

Pumpkin Leaf

Materials

Each Candle

- 2.5-ounce scented candle in round glass container*
- Cuttable craft plastic
- Leading strips*
- Classic gold wax metallic finish*
- Paints for plastic*: green apple, green
- 12" piece yellow 18-gauge plastic-covered wire
- Orange threaded dark-tone paper
- Matte-finish decoupage coating
- ⅛" deerfoot stippler brush

Candle from Star Candle Co.; Readi-Lead Strips, Treasure Gold Wax Metallic Finish and Paint for Plastic, all from Plaid.

Make a Note of It

Most successful craft professionals keep a written record called a creative journal.

As an accounts ledger keeps track of the business side of your endeavor, the creative journal supports its creative aspects. It can include ideas, sketches, creative goals and more.

It doesn't matter if you use a spiral-bound notebook or a legal pad. What is important is that you *start,* and get into the habit of keeping a written record of your creative hopes and goals. **$**

Instructions

1. Referring to pattern, cut one leaf from cuttable plastic. Outline leaf with lead strip, overhanging edge slightly; repeat on second side, sandwiching edges of leaves between leading strips and pressing edges of strips together.

2. Using decoupage coating as glue, cover exterior of candle container with orange threaded paper, tearing paper into pieces as needed. When jar is covered, coat paper with decoupage coating; let dry.

3. Squeeze green apple paint onto plastic surface of leaf; let dry.

4. Using stippler brush, pounce green paint over dry green apple color; let dry.

5. Repeat steps 3 and 4 on other side of leaf.

6. Carefully poke small hole through plastic in stem end of leaf.

7. Rub gold wax finish over leaf (plastic and leading), wire and candle container, following manufacturer's instructions.

8. Wrap wire around neck of candle container; twist to secure. Thread leaf onto one end; secure by twisting. Coil wire ends around paintbrush handle. ✂

Mystique Candleholder

Display this handsome piece with a coordinating candle. You may even want to paint candles with decorative designs to sell as companion pieces.

Design by Joan Fee

Materials

- Magenta/gold multistep painting and finishing kit*
- Gold-leafing pen*
- Metal columnar candleholder

Magenta/gold Mystique multistep finishing kit and gold-leafing pen from Krylon.

Project Note

Familiarize yourself with manufacturer's instructions before beginning and follow manufacturer's instructions while completing the project. A metal candleholder was used for sample project.

Instructions

1. Spray two or three coats of base coat onto candleholder; let dry.

2. Apply two or three coats mid-coat color on candleholder; let dry.

3. Using gold-leafing pen, decorate candleholder as desired; let dry.

4. Spray candleholder with three coats of top coat. ✂

Harvest Seeds Set

Use seeds and legumes with different colors and textures to create these magnificent projects. This colorful fall set is sure to attract attention and garner praise.

Autumn Harvest Balls

Design by Bev Shenefield

Materials

- Plastic foam balls: 2 (2"), 3", 4", 4½" (see Project Notes)
- Hot-glue gun with flat ribbon nozzle*
- Dry black beans
- Small dark red beans
- Dry light red kidney beans
- Dry green split peas
- Unpopped yellow popcorn
- Acrylic craft paints*: Hauser medium green, lamp black, marigold, red iron oxide *or* russet, terra-cotta
- #12 flat paintbrush
- Hair dryer
- Pan or other container
- Gloss-finish varnish

Craft & Floral Pro Glue Gun and Nozzle from AdTech; Americana paints from DecoArt.

Project Note

Discarded play balls, softballs, etc., may be substituted for the plastic foam balls.

Instructions

1. *Paint balls:* 2" black for black beans, 4" green for peas, 2" russet for red beans, 4½" red iron oxide or terra-cotta for kidney beans and 3" marigold for popcorn. Let dry.

2. Glue beans, peas and popcorn to balls:

Black beans: Applying glue in short ribbons, glue a row all around center of 2" black ball, then fill in both sides.

Small dark red beans: Glue onto 2" russet ball as for black beans.

Light red kidney beans: Glue onto 4½" ball as for black beans.

Peas: Apply thin patch of glue to 4" ball and pour peas over it, holding ball over a pan or other container to catch overflow. Press peas into glue with fingers, taking care not to touch the hot glue. Cover entire ball in this manner. Rub off any loose peas and fill in bare spots as needed.

Popcorn: Glue onto 3" ball as for peas.

3. Use hair dryer set on high to remove any glue strings. Conceal any visible glue by painting with matching color.

4. Apply varnish to coat all balls; let dry. Pile balls in basket or display as desired.

Candleholder

Design by Vicki Schreiner

Materials

- Large wooden turned candleholder*
- Medium green acrylic craft paint
- Satin-finish interior varnish
- Permanent craft adhesive
- ½" flat paintbrush
- 3-ply jute twine
- Unpopped yellow popcorn
- Dry green split peas
- Small dry red beans
- Tweezers

Candleholder #11-3616 from Provo Craft.

Project Note

Allow all paints and finish to dry completely between coats.

Instructions

1. Paint entire candleholder with two coats green paint.

2. Refer to Fig. 1 for placement of jute, popcorn, dried peas and beans. For application of each item, begin at back of candleholder (the side with small hole at the bottom). To form each row, apply bead of adhesive, then press jute, bean, pea or popcorn kernel into adhesive. Work rows one at a time, going around and down the holder, filling in sections in the following order: Apply jute to all four areas; apply popcorn; apply peas using tweezers; apply red beans. Let dry for several hours.

3. Reapply one coat green paint to bottom of candleholder if necessary.

4. Apply three coats satin varnish over corn, peas, beans and painted areas of candleholder. ✂

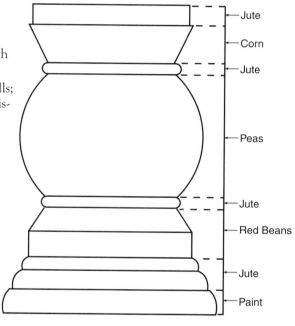

Fig. 1

Labels on figure (top to bottom): Jute, Corn, Jute, Peas, Jute, Red Beans, Jute, Paint

Library of Congress

For a small fee, you can file copyright paperwork for your designs with the Library of Congress. You own the copyright to your work the minute you create it; however, to protect your rights, it's best to consult a lawyer and file the appropriate forms with the government. **$**

Crafting for Charity

By Susan Laity Price

For generations, nonprofit organizations have sold handwork to raise funds for charity. As society has changed, however, so have these fund-raisers.

Today, very few organizations actually make crafts to sell. Instead, most groups hold craft shows and rent booth space to independent crafters. The rental fee covers the costs of running the show and the admission fee charged to the public is donated to the charity.

Leadership Roles

Whether a group makes its own crafts to sell or rents booth space at a show, volunteers are key to a successful effort.

At the top of the list are the *general chairman,* who assigns tasks and ensures that they are completed; the *publicity chairman,* who gets the word out to the public; and the *treasurer,* who keeps financial records and pays the bills.

These positions require dedicated volunteers who have good people skills, are organized and consistently follow through with their assignments in a timely fashion.

Key Volunteers

Supporting these key leadership positions will be volunteers with more narrowly defined roles.

If the group is making their own crafts, responsibilities can be divided along themes—home decor, wearable art, Christmas decorations, bakery, etc. These *department chairmen* coordinate projects made for their areas.

They must work closely with the general chairman and treasurer, especially concerning expenses. If the group reimburses workers for materials, written guidelines must clearly state how much each group can spend.

If, on the other hand, the group rents booth space to independent crafters, one person must be in charge of attracting quality crafters, signing them to contracts and assigning booth space.

Again, these volunteers must work well with people, have excellent organizational skills and good follow-through.

Involve Everyone

Enlist every member of your organization to help. Committees need clerical workers, carpenters, babysitters, antique collectors and gardeners, as well as artists, seamstresses, crafters and cooks.

Step 1: Analyze Your Market

The first step in planning a craft show is to analyze the local market.

- Who is your target customer?
- When are they available to shop?
- What are local decorating trends?
- Are there local interests such as sports, gardening, hunting or sailing to consider?
- What are your potential customers buying locally?
- What magazines are they reading?
- Are other craft sales held in your area? Make sure your show does not conflict with them.
- What types of crafts are sold at other shows?
- How can you make your show stand out from the crowd?

This step takes investigative work. Be sure to analyze the *community* and not just your organization's membership. The whole point of holding a fundraiser is to raise money from *outside* your organization.

Step 2: Analyze Your Organization

- How many members with leadership potential can dedicate themselves to your cause?
- How many helping hands will there be?
- What special talents do your members possess?
- Does anyone have inside contacts with suppliers, sports figures, or space or equipment rentals?

A good way to learn about your membership is to have them fill out an interest survey. One-on-one conversations also reveal helpful data. A good chairman will spend time getting to know everyone in the organization to identify those with "hidden talents," skills and contacts.

Step 3: Choose a Location

Many organizations choose their location based solely on rental costs. Expenses are important, but there are other factors to consider.

- Could you fill a larger space with more booths?
- Are lighting and ventilation satisfactory?
- Is the location easy for customers to find?
- Are loading areas and parking conveniently located?
- Is the building handicapped accessible?
- Is security a problem?

- How far in advance will the owner guarantee availability dates?

Weigh all these factors before signing a rental contract.

Show Day: Make Your Dealers Comfortable

Create an atmosphere that makes dealers *want* to be part of your event.

From your very first contact with them, treat dealers like valued professionals.

Communicate in writing all rules and regulations concerning your event. Explain what your group will do *for* them in addition to what you expect *from* them. Send them detailed maps of the building indicating where they are to check in, unload and park.

Provide volunteers to help exhibitors unload and transport their products to their booth space. Offer booth sitters throughout the show to give crafters working alone periodic breaks. If food is not available in the hall, arrange for carryout orders to be delivered.

At the end of the show, thank the dealers for coming and help them reload their vehicles.

Cater to Customers

Make everything about your event as customer-friendly as possible.

Outdoor signs are very important, especially if your show is in a large building with many entrances. Make signs that are readable from a car. There is nothing more frustrating than parking and then realizing that the entrance is at the other end of the building. Station orange-vested volunteers in the parking lot to direct traffic and answer questions.

Coat and parcel check-in areas keep visitors' hands free to continue shopping. Seating areas allow tired customers to rest and then continue shopping instead of going home.

Having food available will also keep them shopping longer.

Boost Your Attendance

If attendance has been a problem in the past, consider adding free special events spaced throughout the show.

Lectures and demonstrations about crafting, decorating and cooking can attract more visitors. These do not have to be given by well-known experts; simply enlist confident individuals who can hold an audience's attention for 20 minutes.

Local singing groups will bring in grandparents, aunts and uncles who want to hear them. Activities for children such as face painting, clowns and balloons will attract younger families. A promised picture with Santa or the Easter Bunny is popular in season.

Raising Extra Funds

As long as you have attracted a crowd, why not include an additional fund-raiser to make more money for the charity or your organization?

Evaluate your membership to choose the attraction that will work best for your group. Be sure that those renting booth space know exactly what you are planning so that there is no competition.

Consignment sales of items such as packaged gourmet foods, books or holiday greenery offer no financial risk. And you'd need very few volunteers to handle the extra booth.

Other items such as plants can be purchased wholesale, but there may be products leftover.

Bakery sales are always popular. They offer one way to involve members who cannot be there on the day of the show.

Your organization might also have its own booth filled with crafts made by your members. It should be clearly marked that everything is made by the membership and all

proceeds are donated directly to the charity. Make sure your crafts do not compete with those of exhibitors who have rented space. ✂

Be in the Know

Take note of these items when you're checking out a show in which you might like to participate.

- How did you find out about the show? A newspaper ad? Road signs? Word of mouth?
- How are crafters setting up their displays and booths?
- What kinds of displays catch your eye?
- What are the price ranges of different items?
- Are buyers walking around with bags of purchases or are they empty-handed?
- What seems to be selling well? Anything not selling? **$**

You can't help but think of lazy, crazy days of summer when you get a look at these watermelon cuties. Whimsical displays are very tempting to buyers.

Fall Wind Chimes

*Colorful bead embellishments add class and charm
to these tinkling wind chimes. The handsome
combination of rustic colors and fall leaves
makes them a must-have home accent!*

Design by June Fiechter

Materials

Square Chimes
- 6" rusted tin triple square sign*
- Aluminum wind chimes
- 8 small wooden heart cutouts
- Metallic crochet thread

Cylinder Chimes
- Cylinder wind chimes*

Each Project
- 20-gauge gold wire
- Metal "flakes"*
- Metallic pen*
- Glass beads in assorted fall colors
- Die-cut vellum leaves*
- Tacky craft glue
- Clear coating
- Spanish copper rub-on metallic finish*
- #6 flat paintbrush
- Craft drill with small bit
- Needle-nose pliers
- Hot-glue gun

*Rusted tin sign #52-2155 and cylinder chimes #24-6896 from D&CC; Eberhard Faber Flakes Easy Metal #8781-99 and Easy Pen #12394N from Amaco; Paper Reflections Vellum Die Cuts leaves #DIE04245 from DMD Industries; Rub'n Buff Metallic Finish from Amaco.

Project Note

Follow manufacturer's instructions for using metallic pen and applying metallic flakes.

Square Chimes

1. Remove leather and back tin square from sign.

2. Apply copper rub-on finish to heart cutouts; set aside to dry.

3. Color edges of each tin square with metallic pen. While still tacky, apply metal flakes around edges; brush off excess flakes with brush.

4. Trace around green vellum die-cut leaf in center of small tin square; remove leaf and color area with pen. Coat with metal flakes as in step 3.

5. Glue four heart cutouts to back of each tin square, near corners; glue smaller square in center of larger square, aligning large rectangular openings at top and using hearts on back of smaller square as "spacers."

6. Drill six holes ½" apart across bottom edge of larger square.

7. Cut 2¼" piece wire; thread on green bead, orange bead and another green bead; coil wire ends around paintbrush to keep beads in place.

8. Cut 10" piece wire; shape into a circular hanger. Using needle-nose pliers, bend a small loop in each end of wire, but do not join wire ends.

9. Cut two 2" pieces wire; using pliers, firmly attach one end of each to beaded wire (step 7), attaching 2" wires between beads. Feed free ends of 2" wires through holes in metal squares to back; using pliers, securely attach one end to each of the loops in hanger.

10. Lay same vellum leaf used in step 4 on work surface; dab top with pen, patting with finger to remove excess. Coat with flakes, brushing off excess.

11. Apply several large blobs of glue to traced leaf on center of smaller square; lay vellum leaf on top without pressing it down into glue.

12. Dab chimes all over with pen; apply flakes and brush off excess. Suspend chimes from holes in bottom with lengths of crochet thread.

13. Spray entire wind chime with clear coating.

Cylinder Chimes

1. Color top and bottom edges of cylinder with metallic pen. While still tacky, apply metal flakes around edges; brush off excess flakes with brush.

2. Select large orange oak leaf from vellum die-cuts; place on cylinder and trace around it; remove leaf and color area with pen. Coat with metal flakes as in step 1.

3. Lay same vellum leaf used in step 2 on work surface; dab top with pen, patting with finger to remove excess. Coat with flakes, brushing off excess. Glue leaf over traced leaf on cylinder.

4. Cut one 2" and two 4" pieces of wire. Thread assorted glass beads onto wires, kinking and twisting as desired with needle-nose pliers, and twisting loops or coils in ends to keep beads in place.

5. Wrap shorter wire around hanger cord at top of dangling heart charm. Wrap longer strands around hanger just above where it attaches to sides of canister. ✂

Inspiration

Need some inspiration to kick-start your efforts in selling your crafts? There are many ways to overcome a rut or slump in marketing and merchandising.

First, write down your goals— short-term and long-term. Have a good idea of what you hope to accomplish in your designs and how that relates to your productivity and sales.

Expand Your Market

Add a new show or two to your selling plan. Stretch into some new marketplaces and regions. You may decide not to return to a show that was unsuccessful (and depressing!) in the past.

Think about planning a fall home show, creating a Web site or setting up in a craft mall. You might also think about selling directly to retail stores in your area. **$**

Heart-Shaped Leaf Box

Try filling this attractive box with photos for your display, or just let the lovely autumn project speak for itself.

Design by Joan Fee

Materials

- 10" heart-shaped papier-mâché box with lid
- Ivory spray paint*
- Matte-finish decoupage coating
- Rust acrylic paint
- Foam paintbrush
- Paper plate
- Plastic wrap
- Fall leaves

Krylon General Purpose Color Spray Paint.

Instructions

1. Spray-paint box and lid; let dry.

2. Pour puddle of rust paint on paper plate. Scrunch up a wad of plastic wrap and dab into paint; dab off excess on paper plate, then dab plastic wrap all over box and lid. Let dry.

3. Brush decoupage coating onto top of lid; while still wet, arrange leaves on lid as desired. Coat leaves and lid with additional decoupage coating. Let dry.

4. Repeat step 3 on sides of box.

5. For added durability, brush additional coat(s) of decoupage coating over lid and sides of box, letting it dry between coats. ✂

More Niches

Find a niche you enjoy and you'll have a ready-made consumer base.

- Items that highlight occupations—teachers, nurses, engineers, firemen
- Baby items
- Kids' clothing and toys
- Personalized jewelry
- Masculine gifts
- Religious or spiritual items
- Celebrations of hobbies—golf, bingo, fishing, crafting, etc.
- Memory crafts
- Pet items
- Outdoor and garden novelties
- Collector pieces—Santas, teddy bears, dolls **$**

Crafter's Success Story
Jackie Haskell

was born and raised in North Dakota, and I still live there. My specialty has been making polymer clay miniatures.

I have made miniatures since I was a child, when an art teacher at our elementary school showed us how to make little bear ornaments out of dough.

But polymer clay is much more versatile, and allows me to be much more creative. I made the switch about 12 years ago, and my imagination really shifted into high gear!

I started crafting as a hobby. But after I had children, I wanted to do it professionally so that I could stay home with the kids and still bring in some income.

I have sold my miniatures through a magazine and a craft mall, but now I concentrate mostly on craft shows in North and South Dakota and Minnesota. I have been selling at craft shows for about 15 years. I also display some of my miniatures on my own Web page, www.jhminiatures.com.

It is difficult to know what to make and sell when you are starting out. It can be tempting to offer whatever is selling well for someone else. But a lot of other people are thinking that, too—and soon, too many crafters are doing the same thing.

I advise crafters to specialize in something that not so many people are doing. If you don't do it especially well at first, keep practicing! I taught myself without books or classes, but if you can't do that, then learn as much as you can, however you can.

Be prepared for disappointments. I thought my first miniatures were really cute. But now I wonder how I ever sold any!

The turning point for me came when I bought a quarter-page ad in a magazine, which displayed my miniatures in three issues. I really couldn't afford it, but I had a gut feeling. As it happened, everything worked out fine!

The ads gave my miniatures a showcase throughout this country and beyond. I even made a sale to a customer in Sweden!

The ad also led to magazine articles about my miniatures and me. If I hadn't taken that chance, I wouldn't be selling my designs today—and no one besides the people who attend the craft shows where I exhibit would even know about my miniatures. ✂

Acorn Harvest Squirrel on page 122.

Autumn Leaves Pyramid Boxes

These clever boxes give you the opportunity to try different colors and combinations. Fill them with scented potpourri and hang them at your window!

Design by June Fiechter

Materials

- Pyramid gift boxes*
- Raffia: brown, gold, orange
- Hole punch
- Small sharp scissors
- Oak leaves rubber stamp
- Fine- and medium-point black permanent markers
- Colored pencils
- Pin
- Large-tip embossing tool*
- Wavy metallic satin paper*
- Threaded dark-tone paper sheets*: pumpkin, forest green
- Shiny black dimensional fabric paint
- Tacky craft glue
- Waxed paper
- Die-cut vellum fall leaves*
- Caribbean blue spray paint
- Sparkle decoupage coating*
- Dark blue soft chalk
- ¾" flat glaze brush

*All Night Media pyramid boxes #94PMD from Plaid; embossing tool, satin and threaded papers from Embossing Arts Co.; vellum die cuts from DMD Industries and Sparkle Mod Podge from Plaid.

Small Stamped Box

1. Color leaf stamp with black marker; stamp on one side of box. Repeat to stamp a second leaf on that side. Repeat until each side has two stamped leaves.

2. Embellish leaves with marker; color them with colored pencils using red, yellow and green. Color background on box with two shades blue.

3. Perforate box sides around leaves with pin.

4. Turn box over and emboss areas inside pinholes with embossing tool.

5. Punch a hole near tip of each box side. Close box; secure with orange raffia tied in a bow.

Large Green Box

1. Dilute glue with a small amount of water, mixing well.

2. Open pyramid box and lay flat on protected surface, right side up; paint surface of box with a thin layer of glue. Press green paper over glue to cover box; press flat and let dry.

3. Cut away all excess green paper; set aside. Punch a hole near tip of each box side.

4. Cut a triangle of wavy paper to fit on one side, leaving a narrow green border exposed.

5. Cut leaf shape to fit on one side from orange threaded paper; lay leaf right side up on waxed paper and coat right side of leaf with glue mixture; let dry.

6. Assemble box. Glue wavy triangle and leaf to one side as shown.

7. Outline leaf and add details with fine-point black marker.

8. Close box; secure with brown raffia tied in a bow.

Large Blue Box

1. Open large box and lay flat, right side up, on work surface. Mist with blue spray paint; let dry.

2. Glue small vellum leaf to each side of box. Outline leaves and add details with fine-point black marker.

3. Punch a hole near tip of each box side. Assemble box. Rub chalk over edges of box and beside leaves for shadow.

4. Brush decoupage coating over surface of box; let dry.

5. Close box; secure with gold raffia tied in a bow. ✄

The Show Must Go On

It seems arts-and-crafts shows have been a staple market for creative craftspeople and artists since man became creative. Almost every country has some form of marketplace for buyers to browse the wares of the creative.

This type of show can be small—a church bazaar held in the church basement with a dozen tables of wares—or very large—an outdoor show with hundreds of vendors lining the streets of a city or park.

Craft Shows Everywhere!

On any given day, there is at least one craft show happening somewhere in the United States. On some weekends, there can be a handful of shows in the same city.

So how do you choose the best craft show or bazaar in which to participate?

The Right Choice for You

First things first! Attend several craft shows and walk each as a buyer. This will give you a better understanding of how the craft buyer shops.

This marketplace is very broad and it is the main source of income for many professional crafters. Visiting a few shows can really help you get a feel for what is needed to be successful in that venue.

Try to visit different types of shows, including an outdoor event, an indoor show and a juried show. Take notes and see if you prefer one type of show to another. **$**

Wooden Apple Bucket

Use different colors and shades when making a supply of these decorative buckets to give your customers options in matching their home decor.

Design by June Fiechter

Materials
- Wooden bucket with apple cutout*
- Natural raffia
- 3¼" x 4½" aluminum mesh*
- Metal paints*: bing cherry, espresso bean, hunter green
- Celery green acrylic craft paint
- Fine-tip black permanent marker
- Fine-grit sandpaper
- #8 shader paintbrush
- Tacky craft glue

Apple bucket #11-3640 from Provo Craft; aluminum #50023E Modeler's Mesh from Amaco; No-Prep metal paints from DecoArt.

Instructions
1. Paint a very light coat of green acrylic paint over bucket, inside and out.

2. Glue mesh inside bucket to cover apple cutout; let dry.

3. Using brown, paint mesh inside stem cutout; paint also ⅛" border around stem on front of bucket, and inner edges of cutout opening.

4. Using green metal paint, paint mesh inside leaf cutouts; paint also ⅛" border around leaves on front of bucket, and inner edges of cutout opening.

5. Using cherry paint throughout, paint mesh inside apple cutout; paint also ⅛" border around apple on front of bucket, and inner edges of cutout opening; paint wooden bucket handle.

6. Sand all wooden surfaces lightly.

7. Using marker, outline apple, leaves and stem with dashed line.

8. Hold several strands of raffia together and tie them around handle in a bow. ✂

Happy Harvest Pin

Wearing pins you made is a great way to get customers to notice them and want one for their own! Use different fabrics and colors for the scarecrow's necktie to add variety to your display.

Design by Mary Nelson

Materials

- ¼"-thick pine or poplar
- Graphite paper
- Scroll saw
- Fine-grit sandpaper
- Acrylic craft paints*: antique mauve, buttermilk, burnt umber, cool neutral, lamp black, marigold, medium flesh, milk chocolate, Napa red, true ochre
- Paintbrushes: ½" wash, ¼" angular shader, #3 round, #0 and #1 liners, ½" stencil brush
- 1" pin back
- Craft cement
- Masking tape
- Acrylic spray sealer
- Old toothbrush or spatter brush
- ¼" checkerboard stencil
- Fabric scrap
- Cotton-tip swab

Americana paints from DecoArt.

Project Notes

When painting, use largest brush that will fit area to be painted. For shading, lining and spattering, thin paints to an inky consistency with water. Let paints dry between colors.

Instructions

1. Referring to instructions for "Using Transfer & Graphite Paper" (General Instructions, page 190), transfer pattern outline onto wood. Cut out; sand.

2. Cut a piece of masking tape slightly larger than pin back; press onto back of pin where pin back will be attached later. Leave tape in place until project has been painted and sprayed with sealer.

3. Paint all surfaces of pin cool neutral.

4. Lightly transfer pattern lines to front of pin.

5. *Sign:* Stencil pattern of buttermilk checks over sign. Shade sign with milk chocolate. Add lettering and linework around edges with thinned black and liner brush; add dots to ends of letters with liner brush handle dipped in undiluted black.

6. *Hands and face:* Paint face and hands medium flesh; shade with chocolate. Using swab, blush cheeks with mauve. Paint red nose and dot on black eyes with brush handle. Using liner and thinned black, line around hands, finger stitches, mouth, eyebrows and stitches.

7. *Hat and hair:* Paint hat chocolate; shade with burnt umber. Paint hair using alternating strokes of marigold, true ochre and chocolate. Let dry.

8. Spatter pin with buttermilk and black. Add tiny buttermilk highlight dots to cheeks and eyes.

9. Spray front of pin with sealer; let dry. Spray back of pin; let dry.

10. Tie knot in tiny strip of fabric; trim ends; glue to front of pin.

11. Carefully peel tape from back of pin. Apply generous amount of cement to unsealed area and press pin back in place, allowing cement to ooze through holes. Let pin set overnight before wearing. ✂

Happy Harvest Pin

Maid's Day Off?

Keep your display and crafts clean and dust free. Dust is a signal to the customer that your work isn't selling. **$**

Scarecrow Candy Container

This scarecrow invites you to help yourself to a piece or two of candy. Fill him with goodies to treat your customers as they browse your booth.

Design by Mary Ayres

Materials

- 6½" x 5½" x 6" wooden box*
- 2⅞" x 7⅛" wooden slat*
- 24 jumbo craft sticks
- Wooden craft pick*
- Wooden cutouts: ¾" x 1" triangle, 1½" oval
- 1¾" wooden craft disk*
- 1" x 12" torn strip fabric
- Jute twine
- Burlap fabric scrap
- Natural raffia
- Acrylic craft paints*: cadmium yellow, lamp black, pumpkin, sable brown, true red, white wash, wild orchid
- Paintbrushes: #6 and #8 round bristle brushes, #1 and #6 soft rounds
- Craft glue
- Black twin-tip marker*
- Fine-grit sandpaper
- Graphite paper (optional)
- Stylus (optional)

Box from Plaid; wooden slat, pick and disk from Forster; Americana paints from DecoArt; ZIG Memory System marker from EK Success Ltd.

Instructions

1. Cut one jumbo craft stick in half for arms. Cut rounded end of craft pick to 1¾" long for pumpkin stem.

2. Lightly sand wooden pieces as needed; wipe off dust.

3. Referring to patterns and to instructions for "Using Transfer & Graphite Paper" (General Instructions, page 190), transfer top and bottom edges of scarecrow's shirt to wooden slat; transfer cuff line to each arm.

4. Paint box black inside and out. Paint all surfaces of remaining pieces as follows: *red*—triangle (scarecrow's nose); *black*—oval (crow); *white*—23 jumbo craft sticks (fence pickets); *pumpkin*—wooden disk (jack-o'-lantern); *brown*—pumpkin stem and pants area on bottom of wooden slat; *yellow*—head area on slat and hands on arms; *orchid*—shirt area on slat. Let dry.

5. Transfer mouth, cheek dots and eyes to scarecrow face; eyes and beak to crow; and eyes, nose, mouth and cheek dots to jack-o'-lantern.

Rouge scarecrow and jack-o'-lantern's cheeks with red; when dry, add highlight dots to cheeks using brush handle dipped in white; in same manner, dot white eyes onto crow. Paint crow's beak yellow.

6. Using bullet tip of black marker, draw scarecrow's eyes and jack-o'-lantern's eyes and nose.

7. Using fine tip of black marker, draw mouths on scarecrow and jack-o'-lantern; draw buttonhole stitch around edges of nose; outline white fence pickets; add details to pumpkin stem; add pattern of vertical and horizontal lines to sleeves and shirt.

8. Glue nose to scarecrow. Cut raffia

in short pieces and glue along edges of sleeves to overlap hands and along neckline to overlap face. Wrap fabric strip around scarecrow's "neck" for scarf; knot off to right side and trim scarf ends.

9. Cut a 5½" circle from burlap; cut circle in half. Reserve one piece for another use. Fold remaining piece in half, overlapping straight edges, and glue. Glue hat to scarecrow's head with overlapped edges in back. Unravel bottom edge of hat; turn brim up and glue to secure. Tie jute around top of hat; knot in front; trim ends to ¾" and fray ends.

10. Wrap jute around wrists and

Scratch That Niche!

Try to match your crafts to the needs of the marketplace you select. In some cases you may end up with a niche craft item to sell. This simply means that although your craft may not attract every person who sees it, it will be a "must-have" for your niche consumer.

Success in a Niche Market

A good example of a crafter who found a niche market is Nancee McAteer and her business, Wooden Warriors. With a daughter attending West Point,

Nancee was always on the lookout for items related to West Point. But she was disappointed with what she found and decided to design some cadet ornaments herself as a Christmas gift for her West Point parents club.

The ornaments were such a hit that Nancee received requests for them from all over the United States.

Nancee was able to turn a one-time gift idea into a business. She identified a need and created a craft to fill that need within a niche market. **$**

belt; knot on front. Trim ends to ¾"
and unravel.

11. Glue ends of arms to back of
scarecrow; glue crow to left arm. Glue
five fence pickets vertically to front
of box and five more to each side; add
two horizontal crosspieces to front and
sides. Glue remaining pickets to back
of box, one on each side of scarecrow.
Glue stem to back of jack-o'-lantern;
glue jack-o'-lantern to front of box at
bottom right. ✂

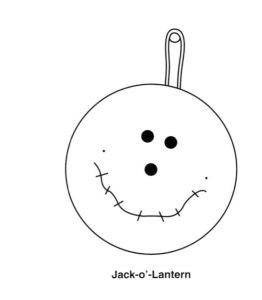

Jack-o'-Lantern

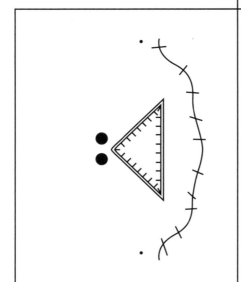

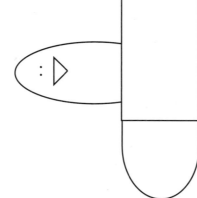

Travel With Ease

If you are traveling with your
display to craft shows, all the
materials and props you use
must fit in your car or trailer.
That means it's best to work
with collapsible items. **$**

Boo Ghost

Boo and his long-legged friends will quickly charm themselves out of your booth and into someone's home. Use plaids or different-colored fabrics for creative options.

Design by Paula Bales for Dow Chemical Co.

Materials

- Plastic foam balls*: 1", 3", 4"
- 3" section of 3/16" wooden dowel
- Serrated knife
- Tea bag
- Man's white tube sock
- Tacky craft glue
- Low-temperature glue gun
- 2" x 13" torn fabric strip
- 3 (½") flat black buttons
- 16 (1") pieces black plastic-coated 24-gauge wire
- Wire cutters
- Acrylic craft paints*: autumn leaves, ivory white, pure black
- Paintbrushes: #2, #6 and #10 shaders, #3 round

*STYROFOAM balls from Dow; FolkArt paints from Plaid.

Project Note

Use tacky glue for gluing unless instructed otherwise.

Instructions

1. *Body:* Using serrated knife, slice off

one-quarter of 4" ball from one side. Set body on its flat base.

2. *Glue head to body:* Poke ends of dowel in 3" and 4" balls to make guide holes. Remove; apply glue to ends of dowels. Place one end in top of 4" ball (body) and other end in 3" ball (head); push balls together and add more glue between them.

3. Cut cuff off sock; reserve for another use. Brew tea bag in water; cool. Soak foot portion of sock in tea until desired color is achieved. Wring sock; let dry.

4. Push assembled foam balls into sock so toe seam runs across top of head. Pull cut edges smoothly to bottom of ghost and glue in place; let dry.

5. Lightly rouge cheeks with autumn leaves. Hot-glue two buttons on for eyes; add highlight dots with paintbrush handle dipped in white paint. Paint autumn leaves nose directly below and between eyes; add black oval mouth and black eyebrows. Let dry.

6. Tie fabric strip around neck for scarf; knot and hot-glue remaining button at knot.

7. *Spiders:* Cut 1" foam ball in half with serrated knife; paint each half-ball black. Let dry.

8. Using end of paintbrush handle, indent two eyes in each spider; dot white paint into indentations. Let dry, then add smaller black dots for pupils; lightly rouge cheeks with autumn leaves; let dry.

9. Shape spider legs from black wire; apply glue to one end of each and poke four legs into each side of each spider. Let dry. Glue one spider to ghost's head and the other to left side. ✄

Ghostly Duo
Wall Hanging

Hang this charmingly "scary" duo with similarly themed projects in a prime location in your booth to increase impulse buying.

Design by Mary Nelson

Materials

- ¾"-thick pine stock
- Acrylic craft paints*: antique mauve, grey sky, Hauser dark green, lamp black, light cinnamon, pumpkin, red iron oxide, white wash
- Paintbrushes: ½" and 1" shaders, ½" angular shader, #0 and #1 liners, spattering brush
- Cotton-tip swab
- Acrylic spray sealer
- Scroll saw
- Craft drill with #53 bit
- Sandpaper
- Graphite paper
- 18" piece black 19-gauge wire
- 2 small fabric scraps
- Raffia: natural and orange
- Hot-glue gun

*Americana acrylic paints from DecoArt.

Project Notes

When painting, use largest brush that will fit area to be painted. For shading, lining and spattering, thin paints

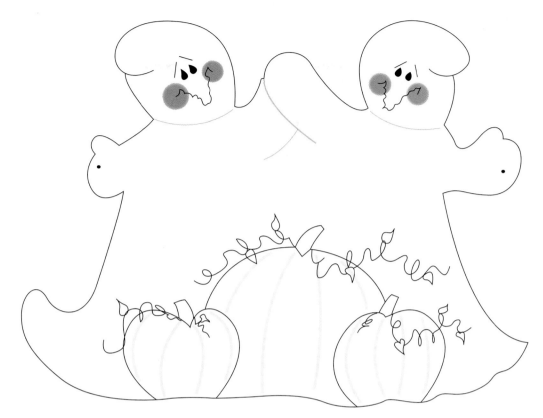

Ghostly Duo Wall Hanging
Enlarge pattern to 200%

to an inky consistency with water. Let paints dry between colors.

Instructions

1. Referring to instructions for "Using Transfer & Graphite Paper" (General Instructions, page 190), transfer pattern outline to wood; cut out and sand edges. Drill holes where indicated by black dots.

2. Transfer main pattern lines to wood.

3. Paint ghosts (including all edges) white; shade with grey.

4. Use cotton swab to blush cheeks with antique mauve. Dot on eyes with black.

5. Using liner, add mouths and eyebrows with thinned black.

6. Add white highlight dots to eyes and cheeks.

7. Paint stems (including edges) cinnamon.

8. Paint pumpkins pumpkin; shade

with red iron oxide.

9. Using liner, add dark green vines; paint dark green leaves. Let dry completely.

Finishing

1. Lightly spatter front with cinnamon, then with black; let dry.

2. Spray front with sealer; let dry. Spray back with sealer; let dry. Repeat.

3. Tie knots in center of two small fabric scraps; trim ends. Sand a small spot under each ghost's chin; hot-glue bows to sanded spots.

4. Fold 18" wire in half; twist to form hanging loop in center. Run ends of wire through holes from back to front; kink wire ends to hold wire in place; twist and kink hanger as desired.

5. Hold together four or five strands each of natural and orange raffia; tie in bow around hanger. ✂

Light It Up!

Check the lighting of your display for dark corners and shadows that may hide your crafts. This isn't always easy to control—especially if you aren't given the option of being near an outlet—but keep lighting needs in mind.

Your display's background colors can help. Lighter colors reflect light and can make it easier to see items. Displaying larger items in the back and smaller items in the front may also help. **$**

Happy Fall Memo Board

Personalize this design with different messages and sayings— or try leaving a few blank. Remember: All projects don't have to be identical. Variety is part of what makes crafting fun!

Design by Paula Bales

Materials

- 12" square ⅜"-thick craft plywood*
- Fine-grit sander*
- 4½" square model railroad cork sheeting*
- Acrylic craft paints*: apricot, black, harvest orange, nutmeg brown, pumpkin, spring green, white
- Medium swirl sponge*
- #4 and #14 shader paintbrushes
- Craft cement
- Black fine-tip marker
- Graphite paper
- Craft saw
- Picture hanger

Plywood, Sup-r Sander and cork all from Midwest Wood Products; Apple Barrel paints and medium swirl Fun Sponge from Plaid.

Instructions

1. Referring to instructions for "Using Transfer & Graphite Paper" (General Instructions, page 190), transfer pattern for pumpkin memo board and three leaves to plywood; cut out.

2. Paint front and back of memo board pumpkin; paint leaves green. Let dry.

3. Apply apricot paint to swirl sponge and stamp randomly over orange surface of pumpkin. Paint stem brown; let dry.

4. Between swirls, dot pumpkin with small white dots and larger orange dots using tips of paintbrush handles dipped in paint; add some small white dots to leaves and small orange dots to stem; let dry.

5. Paint lettering black; let dry.

6. Using marker, outline leaves and add veins. Outline stem and pumpkin; add tendrils and other details.

7. Glue leaves to pumpkin. Glue cork square behind opening. Glue picture hanger to back of bulletin board. ✂

Happy Fall Memo Board
Enlarge pattern to 133%

Vampire Bat Door Hanger

Bright colors and touches of glitter add personality and sparkle to this project. Try a variety of messages to make this bat welcome in any room.

Design by Mary Ayres

Materials

- 3½" x 9½" wooden door hanger with rounded top*
- 5½" x 2¼" wooden sign with jagged edges*
- 1¾" wooden craft disk*
- ⅞" wooden teardrops*
- Craft foam: yellow, black
- Jute twine
- 2 (7mm) round wiggly eyes with green painted eyelids
- Ultrafine crystal glitter
- Stencils*: moon, cloud
- Acrylic craft paints*: cool white, dove grey, festive green, lamp black, lavender, olive green, slate grey, true red, wild orchid
- Glorious gold metallic acrylic craft paint*
- Paintbrushes: ⅜" stencil brush, #6 and #8 round bristle brushes, liner
- Craft glue
- Twin-tip permanent black marker*
- Fine-grit sandpaper
- Light transfer or graphite paper
- Stylus

Door hanger and sign from Lara's Crafts; disk and Woodsies teardrops from Forster; Simply Stencils moon #28209 and cloud #28369 from Plaid; Americana paints from DecoArt; ZIG Memory System marker from EK Success Ltd.

Project Notes

Refer to General Instructions, page 190, for the following: dry-brushing, stenciling and rouging in "Painting Techniques"; and, if transferring designs, in "Using Transfer & Graphite Paper."

If you can't find wiggly eyes with painted eyelids, paint your own; when dry, use fine-point permanent black marker to add line between lids and eyes, and a few tiny lashes.

Instructions

1. Sand wooden shapes; wipe off dust.

2. Paint door hanger orchid; let dry, then dry-brush edges with lavender.

Bat

Lettering Diagram

When sales are down, consider these questions:

1. *Take a serious, unbiased look at where you are selling your crafts.* There are so many marketplaces; is your current marketplace a good match for your craft?

2. *Does your marketplace advertise regularly?* If you are in a craft show or craft mall, make sure *you* advertise yourself and your work too! Part of the responsibility of promotion is on your shoulders. Make sure you have business cards and brochures.

3. *Do you have a customer base or a loyal repeat-customer mailing list?* Keep this group informed of what you are doing and where your crafts are available.

4. *Are you meeting the needs of your repeat buyers?* Add new products or bring in seasonal items for this customer. Make sure you let your repeat customers know how important their business is and how much you appreciate each purchase.

5. *How many new customers are you reaching?* New customers are important too! Be on the lookout for ways to reach more customers. **$**

3. Stencil dove grey clouds on hanger; shade bottom edges with slate and top edges with white.

4. Paint sign olive; let dry, then dry-brush edges with green, pulling color into indentations of jagged edges. Let dry.

5. Referring to lettering diagram, transfer words to sign and go over them with marker's bullet tip.

6. Referring to bat pattern, cut wings in a single piece from black craft foam. With black paint, paint disk for body and teardrops for ears; let dry, then dry-brush edges of body, ears and foam wings with lavender.

7. Transfer facial features to disk as desired; rouge cheeks with red and fangs with white. Let dry. Add cheek dots using toothpick dipped in olive; using liner, outline fangs and add

mouth with lavender.

8. Glue teardrops to back of body so only points show for ears; glue eyes to face. Glue foam wings to back of body.

9. Using stencil as pattern, draw moon on yellow craft foam; cut out and dry-brush edges with gold.

10. Lightly brush glue on clouds, one at a time, and immediately sprinkle with glitter. Repeat around edges of moon and sign; shake off excess glitter.

11. Thread twine through holes in sign; knot on front. Trim ends to ½"; fray ends.

12. Glue moon, bat and sign to door hanger as shown. Add a dab of glue behind wings on both sides of body and prop up wings so they will dry that way. Add bat's legs with marker's fine tip. ✄

Acorn Harvest Squirrel

Making clay figurines for your booth is a great way to offer lower-priced items that will be popular with shoppers. This darling squirrel would be great to display with other fall items!

Design by Jackie Haskell

Materials

- Modeling compound*: black, chocolate, dusty rose, red, sweet potato, tan, white, yellow
- 2 black seed beads
- Straightedge tool for cutting and making lines
- Straight pin
- Pink powdered cosmetic blusher
- Cotton-tip swab
- Ovenproof plate
- Oven

Sculpey III modeling compound from Polyform Products.

Base & Leaves

1. *Base:* Soften and roll one section of tan compound brick into a disk 2" wide and ¼" thick.

2. *Yellow maple leaves:* Roll a marble-size ball of yellow compound; cut into quarters and roll each piece into a ball; use one ball for each yellow leaf. Flatten ball into ½" teardrop with pointed top and wide bottom. Using straightedge, make two evenly spaced cuts in wider end, starting at edge and cutting toward center. Pinch three points onto edge of each section. Add details with straightedge. Repeat to make a total of five yellow leaves.

3. *Orange maple leaves:* Repeat step 2 using sweet potato modeling compound to make five orange leaves.

4. *Red oak leaves:* Roll five pea-size balls red compound; cut each in half. Return one to the block for another use; roll remaining nine pieces into balls and use one for each leaf. Flatten

each ball into ¾" teardrop. Using straightedge, make two evenly spaced cuts on each side of shape, starting at edge and cutting toward center. Slightly elongate top section of each leaf. Add details with straightedge.

5. *Attach leaves:* Alternating colors (yellow, red, orange), loosely attach leaves around edge of base. Attach more firmly when all leaves are in position.

Squirrel

1. Cut one section each from white and black compound bricks; blend thoroughly to make gray.

2. *Body:* Roll ball of gray compound equal to 1¾ marbles; shape into 1" fat teardrop. Pinch fatter end of teardrop to make indentations for legs. Flatten half of a pea-size ball of white compound into ¾"-long teardrop shape; attach to front of body, matching points.

3. *Arms:* Roll two pea-size balls gray compound. Roll each into ¾"-long cone; slightly flatten and round larger ends to form paws. Use straightedge to define paws. Attach smaller ends to body.

4. *Legs:* Roll marble-size ball gray compound; cut in half and use one piece for each leg. Roll each into a ball, and then into a 1" cone; turn up ½" at smaller end to form foot. Flatten larger end of cone to attach to body. Roll two very small balls dusty rose compound for bottoms of feet; flatten each into a teardrop and attach one to bottom of each foot. Use straightedge to define feet. Attach legs to body in sitting position.

5. *Head:* Roll marble-size ball gray compound; cut off one-quarter and shape remaining into egg for head. Push beads on their sides into head

Continued on page 127

Home Shows

A craft home show is like a Tupperware or Mary Kay home party for crafts.

Craft professionals can organize the home show or home party in two ways. The first method is to use the show as the main avenue of sales for your crafts. This means you will have to be booking new shows continually to bring in income.

The second use for the home show is as an additional source of income, with the show scheduled in your own home on an annual, biannual or quarterly basis.

Planning Your Show

If home shows are to be the main source of your crafting income, the market must be consistently promoted and your sales area must expand for growth.

Professional crafters will often hire others to book, prepare and sell at the home shows. The sales help is paid a straight fee or a commission based on total sales.

If home shows represent additional income, an annual or quarterly home show is very easy to handle without additional sales help.

Check the Rules

In any case, the city or county in which the home show will be held must be contacted to make sure there are no statutes prohibiting the exchange of money in a private home for business reasons. Regulations vary widely, so check them out.

Many municipalities think of the annual or quarterly home show in the same category as a garage or estate sale. Most states require that sales tax be collected. The city or county's main concern may be the additional traffic in the neighborhood. Make sure you plan ahead for parking and notify your neighbors when the event will take place.

Plan Ahead!

Consider location, date, hours, inventory, invitations and how you will advertise the home show.

Prepare the home as you would for an open house. Remove all personal property from the rooms in which you will display your crafts. Set up an area for bagging purchases, supplies and collecting money.

A Group Affair

Consider inviting other professionals from non-competing media to join you. This will broaden your show's appeal, allow others to share expenses, and expand your guest list.

If you are working with others, plan ahead on how to keep money separate so there will be no confusion or frustration when the show ends. Consider using tags of different colors, or separate written receipts.

You will literally transform the rooms into sales showrooms. This marketplace allows you to display your work as your potential buyer can use it.

Hang wreaths on the wall. Place dolls on the mantel or shelf. Take every opportunity to show guests how your crafts will brighten their own homes.

Displaying crafts in a home lends comfort and warmth to shoppers who are tired of pushing and shoving their way around the mall.

To-Do List

Decide on a location, date and hours. Prepare invitations and fliers to mail and post around town with all the important information, a map and phone number.

Because this show takes place in a private residence, you may only want to include friends, local schoolteachers, your business mailing list and others with whom you are familiar.

Word-of-mouth helps attendance grow each year. Send out invitations giving customers enough time to schedule your event.

Serve refreshments like punch and cookies.

Reward Loyal Customers

This is a time to show your loyal and important buyers how much their patronage means to you.

Offer them a one-time discount, a free item or door prizes.

Give them 5 percent off for each guest they bring. Keep your guest book handy to record the new names—and then add them to your mailing list.

When an item is purchased, replace it in the display immediately. If an item has sold out, condense the display. Don't allow any part of your display to look picked over or empty. **$**

Pumpkin Coaster Set

These hand-painted autumn coasters will sell themselves. Decorative and affordable, these are sure to be among your most profitable crafts.

Design by Paula Bales

Materials

- Model railroad cork*
- Glossy indoor/outdoor paints*: black, bright red, real brown, real green, real yellow, spring green, tangerine
- Tip pen set*
- Paintbrushes: #4 and #10 shaders, #8 round
- Graphite paper
- Stylus

Cork from Midwest Wood Products; Indoor/Outdoor Gloss paints and tip pen set from Plaid.

Instructions

1. Referring to pattern, cut four pumpkin shapes from cork.

2. Paint shapes tangerine on front and back, applying two coats if necessary; let dry.

3. Transfer leaves and other details to painted pumpkins (see "Using Transfer & Graphite Paper," General Instructions, page 190).

4. Use bristle brush and a pouncing motion to shade each pumpkin with red and highlight each with yellow. Paint stems brown. Paint leaves real green; highlight with spring green. Let dry.

5. Using tip pens and black paint, add outlines and details. ✂

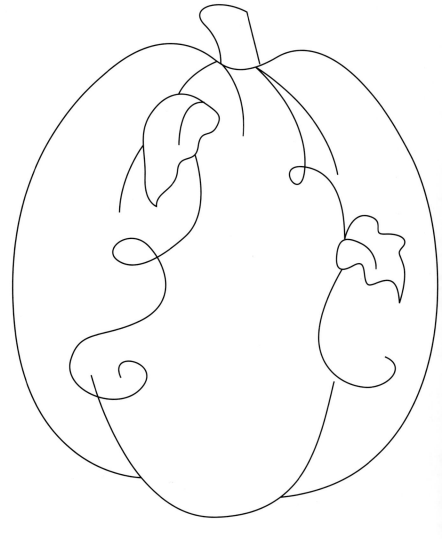

Pumpkin Coaster

Painted Cloth Pumpkins

This charming trio is great for fall decorating. Different sizes make this project all the more appealing.

Design by Karen de la Durantaye

Materials

Set of Three

- 2 yards muslin
- 2½ yards 48"-wide 16-ounce poly-ester batting (see Project Notes)
- Natural raffia
- Natural jute twine
- 3 (¾") dark green buttons
- Heavy crochet thread or string
- Interior flat latex or acrylic paints: orange, rust, yellow, green, brown
- Flat paintbrush
- Hot-glue gun
- Pinking shears (optional)
- Sewing machine
- Natural sewing thread
- Chenille needle or other large-eye needle
- Sea sponge
- Spray bottle for water
- Spring clothespins

Project Notes

Familiarize yourself with all instructions before beginning.

Batting layer should measure 1"–1½" thick; 8-ounce batting may be doubled.

Large Pumpkin

1. Launder muslin without using fabric softener; dry and press as needed to remove wrinkles.

2. Cut two 21½" x 17" pieces muslin and four 8" strips batting.

3. Using ¼" seam allowance, machine-sew muslin panels together along both long edges to make a fabric tube.

4. By hand, sew running stitch ¼" from edge of one open end; pull thread tight to close completely; knot and turn pumpkin right side out.

5. Stack batting strips, edges even, and roll up. Insert in open end of pumpkin. Strips should fit very snugly; add another strip of batting if necessary.

6. Gather excess fabric at open end in your hand. Leaving an 8" tail, wrap jute around excess fabric a couple of times to close top of pumpkin as close to batting as possible; tie double knot but *do not cut jute.*

7. Beginning at a seam, wrap jute very tightly around pumpkin from top to bottom to create six sections. Tie knot; again, *do not cut jute.*

8. *Stem:* Tightly wrap remaining jute upward around excess fabric; when you reach top, wrap jute back down. Wrap jute around base of stem one more time and tie double knot. Clip off excess jute.

Leaves

1. Cut two 8" squares muslin and one 8" square batting.

2. Trace large leaf onto one muslin square. Sandwich batting between muslin with leaf pattern on top; pin layers together at corners.

3. Machine-sew along traced line.

4. Trim excess fabric within ¼" of stitching, using pinking shears if desired.

Painting

Note: Before painting, dilute paints

Large Leaf

Medium Leaf

Keep It Fresh!

63

Change your display frequently. Regular customers are always looking for something new even if they don't ask. If your display of work never changes, the customer gets used to the "look" of your display and eventually stops looking.

You don't have to have new items to change the display. Often just rearranging your work or moving it to a different location in your display is enough to catch a customer's eye.

Try changing the table dressing or adding a lace runner. Even modest changes can pique customers' interest.

Take the time to see how others display their work. If all displays in a craft mall use the same props and colors, individual exhibits all melt together in a customer's mind. Display your work differently to attract buyers. **$**

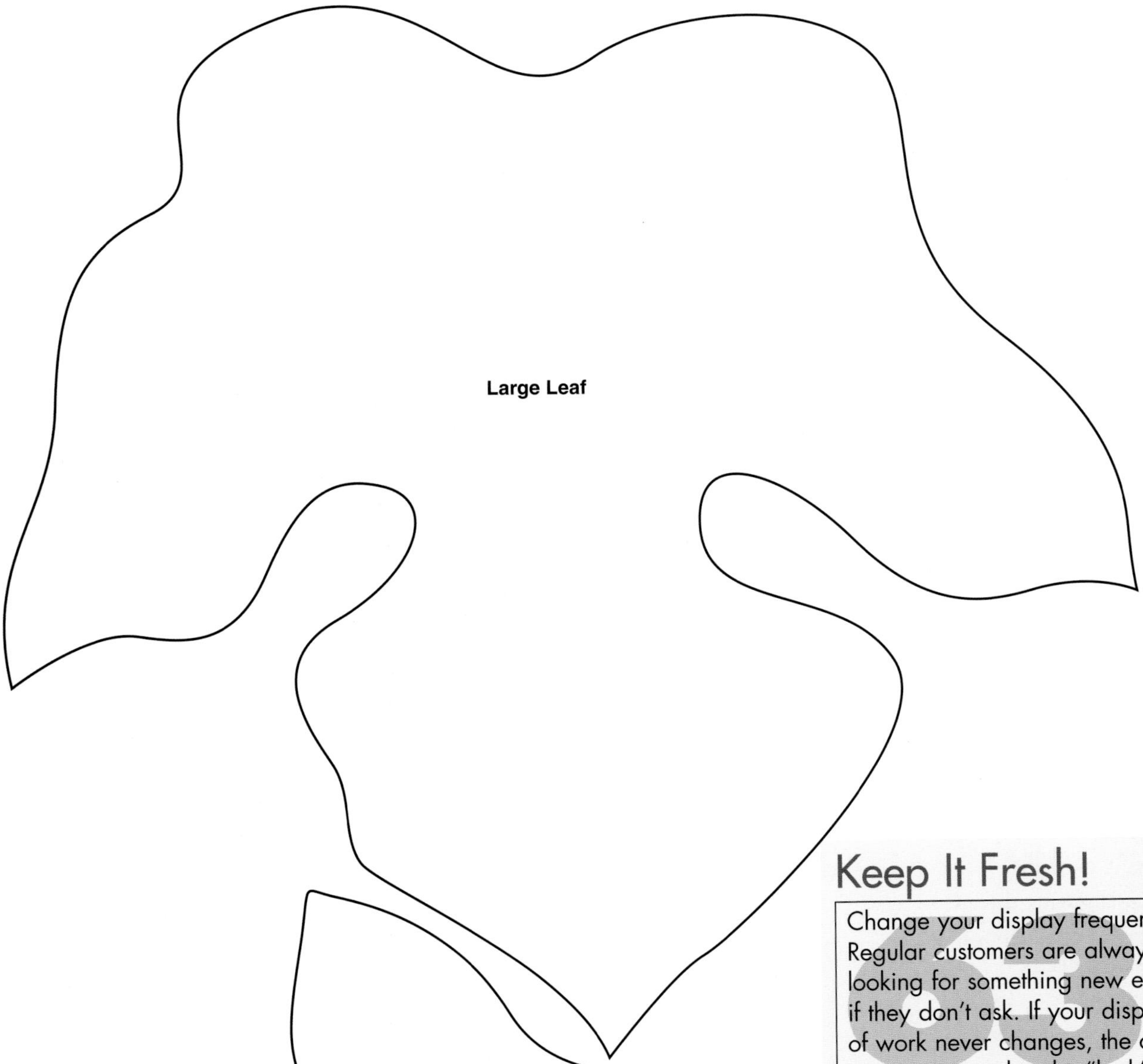

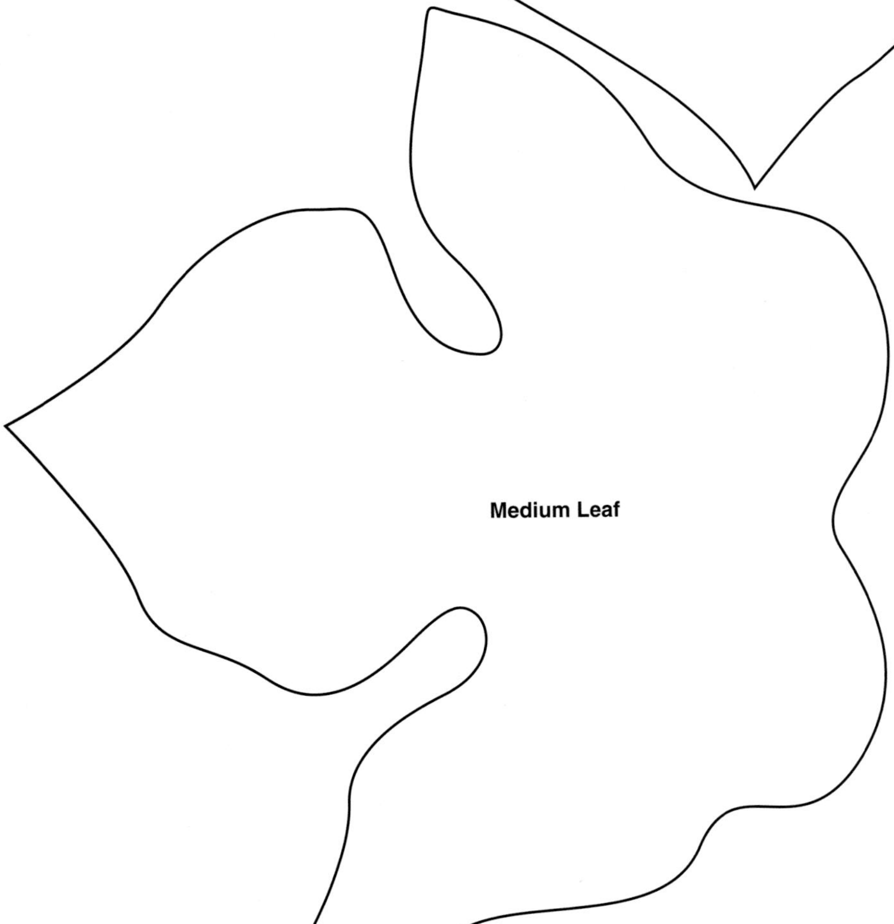

with water to a fairly thin consistency. Experiment to find the consistency that works best.

1. Fill spray bottle with water; spray pumpkin to get it wet.

2. Wet sea sponge with water. Use sponge to apply orange paint to entire pumpkin except stem. While still wet, sponge some rust here and there; repeat with yellow.

3. While still wet, use flat brush to apply green paint along indentations created by wrapping jute around pumpkin.

4. Spray both sides of leaf with water. Sponge green paint on both sides. *Note: Using clothespins, hang leaves to dry over newspapers to catch drips.*

5. Paint stem brown with sponge.

6. Let pumpkin and leaves dry thoroughly; it might take a day or so.

Assembly

1. Glue leaf to stem.

2. Tie raffia bow; glue to leaf.

3. Thread chenille needle with heavy crochet thread; sew thread through buttonholes and knot ends on front of button. Glue button in center of raffia bow.

Medium Pumpkin

Follow all steps for large pumpkin, substituting two 17" x 13½" pieces muslin and four 6" strips batting. For leaf, cut two 7" squares muslin and one 7" square batting; use pattern for medium leaf.

Small Pumpkin

Follow all steps for large pumpkin, substituting two 14" x 12" pieces muslin and four 5" strips batting. For leaf, cut two 5" squares muslin and one 5" square batting; use pattern for small leaf. ✂

Small Leaf

Acorn Harvest Squirrel

Continued from page 122

for eyes until none of hole can be seen. Use straightedge to make small line down center of smaller end. Roll a tiny ball of dusty rose; attach above line for nose. Using pointed end of straightedge tool, make small mouth. Roll very small ball white compound; shape into triangle for teeth. Attach

teeth in mouth. Use straight pin to define teeth, eyelashes and eyebrows. Apply pink blusher to cheeks with cotton swab. Attach head to body.

6. *Ears:* Roll two small balls—about 1/16-pea size—gray compound; slightly flatten each into teardrop shape. Use straightedge tool to make tiny line in each, from broad end almost to *but not through* point. Attach ears to head.

7. *Tail:* Roll ball of gray compound equal to 1½ marbles; shape into 1½" cone. Slightly flatten and round larger end. Scratch lines into tail with straight pin. Curl tail back slightly and attach narrow end to base of body. Attach squirrel to base.

Acorns

1. Combine marble-size ball of tan compound with pea-size

ball of chocolate compound; blend thoroughly.

2. Cut three portions each equal to ¼ marble; form each into an acorn, forming point at bottom.

3. Roll three pea-size balls chocolate compound; use one for each acorn cap. Place each ball on thumb while forming cap to indent caps. Pinch top to form tiny stem.

4. Attach caps to acorns. Use straightedge tool to add detail lines to caps.

5. Attach one acorn between squirrel's hands; attach remaining acorns to side of base with leaves.

Baking

Bake squirrel on ovenproof plate in preheated 275-degree Fahrenheit oven for 10 minutes; let cool completely before handling. ✂

Denim Pumpkin Shirt

Bring the autumn season to life with this fun wearable project. Make several in children's sizes, too.

Design by Angie Wilhite

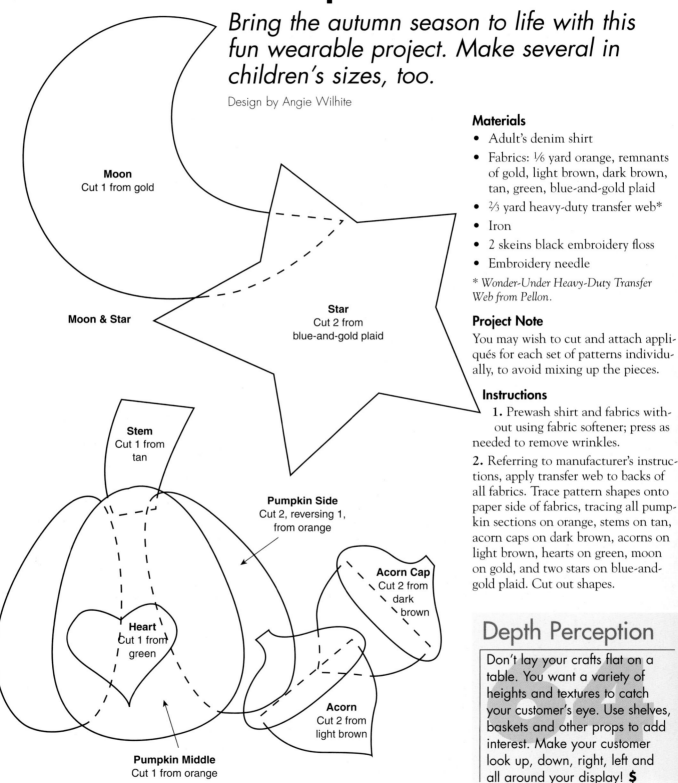

Moon
Cut 1 from gold

Moon & Star

Star
Cut 2 from
blue-and-gold plaid

Stem
Cut 1 from
tan

Pumpkin Side
Cut 2, reversing 1,
from orange

Acorn Cap
Cut 2 from
dark
brown

Heart
Cut 1 from
green

Acorn
Cut 2 from
light brown

Pumpkin Middle
Cut 1 from orange

Back Pumpkin Cluster

Materials

- Adult's denim shirt
- Fabrics: 1/6 yard orange, remnants of gold, light brown, dark brown, tan, green, blue-and-gold plaid
- 2/3 yard heavy-duty transfer web*
- Iron
- 2 skeins black embroidery floss
- Embroidery needle

* Wonder-Under Heavy-Duty Transfer Web from Pellon.

Project Note

You may wish to cut and attach appliqués for each set of patterns individually, to avoid mixing up the pieces.

Instructions

1. Prewash shirt and fabrics without using fabric softener; press as needed to remove wrinkles.

2. Referring to manufacturer's instructions, apply transfer web to backs of all fabrics. Trace pattern shapes onto paper side of fabrics, tracing all pumpkin sections on orange, stems on tan, acorn caps on dark brown, acorns on light brown, hearts on green, moon on gold, and two stars on blue-and-gold plaid. Cut out shapes.

Depth Perception

Don't lay your crafts flat on a table. You want a variety of heights and textures to catch your customer's eye. Use shelves, baskets and other props to add interest. Make your customer look up, down, right, left and all around your display! **$**

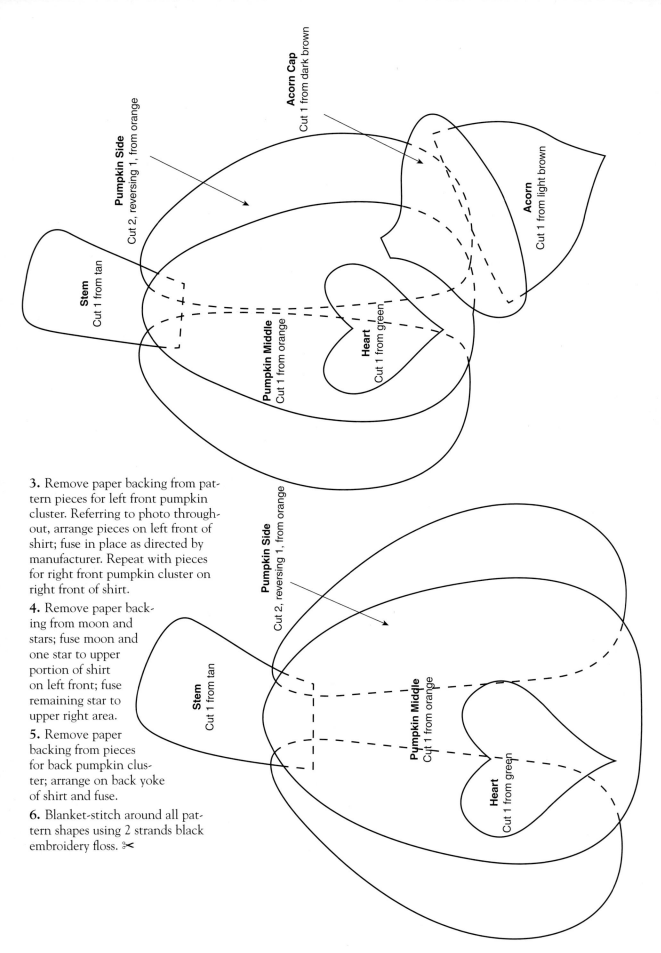

Pumpkin Side
Cut 2, reversing 1, from orange

Acorn Cap
Cut 1 from dark brown

Acorn
Cut 1 from light brown

Stem
Cut 1 from tan

Pumpkin Middle
Cut 1 from orange

Heart
Cut 1 from green

Right Front Pumpkin Cluster

Pumpkin Side
Cut 2, reversing 1, from orange

Stem
Cut 1 from tan

Pumpkin Middle
Cut 1 from orange

Heart
Cut 1 from green

3. Remove paper backing from pattern pieces for left front pumpkin cluster. Referring to photo throughout, arrange pieces on left front of shirt; fuse in place as directed by manufacturer. Repeat with pieces for right front pumpkin cluster on right front of shirt.

4. Remove paper backing from moon and stars; fuse moon and one star to upper portion of shirt on left front; fuse remaining star to upper right area.

5. Remove paper backing from pieces for back pumpkin cluster; arrange on back yoke of shirt and fuse.

6. Blanket-stitch around all pattern shapes using 2 strands black embroidery floss. ✂

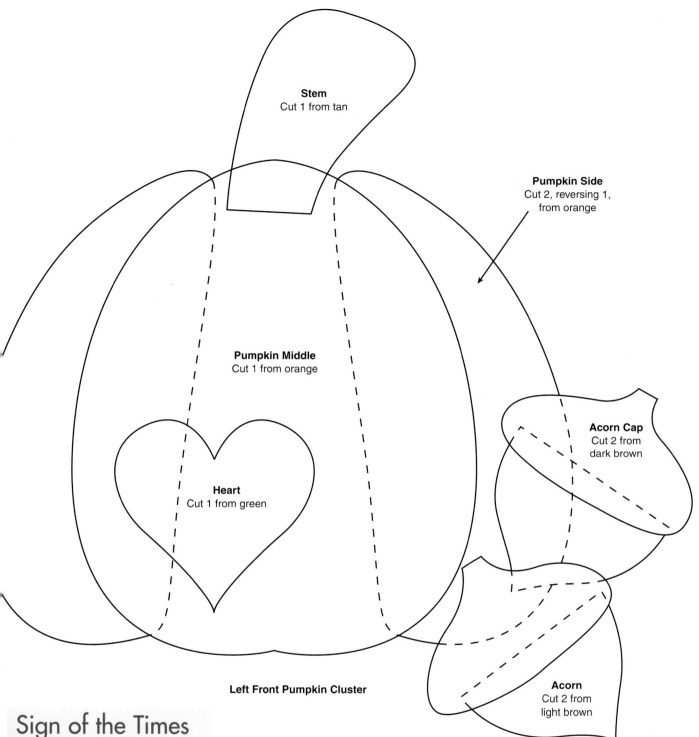

Stem
Cut 1 from tan

Pumpkin Side
Cut 2, reversing 1,
from orange

Pumpkin Middle
Cut 1 from orange

Acorn Cap
Cut 2 from
dark brown

Heart
Cut 1 from green

Acorn
Cut 2 from
light brown

Left Front Pumpkin Cluster

Sign of the Times

Help out customers with signs that explain your craft. Keep signs neat, concise and brief.

But avoid words like "SALE" and "MARK DOWN"; most handcrafted items are undervalued and you don't want customers to think you can't sell the work at retail prices. If you do decide to lower a price, just do so without drawing attention to it. **$**

Make Color Work for You

Color plays an active role in any craft display. Coordinate and contrast colors of backdrops and coverings with your work. A shock of bright color attracts the eye of a potential customer.

Color marketing experts suggest refined colors of blue, green, gray and black help sell higher-priced items. Lower-priced items sell faster with vivid shades of yellow, orange and red.

Darker shades make big spaces look smaller and more comfortable while lighter shades open up a small space. A warm neutral or pastel is said to put the customer in the mood for buying. **$**

Felt Autumn Pillow

Make pillows in different colors and stitch on these charming pumpkins for decoration.

Design by Chris Malone

Materials

- Felt*: ½ yard 36"-wide sage, 10" square sandstone; 9" x 12" sheets cinnamon and coral dawn
- Cotton embroidery floss: black, gray-green
- Embroidery needle
- 16" square pillow form
- 3 yards ³⁄₁₆" twisted beige cord trim
- Seam sealant
- Sewing machine
- Sage sewing thread

Kunin Rainbow Felt Classic.

Instructions

1. From sage felt cut one 17" square and two 17" x 12" rectangles.

2. Referring to patterns, cut one pumpkin and one pumpkin center from coral dawn, one stem from sage, and three leaves, reversing one, from cinnamon.

3. Pin pumpkin, stem and two top leaves to sandstone square as shown in photo. Using 2 strands black floss, blanket-stitch around all appliqués.

4. Pin sandstone square in center of sage square; using 3 strands green floss, blanket-stitch around edge of sandstone felt.

5. Pin remaining leaf to side of pumpkin as shown, overlapping squares; blanket-stitch in place with 2 strands black floss.

6. Using 3 strands green floss, blanket-stitch along one long edge of one sage rectangle. Pin rectangle to top half of pillow front, right sides facing, matching unstitched long edge to top edge

of pillow front.

7. Pin remaining rectangle across bottom of pillow, right sides facing, matching one long edge to bottom of pillow front and overlapping first rectangle section; pin sides.

8. Machine-sew all around pillow. Trim corners; turn pillow cover right side out. Insert pillow form through opening formed by overlapping flaps on back.

9. Cut cord trim into four equal pieces. **Note:** *To prevent raveling, wrap a small piece of tape around each end and at each place where cord will be cut; cut through tape and cord.* Knot each end of each cord. Apply seam sealant solution liberally to each cut end and let dry before cutting off tape.

10. Wrap one cord around each corner of pillow; tie in bow on front. ✂

Color Me Creative!

Color trends are an interesting blend in the 21st century.

Two branches of color hues are predicted to influence the consumer. One is soft, pale, weathered, washed-out true colors. The other is bold, rich, clean, true colors.

"True color" means there is little or no shading in tones of blue, gray or black.

Both distinct color spectrums are in demand and both will be highlighted in fashion and home decor. Gray will be the popular neutral while soft green, light tan and off-white will also serve as neutrals. **$**

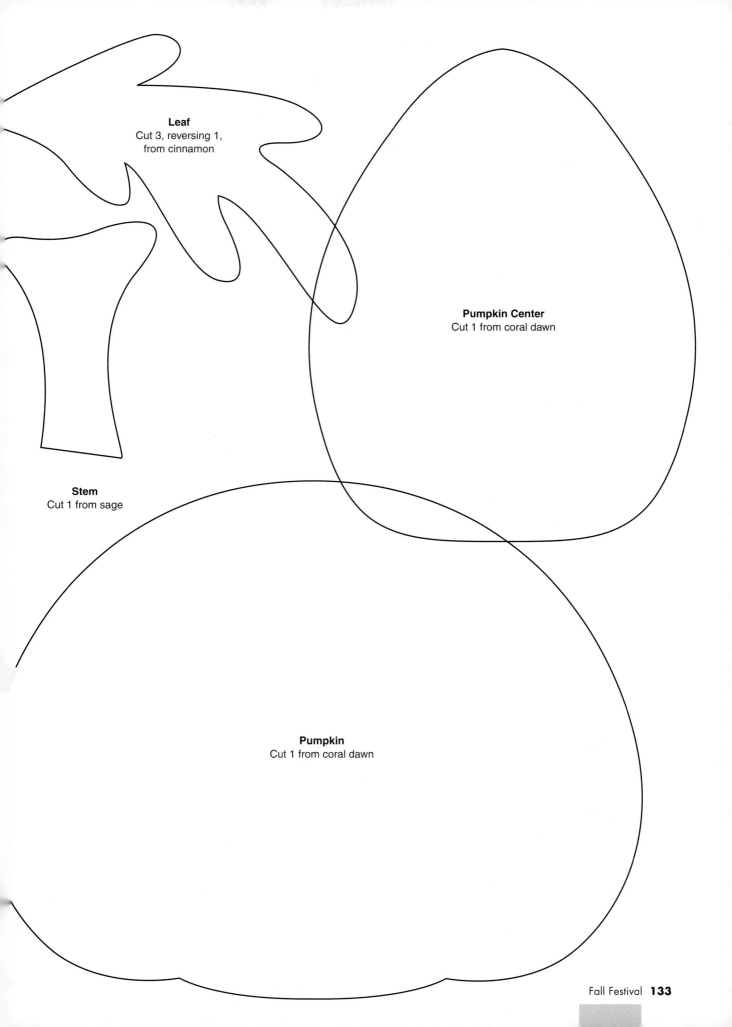

Leaf
Cut 3, reversing 1,
from cinnamon

Pumpkin Center
Cut 1 from coral dawn

Stem
Cut 1 from sage

Pumpkin
Cut 1 from coral dawn

Fall Floral Steppingstone

Attract customers who want to brighten their yards and gardens with this vibrant outdoor accent. Use the techniques described here to make stepping-stones with designs to fit every season.

Design by Margaret Hanson-Maddox

Materials

- Concrete mix
- 14" round steppingstone mold
- Palette paper or foam plate
- Water basin
- Cellulose household sponge
- Acrylic indoor/outdoor paints*: antique mum, daisy cream, cloud white, fiesta yellow, golden honey, holly berry red, light sage green, pine green, sprout green, tiger lily orange, woodland brown, wrought iron black
- Paintbrushes: #4 and #12 flat shaders, #4 filbert, #10/0 liner
- Graphite paper and stylus
- Tracing paper

*Patio Paints from DecoArt.

Instructions

1. Follow concrete manufacturer's instructions for making stepping-stone in round mold. **Note:** *For easier removal, wipe inside of mold lightly with cooking oil before pouring in concrete mixture.*

2. Let stone cure as directed, then wipe smooth side of stone with paper towel to remove dust.

3. Tap household sponge into cream, mum and brown. Tap paint-filled sponge over surface of stone using an up-and-down motion. Let dry.

4. In same manner, sponge sprout green over stone where pattern will be placed to form foliage behind flowers. Think of your steppingstone as a clock and sponge paint from the 11 o'clock position down to the 7 o'clock position. Let dry.

5. Use photocopier to enlarge pattern 133 percent. Referring to directions for "Using Transfer & Graphite Paper" (General Instructions, page 190), transfer design onto painted stone.

6. *Leaves:* For yellow leaves, tip one edge of #12 flat shader into yellow and the other edge into orange; blend on palette before painting surface. For brown leaves, tip one edge into brown and the other into orange, again blending before painting. Add vein and stem to each leaf using liner brush and red.

7. *Mums:* For each petal, tip #4 filbert into both yellow and honey. Using liner, add stem in light sage and pine.

8. *Forget-me-nots:* Tip one edge of #12 flat shader into red and the other edge into orange; blend on palette before painting each petal. Using stylus dipped in yellow, dot center onto each flower.

9. Using stylus dipped in white, add dots throughout arrangement.

10. *Lettering:* Using #4 flat shader and black, add lettering.

11. Let paint dry and cure as directed by manufacturer. ✂

Fall Floral Steppingstone
Enlarge pattern 133% before transferring

Winter Floral Arrangement

Made with pine and berries, this beautiful centerpiece can accent your home throughout the long winter months. Display this project with your other winter-themed items.

Design by June Fiechter

Materials

- Classic urn vase*
- 1 block floral arranging foam*
- Basil-color floral spray*
- 7 sprays imitation blue spruce
- 12 sprays red berries
- 8 cinnamon sticks
- 7 pinecones
- 11 sprays tiny white flowers
- 18–20 stems eucalyptus
- Sponge-on bronze patina kit*
- Acrylic craft paints*: earth brown, honey brown, milk chocolate
- Sea sponge
- Small paintbrush
- Foam glue*
- varnish*
- n floral picks
- ıpe

ssics vase #BRC80004 and
Foam from Dow Flora Craft;
Colortool floral spray; Bronze Patina Sponging Kit, Heavenly Hues and Americana acrylic paints and DuraClear Varnish, all from DecoArt.

Painting Vase

1. Wipe vase clean with cloth. Randomly sponge on chocolate and honey brown to cover vase; let dry.
2. Following manufacturer's instructions, use patina sponge kit to add bronze patina, leaving some of the brown base-coat showing through.
3. Using paintbrush, add earth brown "antiquing" in crevices; let dry.
4. Coat vase with varnish; let dry.

Arrangement

1. Glue foam in vase; let dry.
2. Spray blue spruce lightly with basil floral spray; let dry.
3. Referring to Figs. 1–3 throughout, arrange blue spruce, then berries, then cinnamon sticks in foam, taping pieces first to floral picks as needed to give them desired height and dimension.
4. Fill in empty spaces with pinecones, white flowers and eucalyptus. ✂

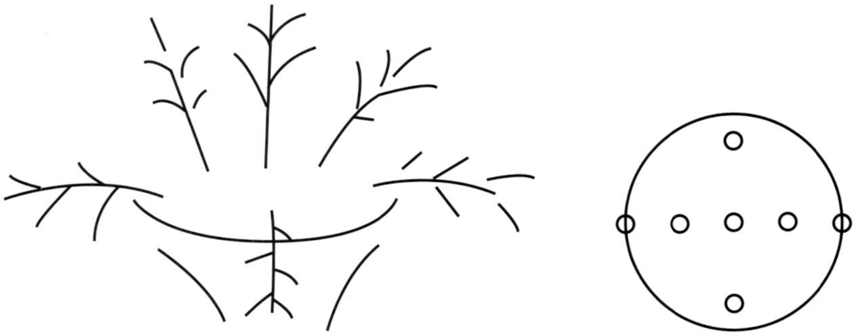
Evergreen
Top View

Fig. 1

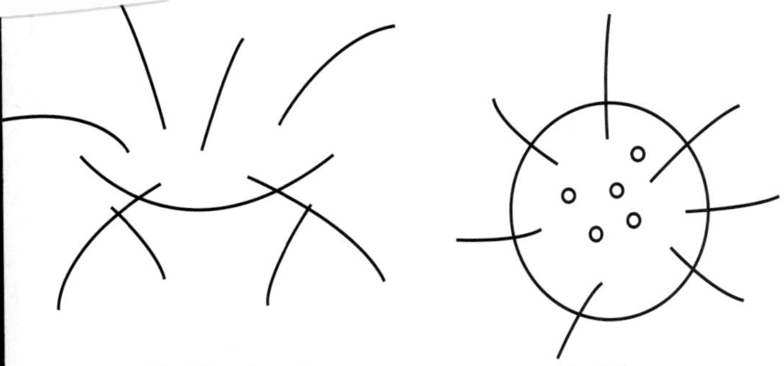
Red Berries
Top View

Fig. 2

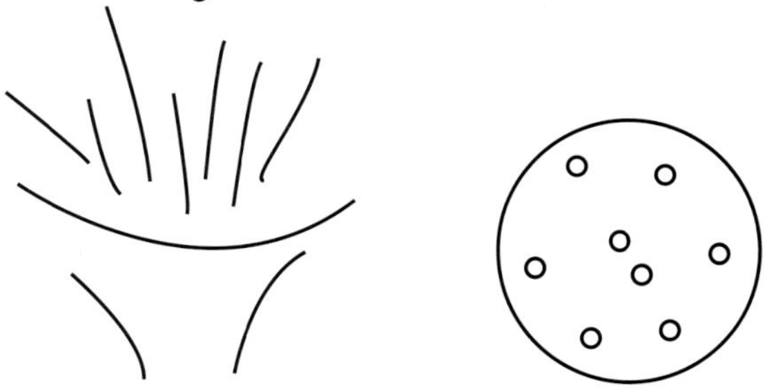
Cinnamon Sticks
Top View

Fig. 3

Take Advantage of Holiday Spirit

Christmas boutiques are the most popular and successful home shows. Play music, light scented candles, decorate a tree with lights, serve punch and cookies, and hire a baby sitter for the kids so Mom and Dad can browse without distractions.

The idea is to invite the customer to bring a gift shopping list and stay awhile. Offer gift-wrapping and handmade gift tags. Have an area of lower-priced items so children can purchase gifts for Mom and Dad.

Make It Fun!

Offer a free ornament or percentage off one item if your customer brings a new guest for your mailing list. Personalize items on site. Teach bow making or have another small craft for guests to make.

This can be a fun celebration of crafting, so get creative and show off. If held at the end of your fiscal year, there is the added bonus of reducing your inventory, making inventory much easier to handle at tax time. **$**

Kissing Ball

Make this kissing ball in several different shades to really let your creative flair shine. Touches of glitter add sparkle and beauty.

Design by June Fiechter

Materials
- Approximately 26 mini red dried or silk roses
- Approximately 28 small mauve dried or silk flowers
- Approximately 30 small white dried or silk flowers
- Small pieces of eucalyptus
- Light green leaves for filler
- Craft glue
- Silver stiffening spray*
- 25" 1½"-wide sheer white and silver wire-edge ribbon
- Gold cord for hanging loop
- 2 wooden floral picks
- Toothpick
- 4" plastic foam ball

Sparkling Stiffen Stuff from Beacon.

Instructions
1. Attach hanging loop of gold cord to one wooden pick; dip tip of pick in glue and press pick into top of plastic foam ball.

2. Trim all stems to be inserted in ball to ½".

3. For each piece inserted in ball, pierce ½" hole into ball with toothpick; squeeze glue into hole, then insert stem. Position same pieces opposite one another, then move on to another floral product. Cover entire ball in this fashion, filling spaces with green leaves.

4. Tie ribbon in bow; attach to remaining floral pick and press pick into ball beside first pick, securing with glue as needed.

5. Spray ball with silver stiffening spray. ✂

My Best-Selling Item
By Missy Becker

One year my mother and I were shopping the after-Christmas sales when I spotted a Victorian teardrop ornament. When I held it up and asked if she thought it resembled anything, we both agreed it looked like a light bulb. Then we shared a good laugh about how funny it would look to cover a tree with light bulbs!

Over the next few months, I played around with the idea as a joke to play on my mom. Finally it hit me: What if I painted the light bulb to look like Santa?

The "Joke" Takes a Life of Its Own
After a few test runs, I came up with a face that I liked. When I added some ribbon, mini lights and beads, I had a really cute ornament. I decided to show it to my mom early so I could start making them to sell.

They became the hottest item at my shows. I had everyone I knew saving their burned-out light bulbs for me!

I then expanded the line to include a reindeer, a cow and a pig, which only increased the demand. The closer we got to Christmas, the more light bulbs I needed.

Buying in Bulk
Soon I needed many more light bulbs than I could collect from my friends, so I started buying them at a local discount store. I loaded a shopping cart with light bulbs each time I went in!

People gave me strange looks when I lined up with a cart full of light bulbs. But I had fun with it, and enjoyed making up excuses for needing so many. I told people that I was opening my own casino, or that my kids flicked the lights on and off, making the bulbs burn out faster!

To this day, these light-bulb ornaments are still my biggest sellers. And it all started as a joke! ✂

Holly Vase & Candleholder

Holly leaves and berries adorn this wintry set. Try filling the vase with holiday treats for your home craft display.

Design by Mary Ayres

Holly

Materials

- 8" clear glass vase
- Clear glass votive candleholder
- Gold leading*
- Glass paints*: leaf green, lemon lime, primary red, tickled pink, white pearl
- Styrene painting blank*
- Masking tape
- White paper
- Craft knife

Liquid Rainbow leading, paints and painting blank from DecoArt.

Instructions

1. Trace holly pattern 10 times onto white paper. Tape to underside of painting blank.

2. Trace pattern outlines directly onto painting blank with gold leading, keeping tip of tube above blank and allowing paint to flow from tube. Mistakes or unwanted blobs of paint can be cut and peeled away with a craft knife after leading is dry. Let leading dry 1–2 hours.

3. Working on one pattern at a time, apply a line of leaf green inside leaf edges and on left side of each center vein. Fill in leaves with lemon lime.

4. Painting one berry at a time, apply a line of red inside berry outline, then fill in center of berry with pink. Let dry.

5. Apply a dot of white in center of each berry; let dry for 24 hours.

6. Carefully peel painted designs off painting blank. Apply one to front of votive candleholder; arrange remaining motifs on vase as desired, spacing them evenly and pointing leaves in different directions. ✄

Beaded Porcelain Ornaments

Display these elegant ornaments in a prime location at your booth. These simple yet exquisite projects will also add a classy touch to your home.

Designs by Vicki Schreiner

Don't Fade Into the Background

Make sure the colors you select for your display don't blend in with the colors in your products. Color is meant to enhance the product and make it stand out.

Step back from your display and look at it as a customer would. Does it entice you to take a closer look? **$**

Materials
- White porcelain ornaments*: lace-edge star, heart lace
- Round pearl beads: 13 (3mm) mint green, 10 (5mm) mint green, 5 (6mm) mint green, 39 (4mm) white, 25 (5mm) white
- Acrylic craft paints*: barn red, butter cream, dark foliage green, dusty mauve, eucalyptus, mocha brown, village green, white
- Clear glaze base*
- Clear satin glaze*
- Paintbrushes: #4 flat, #3 round, #1 liner
- Craft adhesive
- 2 (8") pieces ¼"-wide gold metallic ribbon

- White nylon bead string
- Beading needle
- Dark graphite transfer paper
- Ballpoint pen
- Old paintbrush handle
- Toothpick
- Removable tape

Ornaments from Provo Craft; Ceramcoat paints, Clear Glaze Base and Perm Enamel Clear Satin Glaze, all from Delta.

Painting

1. Referring to directions for "Using Transfer & Graphite Paper" (General Instructions, page 190), transfer heart and star outlines and stripes onto ornaments, tracing over designs with ballpoint pen and using removable tape to hold patterns in place. Do not transfer stippling dots; these are for your reference in shading.

2. Using #4 flat brush and referring to directions for base-coating under "Painting Techniques" in the General Instructions, base-coat stripes in village green and butter cream; let dry.

3. Transfer design details to ornaments.

4. Referring to Fig. 1 throughout, paint rosebuds on heart with mauve. Paint leaves on star with eucalyptus.

Fig. 1

5. Mix equal parts glaze base with each color, then shade, working on a small area at a time. Load brush with small amount of paint mixture, apply to area to be shaded, then quickly dry brush on paper towel and pat applied paint with dry brush to blend and soften. Shade edges of star and heart with mocha; shade leaves with dark green.

6. *Complete painting:*

Star: Using liner and dark green, add vein to each leaf; let dry. Using paintbrush handle dipped in mauve, dot on holly berries; let dry. Using toothpick dipped in white, add highlight to right side of each berry; let dry.

Heart: Using liner and dark green, line stems and leaves; using liner and barn red, place medium dot at top of each mauve rosebud; let dry. Using toothpick dipped in white, add highlight in center of each red dot; let dry.

7. Apply two coats satin glaze to painted designs, letting glaze dry 15 minutes between coats.

8. *Hanger:* Loop a piece of ribbon through hole in top of each ornament; knot.

Beading

1. *Star:* Work first in outermost row of holes, using 5mm white pearls: Thread beading needle with 2 yards bead string. Push through first hole from back to front; string on pearl, leaving 6" tail on back. Push needle back through same hole and pull until taut; knot using tail. Do not trim tail. Take needle through next hole, thread on pearl, take needle back through, pull until taut, come up through next hole, thread on bead, etc. Work around outermost row in this fashion. After attaching last white bead, knot string ends using original tail; trim excess.

2. In same fashion, bead remaining holes, using 6mm mint pearl in point of each triangle and 5mm mint pearls in remaining holes.

3. *Heart:* Using same procedure as for star, bead outermost row with 4mm white pearls and inner row with 3mm mint pearls.

4. Trim tails of string; apply dot of adhesive to each knot. ✂

Star

Heart

Overcoming Creative Burnout

Many professional crafters suffer a "midlife crisis" after five to seven years of selling crafts. Hobbyists often experience the same thing after making a specific item for what seems like the 100th time.

Creative burnout is normal. It just means you need to take a healthy break to recharge.

Ways to Rejuvenate

- Teach a craft at a craft store or other community event.
- Take a craft class.
- Research your craft on the Web.
- Visit a gift or card shop.
- Spend a day really looking at your finished inventory.
- Relax and enjoy a day without crafting even for one second!
- Invest in a new tool or craft book.
- Call a crafting friend and talk about the weather.
- Call a friend who says he/she has no creative talent and talk about crafting.
- Donate old inventory (or slow-moving items) to a charity.
- Put on lively music and listen to it while you craft.
- Put on lively music and dance.
- Watch or tape several craft or home-decor TV programs.
- Daydream about how you can spend your fall income.
- Read any book by SARK.
- Start an ornament exchange.
- Browse through all your patterns and old books.
- Change your favorite pattern.
- Visit a quilt shop, cake-and-candy shop or rubber-stamp store.
- Finger-paint and explore color combinations.
- Finger-paint with a child.
- Sprinkle flower seeds randomly in a flowerpot and watch what happens!
- Work near a big window.
- Change your work area set-up.
- Start work an hour early and stop working an hour early.
- Catch up on all your paperwork *now.*
- Make a work list and check off items as you complete them.
- Make a work list, rip it to shreds and burn it.
- Remember why you started your business and smile.
- Remember the best compliment a customer gave you.
- Remember the first time you sold out of an item.
- Forget everything and take a warm bubble bath.
- Always remember the joy crafting brings to your life. **$**

Santa Candleholder

Jolly St. Nick adds holiday cheer to your booth as he greets your customers with open arms. This candle-holder is a wonderful holiday piece for your home.

Design by Mary Ayres

Materials

- 7¼" x 2¹³⁄₁₆" wooden slat*
- 3¼" x 5¼" x ¾" rectangular wooden base
- ½" round wooden plug
- Craft foam: red, white
- Acrylic craft paints*: cranberry wine, lamp black, mocha, slate grey, true red, white pearl, white wash
- Glorious gold metallic acrylic craft paint*
- Paintbrushes: #5 and #8 natural bristle brushes, #6 round
- Craft glue
- Utrafine crystal glitter
- Twin-tip black permanent marker*
- Mini-pinking, decorative-edge scissors*
- Votive candleholder
- Fine sandpaper
- Tack cloth
- Transfer or graphite paper
- Stylus

Slat from Forster; Americana and Dazzling Metallics paints from DecoArt; ZIG Memory System marker from EK Success Ltd.; Fiskars scissors.

Instructions

1. Sand slat and base; wipe off dust with tack cloth.

2. Referring to instructions for "Using Transfer & Graphite Paper" (General Instructions, page 190), transfer outline of face, beard, belt and buckle to wooden slat.

3. Paint wooden plug mocha for nose; paint beard white, belt and rectangular base black, and buckle gold; paint remainder of slat red; let dry.

4. Referring to directions for dry-brushing under "Painting Techniques" in General Instructions, dry-brush side edges of beard and edges of base with grey and edges of coat with cranberry. Let dry.

5. Referring to directions for rouging under "Painting Techniques," rouge cheeks and nose with red; let dry. Using end of paintbrush handle dipped in white, add highlight dots to cheeks and nose. Using side of marker's bullet tip, add eyes; using fine tip, outline face, beard and buckle with dashed line.

6. Using regular scissors, cut hat and arms (including mittens) from red craft foam, and mustaches from white; using pinking edgers, cut cuffs, hat brim and pompom from white craft foam.

7. Paint cuffs, brim and pompom with pearl; dry-brush edges with gold. When dry, brush glue over painted foam and sprinkle with glitter; shake off excess and let dry.

8. Dry-brush edges of mustaches with gray. Paint mittens black; dry-brush edges of mittens with white; dry-brush edges of sleeves and hat with cranberry; let dry.

9. Glue arms to back of slat; glue cuffs at wrists. Glue hat and mustaches to front of slat; glue brim and pompom to hat; glue wooden plug to mustache for nose. Let dry.

10. Glue bottom edge of Santa to short end of base; let dry. Set votive candleholder on base. ✄

Snowflake Candle-holder

Icy shades of blue make this decorative candle-holder a perfect winter addition to your home. Light a scented candle while you're displaying this project.

Design by Sharon Tittle

Materials

- 3¼" square wooden candleholder with snowflake cutout and wire-and-wood handle*
- Votive or 1¾"-diameter pillar candle
- Stencils: snowflakes, snowy village*
- Stencil spray adhesive*
- Acrylic craft paints*: blue jay, navy blue, white
- Gloss varnish
- Paintbrushes: ¾" flat wash, #6 shader
- Stencil accessory kit with wand, sponge and shield*
- Sea sponge

Candleholder from D&CC; stencils, adhesive, Ceramcoat paints, Stencil Buddy accessory kit from Delta.

Instructions

Note: *Never leave burning candles unattended.*

1. Using ¾" brush, paint exterior of candleholder navy; paint interior white.

2. Using #6 brush, paint two outer sections of handle navy blue; paint center section white. Let dry.

3. Combine three parts blue jay with one part white. Lightly sponge interior of candleholder with mixture.

4. Using #6 brush, paint edges of cutout with blue jay; let dry. Referring to instructions for dry-brushing in "Painting Techniques" (General Instructions, page 190), dry-brush edges of cutout in a few places with white. Let dry.

5. Combine four parts white with one part blue jay. Following manufacturer's instructions, stencil both sizes snowflakes from both stencils all around candleholder with mixture, using wand and sponge.

6. Pounce sponge into pure white; pounce of some paint onto palette, then pounce around edges and corners of candleholder and handle; let dry.

7. Spray candleholder inside and out with varnish. ✂

Bejeweled Gel Votives

Lighted or not, these little candles are dazzling showstoppers! Stir in glitter for extra shimmer.

Design by Cheryl Ball for Delta Technical Coatings

Materials
- Topaz candle gel*
- 6" gel candlewick*
- Iridescent candle glitter*
- 2" round glass votive candleholder
- Nonstick saucepan
- Bamboo skewer
- Large metal spoon
- Assorted flat-back acrylic jewels
- White craft glue

Gel Candles Tub, Wick and Special Effects Iridescent Glitter, all from Delta.

Instructions

1. Review all instructions on product packaging.

2. *Prepare wick:* Roll excess wick around skewer so metal disk will lay flat in bottom of candleholder when skewer is laid across rim.

3. Cut gel into 2"–3" chunks. Place in saucepan and melt over low heat; do not allow gel to steam. Remove immediately from heat.

4. Dip metal end of wick in melted gel; press in place in bottom of candleholder, laying skewer across top to hold wick up straight.

5. Immediately pour some glitter into melted gel in saucepan, stirring in with spoon. Add more glitter until desired effect is achieved.

6. Fill candleholder with melted gel, pouring it slowly from saucepan to minimize bubbles; wipe any drips off side of saucepan with paper towel. Let cool, then trim excess wick to ½".

7. Glue jewels around candlholder as desired. **Note:** *Substitute glass cement for craft glue if you want candleholder to be washable.*

8. Follow package instructions regarding care and use of candle. ✂

Selling Cheat Sheet

Take a minute to complete this creative exercise.

Place your craft in front of you. Now, write down a list of reasons why a customer should buy your item.

Now, turn the paper over and close your eyes for a few seconds. When you open your eyes, pretend that the craft item in front of you was made by someone you respect (like your mom or best friend). Again make a list of all the wonderful aspects of this craft and why someone should buy it.

For many, the second list is longer.

Leave Your Booth!
Creative people tend to be highly critical of their own work while seeing all the positives in another's work. To be comfortable selling your own work, you may need to take "yourself" out of the picture.

Pretend you are selling your mom's or best friend's work from your booth. With some practice, you'll soon become more comfortable selling your crafts.

And while it may seem that your ego or self-esteem is on the line, remember this: It's nothing personal! It just may be that the individual doesn't need your product at that time.

Memorize the High Points
Make a list of all the positive aspects of your crafts and memorize it. You might also write a selling script. Rehearse your "sales pitch" until you feel relaxed with it. You don't have to repeat it word for word, but remember the key points.

Another good icebreaker is to tell customers about the craft itself (like quilting, decorative painting, woodturning, candle making). You will not be talking about yourself, but rather the fun and interesting aspects of your craft. **$**

Jewels & Pearls Candles

Rich, jewel-colored cubes swimming in creamy, pearlescent swirls make for an eye-catching trio of candles. Their vibrant colors are sure to attract plenty of attention from prospective customers.

Design by Cheryl Ball for Delta Technical Coatings

Materials

Each Candle

- Tubs of candle gel*: crystal clear *plus* emerald, garnet or sapphire
- 6" gel candlewick*
- Pearl candle powder*
- 3"–4" square glass votive candleholder
- Nonstick saucepan
- Bamboo skewer
- Large metal spoon

Gel Candles Tubs, Wicks and Special Effects Pearl Powder, all from Delta.

Instructions

1. Review all instructions on product packaging.

2. Cut emerald, garnet or sapphire gel into approximately ¾" cubes.

3. *Prepare wick:* Roll excess wick around skewer so that metal disk will lay flat in bottom of candleholder when skewer is laid across rim.

4. Cut clear gel into 2"–3" chunks. Place in saucepan and melt over low heat; do not allow gel to smoke. Remove immediately from heat.

5. Dip metal end of wick in melted gel; press in place in bottom of candleholder, laying skewer across top to hold wick up straight.

6. Immediately pour entire package of pearl powder into melted gel in saucepan, stirring with spoon.

7. Position a few gel chunks around wick in candleholder.

8. Alternately add melted gel and gel cubes to fill candleholder. Pour the melted gel slowly to minimize bubbles; wipe drips off side of saucepan with paper towel. Position cubes along sides of container so they are visible from the outside. As candle fills, add a few more cubes to very top layer.

9. Let candle cool, then trim excess wick to ½".

10. Follow package instructions regarding care and use of candle. ✂

Display With a Purpose

For an eye-catching display, you should strive to enhance your work without overwhelming it.

Avoid clutter. Have a focal point—one piece or area to which the customer's eye travels first.

Step back from your display, close your eyes for a few seconds, then open them.

What catches your eye first? Is that what you want as the centerpiece?

Give each item enough space to let customers view it clearly. Place several smaller crafts around one or two larger pieces or group items by color or use. **$**

Give Them Ideas

Your display should also show customers how they can use your crafts in their own homes. If you are selling handmade soap dishes, fill one with decorative soaps to show the buyer how to display her purchase. If you are selling your own unique line of eyeglasses cases, display at least one with sunglasses or reading glasses peeking out.

Never assume that the customer knows how to use your craft. New generations of customers enter the markets continually and may not have your knowledge or creative insight. **$**

Musical Chairs

An adjustable chair is recommended if you craft more than 20 hours per week. The chair should be padded and support your back and legs while your feet rest comfortably on the floor without dangling or curling under.

Swivel chairs are a bonus; they allow easier access to all your workspace. The best investment you can make is an ergonomically correct chair. Office supply stores that carry furniture usually have several models to try. **$**

This display creates a scene or vignette that is appealing to the eye. It groups similiar items with an apple theme and the warm color red to bring you in for a closer look.

Stained Glass Snowman

*Let this snowman catch your customer's eye
by hanging him in a prominent location. Stained
glass projects are always beautiful and sell quickly.*

Design by Mary Ayres

Materials

- Blank 6" round hanging glass panel*
- Glass paints*: black leading, blue cloud, lemon lime, lively lavender, lollipop orange, pewter leading, primary blue, snow-flake white
- Craft pick or toothpick
- Craft knife (optional)
- Paintbrush

*Glass panel from Provo Craft; Liquid Rainbow Paints from DecoArt.

Instructions

1. Place pattern under glass, positioning hanger at top. Trace pattern lines directly onto glass with pewter leading, keeping tip of paint tube slightly above glass and allowing paint to flow from tube. Let leading dry for 1–2 hours. Any excess paint can be cut away with craft knife and peeled away when paint is dry.

2. Following manufacturer's instructions, fill nose with orange; face and body with white; scarf, hat pompom and every other section of hat brim with lavender; remainder of hat and brim with lemon lime; and sky background with blue cloud. While paint is still wet, add evenly spaced dots of primary blue atop blue cloud and swirl with craft pick. Let dry for several hours.

3. *Add eye and mouth dots:* Squirt black leading onto disposable plate. Dip end of paintbrush handle into black paint and dot onto face. Redip brush handle before each dot so all dots are the same size. Let paints dry until colors are completely transparent. ✂

Stained Glass Snowman

Salesmanship 101

Actually selling your crafts may seem intimidating. Don't feel alone; 80 percent of crafters don't like the idea of having to sell their crafts one-on-one to the public.

Most of us find it hard to self-promote, to "brag" about our products. We were taught to be humble and modest about our skills. Selling your crafts, however, is one case in which it is very important that you feel comfortable expressing your love of your craft.

In most cases, your crafts will sell themselves without much effort on your part, but you can't assume that is the situation. The more customers hear and see your love of creativity, the more they will want to buy your work. **$**

Holiday Earthenware Ornaments

Sell these classic holiday ornaments individually, in pairs or as a set. Your customers will love the icy shades of blue and attention to detail.

Designs by Shelia Sommers

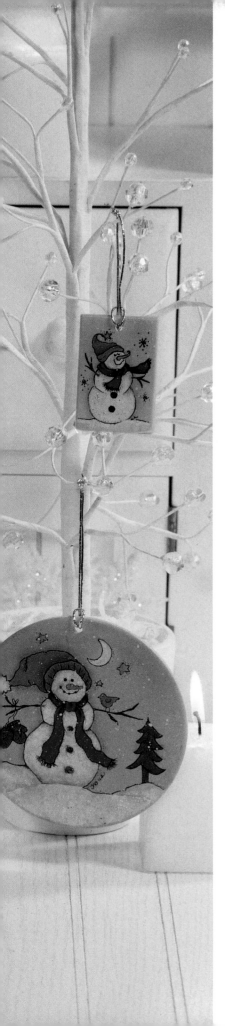

Materials

- Earthenware ornaments* with Santa and snowman designs: 2¾" and 3¾" disks and 1¼" x 2" rectangles
- Acrylic craft paints*: autumn brown, black, chocolate cherry, Lisa pink, medium flesh, medium foliage green, opaque red, opaque yellow, periwinkle blue, phthalo green, poppy orange, pumpkin, purple smoke, Santa flesh, soft gray, white
- Acrylic sparkle glaze*
- Glossy-finish varnish
- Paintbrushes: ½" flat, ¼" angular, 10/0 liner, #4 and #6 filberts, old flat brush with bristles flared out (the more the better)
- Old toothbrush
- Ultrafine-point permanent black pen*
- Thin metallic silver cord

*Cridge Ware ornaments; Ceramcoat paints and Sparkle Glaze from Delta; .01 micron pen from Sakura.

Project Notes

These ornaments come with the patterns imprinted on them.

Thin each color of paint slightly with water before painting. Apply washes of color, allowing line work to show through.

Santas

1. Thin periwinkle with water to produce a *very* transparent shade. Use ½" flat brush to apply a wash to back and edges of each ornament. Apply wash of color to the front of each piece, painting around design. Continue to add layers of color until you have achieved desired shade.

2. Paint face (and lip on round ornament) Santa flesh.

3. Referring to instructions for shading under "Painting Techniques" (General Instructions, page 190) throughout, shade under hat, bottom of nose and lip with medium flesh.

Round ornament: Thin Lisa pink with water; add half-circles for cheeks. Referring to instructions for highlighting under "Painting Techniques" throughout, highlight top of nose and lip with pink. Paint eyes black; add

tiny white highlight dots; add two thin black eyelashes to each eye.

4. Paint beard, mustache, space under nose and eyebrows (on round ornament) soft gray; shade under mustache with a whisper of black.

5. Using liner, add several thin white lines to eyebrows, beard and mustache.

Round ornament: Load liner with white and trace swirls on beard.

6. *Round ornament:* Paint hat and berries red; shade with chocolate cherry; highlight top of hat and each berry with Lisa pink.

Rectangular ornament: Paint hat and coat red; shade with chocolate cherry; highlight top of hat with Lisa pink.

7. Paint all fur on hats and coat white.

8. Paint jingle bell and stars yellow; shade with pumpkin.

9. *Round ornament:* Paint holly leaves medium foliage green; shade with phthalo green.

Rectangular ornament: Paint tree trunk and mittens autumn brown. Paint tree medium foliage green; shade with phthalo green. Add very transparent wash of black to shoes.

10. Let paints dry completely, then re-ink details with ultrafine-point black pen.

Snowmen

1. Repeat step 1 as for Santas *except* paint washes of color right over snowmen designs and ground underneath.

2. Using old flat brush, pounce white onto each snowman and ground underneath them, avoiding imprinted pattern lines. Shade with periwinkle.

3. Thin Lisa pink with water; add left cheek to each snowman; let dry.

4. Paint sparkle glaze over pounced snow; let dry.

5. Paint noses pumpkin; shade larger noses with poppy. Paint scarves red; shade with chocolate cherry.

Large round ornament: Paint eyes and mouth black; add tiny white highlight dots to eyes and add two thin black eyelashes.

6. *Hat pompoms, all stars, moon:* Pounce pompoms with white using old flat brush; paint stars yellow and shade with pumpkin; paint moon

Continued on page 153

Winter Village Candleholder Collection

Add luminance to your booth by lighting candles for display in this winter-themed trio. Gold and glitter accents will make these elegant home decor pieces.

Designs by Shelia Sommers

Materials

- Porcelain candleholders* with village motifs: large dome on column, small dome on base and votive holder with ornamental disk
- Acrylic craft paints*: autumn brown, chocolate cherry, dark burnt umber, dark jungle green, empire gold, medium foliage green, oasis green, periwinkle blue, phthalo green, purple smoke, tomato spice, white
- Acrylic sparkle glaze*
- Paintbrushes: ½" flat, ¼" angular, 10/0 liner, #4 and #6 filberts, old flat brush with bristles flared out (the more the better)
- Gold foil and foil adhesive*
- Glossy-finish varnish
- Old toothbrush

*Winterberry Village #81-6959, Village Dome #81-6941 and Village Votive #81-6944, all from Creative Xpress; Ceramcoat paints and Sparkle Glaze, foil and adhesive, all from Delta.

Surface Preparation

Apply two coats of spray varnish to outside of each piece. Porcelain is a slick surface, and varnish will provide sufficient "tooth" for paints to grab onto as you apply colors.

Painting

1. Paint outside of each piece—including bottoms—with purple smoke; do not paint insides of large or small domes.

2. Paint trees medium foliage green; referring to instructions for shading under "Painting Techniques" (General Instructions, page 190) throughout, shade under each bough with phthalo green.

3. Paint houses and churches in a pleasing combination of colors; tomato, gold, oasis green and periwinkle were used on sample, with brown roofs. Shade tomato with chocolate cherry; gold with brown; oasis green with dark jungle green; periwinkle with purple smoke; and brown with dark burnt umber.

4. Paint trim and doors on houses using colors of your choice.

5. Paint windows gold; paint a few windows with a wash of dark burnt umber to indicate that no lights are on in that part of the house.

6. Paint chimneys tomato, adding dark burnt umber cap to top.

7. Highlight edges of roofs and trees with white; using liner, dab white on very edges of these same areas.

8. Using old flat brush, pounce white onto ground under houses, adding color until it looks "fluffy." Let paint dry, then shade between hills with purple smoke.

9. Using liner, paint raised snowflakes white; add dots to ends with stylus or blunt pencil dipped in white. Let dry.

10. Apply sparkle glaze to edges of roofs and to ground beneath houses.

11. Slightly moisten old toothbrush with water; load bristles with white and spatter around outside of largest dome, smaller dome and disk on votive. Do not speckle bases.

12. *Large candle dome:* Paint branches of greenery around columnar base autumn brown. Paint leaves medium green; shade with phthalo green. Paint berries tomato; shade with chocolate cherry. Let dry.

Foil Accents

1. Referring manufacturer's instructions, apply two coats of foil adhesive to areas where you want to apply foil. Adhesive is dry when it is clear, not milky. Adhesive will dry to a tacky touch.

2. Cut 1" strip of foil. Place shiny side down on adhesive and rub with fingers. As you lift plastic backing, foil will adhere to candleholder.

Finishing

To keep paints and foil from rubbing off, spray each piece with three or four coats varnish, allowing varnish to dry between coats. ✂

Holiday Earthenware Ornaments

Continued from page 151

Continued from page 151

white; shade with yellow.

7. Paint arms autumn brown. Paint buttons with a wash of black.

8. Paint mittens including cuffs medium foliage green; paint hearts on mittens with wash of red.

9. Paint hats periwinkle; shade with purple smoke.

10. Paint tree trunk autumn brown. Paint tree medium foliage green; shade with phthalo green.

11. Paint bird's beak yellow; paint body periwinkle.

12. Shade around edges of snowmen with periwinkle using tiny black dots as your guide.

13. Let paints dry completely, then re-ink details with ultrafine-point black pen, adding tiny dots.

Finishing

1. Load old toothbrush with white; speckle or spatter each ornament. Let dry for 2–4 hours.

2. Apply coat of varnish to all surfaces.

3. String loop of silver cord through hole for hanger. ✂

Help Your Crafts Sell Themselves

- Clearly tag all items so customers don't have to ask the price.

- Pack up your customers' purchases in clear bags. They allow others to see what that customer bought and often spur additional sales.

- Demonstrate your skills. When selling painted signs, have a few on hand to paint while customers watch. People love demonstrations; it reinforces the fact that your crafts are handmade. It also helps form a crowd, and people are attracted to crowds—they want to see what everyone is looking at!

- Eyes are attracted to movement. Who can resist whirlygigs? Is there any movement in your crafts? Toy cars can be set up to move back and forth. Position flags so that any breeze will set them aflutter.

- Sound captures attention, too. Incorporate a CD player playing seasonal music into your display. Keep it out of sight and keep the volume soft enough so that it will not disturb other exhibitors. Wind up a music box every few minutes to entice the buyers.

- Use signs to explain pricing, uses and messages to your customers. If you are selling jewelry or decorated T-shirts, wear samples! **$**

Rag Doll Ornaments

These ornaments are too darling to enjoy only during the holidays. Wooden pieces always make a nice addition to your ornament collection.

Designs by Joyce Atwood

Materials

- ¼"-thick wood stock
- Craft saw
- Sandpaper
- Tack cloth
- Graphite paper
- Stylus
- Acrylic craft paints*: Black Forest green, black green, black plum, blue haze, burnt umber, Delane's cheek color, gingerbread, lamp black, light cinnamon, mink tan, peach sherbet, Rookwood red, sand, soft peach
- Paintbrushes: ¼" angular, ¾" glaze/wash, #2, #4 and #8 shaders, #0 liner, #10 sable
- 2 (4") rusty wings*
- Rusty tin wire*
- Small craft drill with bit
- Craft cement
- Matte-finish spray sealer/finish

*Americana acrylic paints from DecoArt; TinTiques rusty tin and wire from D&CC.

Preparation

Referring to instructions for "Using Transfer & Graphite Paper" (General Instructions, page 190), transfer pattern outlines to wood. Cut out; sand and wipe off dust with tack cloth.

Girl Ornament

1. Referring to instructions for base-coating under "Painting Techniques" in the General Instructions, base-coat dress and hat with Black Forest green, cuffs and hair with red, star with tan, face and hands with peach sherbet and shoes with lamp black.

2. Referring to instructions for shading and dry-brushing in "Painting Techniques" in the General Instructions, shade hair with black plum and dry-brush cheek color highlights into hair.

3. Shade face and hands first with gingerbread and then with cinnamon for darker shading. Dry-brush with soft peach to add highlights.

4. Paint nose red; shade edges with black plum. Dot on eyes with stylus dipped in lamp black; add lamp black eyebrows and mouths.

5. Dot tiny sand highlights onto eyes; dry-brush cheeks with cheek color.

6. *Dress:* Shade with black green; add dry-brushed highlights to dress and highlight around hat with blue haze. Shade cuffs with black plum; add dry-brushed highlights with cheek color.

7. *Star in hands:* Shade with cinnamon; dry-brush sand highlight; darken shading next to hands with burnt umber.

8. *Stars on clothes:* Highlight left edges of stars with sand; shade right edges with cinnamon.

9. *Shoes:* Highlight with blue haze.

Boy Ornament

1. Base-coat coat with Black Forest green, cuffs, pants and hair with red, star with tan, face and hands with peach sherbet and shoes with lamp black.

2. Repeat steps 2–5 for girl.

3. Highlight around coat and arms and along top of hat and brim with blue haze; shade next to brim with black green. Shade cuffs and pants with black plum; add dry-brushed highlights with cheek color.

4. Repeat steps 7–9 for girl.

Finishing

1. Drill small hole through top of each head. Form hanger loop from rusty wire and thread ends through hole; twist ends to secure.

2. Glue wings to back of each ornament.

3. Spray with matte spray. ✂

Rag Doll Ornaments

Patriotic Santa Pin

Let your patriotism soar year-round with this holiday pin. Small pins are always popular at craft shows and sell quickly.

Design by Mary Nelson

Materials
- ¼"-thick pine or poplar stock
- Graphite or transfer paper
- Scroll saw
- Fine sandpaper
- Acrylic craft paints*: antique mauve, black plum, buttermilk, deep midnight blue, flesh tone, forest green, lamp black, Napa red, sable brown, Santa red, true ochre
- Paintbrushes: ½" wash, ¾" angular shader, #3 round, #0 and #1 liners
- Old toothbrush or spatter brush
- Acrylic spray sealer
- Masking tape
- 1¼" pin back
- Craft cement

Americana paints from DecoArt.

Project Notes
When painting, use largest brush that will fit area to be painted. For shading, lining and spattering, use paints that have been thinned with water to an inky consistency. Let paints dry between colors.

Instructions
1. Referring to instructions for "Using Transfer & Graphite Paper" (General Instructions, page 190), transfer pattern outline onto wood. Cut out; sand.

2. Cut a piece of masking tape slightly larger than base of pin back; press tape onto back of pin where pin back will be attached later. Leave tape in place until project has been painted and sprayed with sealer.

3. Paint all surfaces of pin buttermilk; when dry, lightly transfer pattern lines to front of pin as needed.

4. Paint face flesh tone; blush cheeks with antique mauve. Shade around edges of hat brim, pompom, beard, mustache and face with sable. Dot on lamp black eyes and Napa red nose with brush handle. Paint eyebrows buttermilk.

5. Paint hat and coat Santa red; shade with black plum. Paint stripes on flag Napa red; shade with sable. Paint field in upper left midnight blue; add ochre stars. Paint gloves forest green; paint shoes black.

6. Spatter dry pin lightly with sable, then lamp black.

7. Spray front of pin with sealer; let dry. Spray back of pin; let dry.

8. Carefully peel tape from back of pin. Apply generous amount of cement to unsealed area and press pin back in place, allowing cement to ooze through holes. Let pin set overnight before wearing. ✂

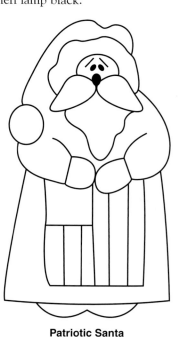

Patriotic Santa

Sweet Gingerbread Heart Wall Hanging

Projects with bright colors and glitter always make eye-catching additions for your booth. These adorable gingerbread friends are equally festive hanging on the wall or from a pegged shelf.

Design by Mary Ayres

Materials

- 6" x 4½" wooden heart with predrilled holes*
- 2 (3⅜" x 3⅞") wooden gingerbread men*
- Wooden shapes: 4 (⅜") circles, 2 (⅜") stars, 2 (1¾") candy canes
- Acrylic craft paints*: honey brown, light cinnamon, primary yellow, spice pink, true red, white wash
- Glorious gold metallic acrylic craft paint*
- #5 and #8 natural bristle paintbrushes
- Black twin-tip permanent marker*
- Opaque white extra-fine–tip permanent marker*
- Red bullet-tip permanent marker*
- Iridescent ultrafine glitter
- Craft glue
- 2 (9") pieces white ⅛"-wide wire-edge ribbon
- 11" 20-gauge gold wire
- Fine sandpaper

Heart and gingerbread men from Lara's Crafts; Americana and Dazzling Metallics paints from DecoArt; ZIG Memory System markers from EK Success Ltd.

Instructions

1. Sand wooden pieces as needed; wipe off dust.

2. Paint heart and circles (cheeks) pink; let dry. Referring to instructions for dry-brushing under "Painting Techniques" (General Instructions, page 190), dry-brush edges with red. Dip tip of paintbrush handle in white and dot highlight onto each cheek.

3. Paint gingerbread men brown; let dry, then dry-brush edges with cinnamon.

4. Paint stars yellow; let dry, then dry-brush edges with gold.

5. Paint candy canes white, reversing one; let dry, then dry-brush edges with gold. When dry, add stripes with red marker.

6. Dilute glue with a little water. Working with one piece at a time, paint mixture over tops of stars, candy canes and cheeks. Quickly sprinkle with glitter while glue is still wet. Shake off excess; let dry.

7. Using side of bullet tip on black marker, add eyes and buttons to gingerbread men. Glue on cheeks; using fine tip of black marker, add running-stitch smiles, extending lines onto cheeks. Using white marker, add running stitch around edges.

8. Using fine tip of black marker,

Continued on page 163

Naughty Cat Ornament

Make your customers smile with this mischievous felt cat ornament. You can easily make dozens of these in an afternoon.

Design by Helen Rafson

Materials

- Antique gold felt
- Burnt sienna acrylic craft paint
- 5mm pink pompom
- Sponge
- 2 black 4mm round beads
- Cotton-tip swab
- Pink powdered cosmetic blusher
- 10" ⅛"-wide gold braid
- 6½" ¼"-wide green satin ribbon
- 8mm mini light-bulb garland*
- Brown embroidery floss
- Black sewing thread
- Needle
- Tacky craft glue
- Seam sealant

Light-bulb garland from Darice.

Instructions

1. Cut two cats and two tails from felt; glue tails together. Set aside tails and one cat for backing.

2. Use damp sponge to apply a little burnt sienna paint randomly over surface of cat front; let dry.

3. Using 3 strands embroidery floss, backstitch legs and mouth; using 2 strands, straight-stitch to outline centers of ears.

4. Sew on beads for eyes using black thread; blush cheeks with blusher and cotton swab.

5. Cut 3" piece embroidery floss. Tie knot in middle, then separate strands with straight pin. Glue knot to cat's face for whiskers; glue pompom over knot. When dry, trim whiskers.

6. Tie ribbon in bow; trim ends and coat with seam sealant; let dry. Glue bow to cat's neck; let dry.

7. Sandwiching tail between cat pieces, glue cat halves together; glue ends of gold ribbon to back of cat's head and tail for hanger. Let dry.

8. Wrap garland around cat, gluing ends to wrong side. Trim away any bulbs on wrong side. Apply tiny dots of glue several bulbs on front of cat to help hold garland in place. Let dry. ✂

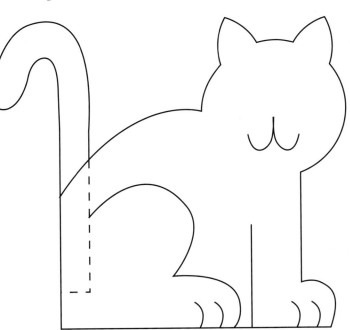

Naughty Cat
Cut 2 from
antique gold felt

Bear Pocket Ornaments

Angelic teddy bears adorn these felt ornaments to add country charm to your tree and packages.

Design by Angie Wilhite

floss, blanket-stitch around wings, bear and muzzle; add French knot eyes and nose, and backstitch ¼" line down center of muzzle.

6. Using pocket pattern, cut one piece fusible stabilizer; fuse to back of pocket front.

7. Using 2 strands black floss, blanket-stitch across top edge of pocket front. Hold pockets together and blanket-stitch down sides and across bottom.

8. Paint star yellow; let dry. Outline with "running stitch" using black marker. Glue to top right corner of pocket.

9. Knot ends of twine; glue one knot inside each top corner of pocket. ✂

Materials

Each Ornament

- Felt: 8" x 10" red or green, 5" square cashmere tan, 3" x 4" antique white
- Scrap of green or red tiny-print fabric
- Black embroidery floss
- ⅛ yard fusible transfer web*
- 4" square heavy-duty transfer web*
- ⅛ yard fusible interfacing*
- 5" square fusible stabilizer*
- Pressing cloth
- Small wooden star cutout
- Yellow acrylic paint
- Small paintbrush
- Permanent craft adhesive
- Fine-point black permanent marker
- 7" fine jute twine

*Wonder-Under and Heavy-Duty Wonder-

Under fusible web, Sof-Shape fusible interfacing and Craft-Bond fusible stabilizer all from Pellon.

Instructions

1. Cut two pockets from red or green felt.

2. Following manufacturer's instructions and using a pressing cloth throughout, apply fusible products to back of felt and fabric pieces in order: interfacing to back of white felt; transfer web to back of white felt just fused and tan; heavy-duty transfer web to back of fabric scrap (red for green pocket, green for red).

3. *Cut pattern pieces from fused felt and fabric (page 163):* bear and oval muzzle from tan, wings from white; heart from red or green fabric.

4. Fuse wings, bear, muzzle and heart to front pocket.

5. Using 2 strands black embroidery

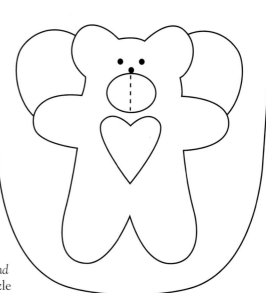

Pocket
Cut 2 pockets
from red or green

Patterns continued on page 163

Christmas Tree Pins

The possibilities for embellishing these funky pins are endless! Use your creativity and watch how quickly they sell.

Designs by Kathy Wegner

Instructions

1. Cut two triangles from felt.

2. Glue cinnamon stick to center bottom on wrong side of one felt triangle so that about 1" protrudes from bottom; glue triangles together along sides, wrong sides facing, leaving bottom open. Let glue dry.

3. Place small amount of fiberfill inside tree around cinnamon stick; glue bottom closed.

4. Using toothpick to apply glue to decorations, decorate tree as desired. Glue pin back to back; let dry. ✁

Where's That Receipt?

Keep details of any income and expenses. Don't just write $100 in the income column of your bookkeeping, but include where the income came from—like the name of a customer, name of a show or the name of the craft mall plus the date you received the income.

In some cases you will not be writing out a receipt but the other party will give you a receipt (an invoice from a co-op or craft mall, for instance). But you should have a receipt for every penny of income.

You should also have an invoice or receipt for every expense. If the receipt doesn't have the details, note on the receipt what was purchased, where and on what date. **$**

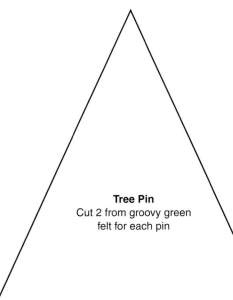

Tree Pin
Cut 2 from groovy green felt for each pin

Materials

Each Pin

- 4" x 5½" groovy green shaggy plush felt*
- 2" cinnamon stick
- 1½" pin back
- Decorations of your choice: mini tree lights and garland, punched decorations from craft foam, spangles, bangles, confetti, sequins, etc.
- Small amount polyester fiberfill
- Thick tacky glue
- Toothpick

Shaggy Plush Felt from Kunin.

Crafter's Success Story
Cheryl Seslar

was little when I began watching my mother—who says she doesn't have a creative bone in her body—paint beautiful watercolor greeting cards with mushrooms and little mice, and crochet baby blankets to take to local shops to make a few extra dollars.

I especially remember the day she picked up her check and bought a new color TV set. I was 6 years old, but I decided at that very minute that when I grew up, I was going to "make things" just like Mom!

Looking for "My" Craft
As I grew up, I jumped from craft to craft, searching for my "niche." I drew, sculpted with clay, made jewelry from magazine scraps—I did it all, and I was even good at some of it.

I attended local craft shows and even consigned a few things to a local market. I usually made enough to buy more supplies and maybe a few groceries.

But it wasn't until I was 27 years old that I found what I believe I was truly meant to do!

Desperate Times
A trip to the doctor's office revealed that that lump on my husband's knee was a tumor. The surgeon set a date to remove it—six weeks before Christmas.

What were we going to do? It was right before the holidays with no income, and we had a 3-year-old daughter for whom we wanted to buy presents. My husband's unemployment check would barely cover the rent.

A few weeks after his surgery, my husband was well enough to hobble around and we took a trip to the

library. That's where he found the pattern for a doll-size rocking horse.

We borrowed $110 from my parents and bought a scroll saw—and the cutting of rocking horses commenced.

Creative Measures
After he cut one out, my husband said, "Honey, do you think you could paint this for me?"

Though I had always considered myself creative, the last time I had picked up a paintbrush, I had been a kid, helping my father part time during the summers. Even then, I only went with him because he bought me lunch!

But to make a long story short, I got hooked! And people liked our rocking horses. I was amazed when we began receiving orders. In fact, we made $2,000 before Christmas!

The Hobby Takes Off
I bought every book on decorative painting I could find. Soon I was cutting my own designs and painting into the wee hours of the morning.

I attended all the local craft shows. Not only did I make enough to buy supplies and a few groceries, but I paid a few bills, too!

I finally took the huge step of contacting a publisher. To my delight, they published three books filled with my decorative painting designs!

Even though I now design full time, I can't resist the allure of some of the local shows and consignment shops. I love the hustle and bustle of the holiday shows, and how customers' eyes twinkle over my latest creations.

I took to dipping candles, making swags and stitching pillows to give

my craft booth a warm, homey feel. Customers love that! And it really can increase sales when they see groupings of different items displayed together.

Advice for Beginners
My advice to anyone starting to sell her own creations is to find something you love. Practice and expand. Have faith in yourself. Talk to people. Share your stories.

And don't forget to smile! It's amazing how much even grumpy people will buy if you take the time to talk for a moment and add a little cheer to their day! ✂

Share the Joy
Learn some trivia about your craft or a little about its history to share with customers.

Fern Le Furgah, a professional decorative painter from Bent Oak Farms in King George, Va., was surprised when her sales doubled and tripled after she started sharing the fact that the slate she painted was rescued from a demolished church that had been built in the early 1800s.

That little fact added incredible value to her designs in the eyes of her buyers. $

Snowman Glass Candy Jar

Display this adorable jar with a selection of holiday candy. Glitter and polar fleece will make this a popular bazaar item.

Design by Debra Quartermain

Materials

- Glass rose bowl with fluted edge
- Slightly smaller round glass "fish bowl"
- 13" x 18" piece blue fleecy fabric
- 2" white pompom
- 8 assorted coordinating flat ½" buttons
- White glass paint
- Black acrylic craft paint
- Paintbrushes
- Sparkle varnish*
- Hot-glue gun

Plaid Sparkle Varnish.

Instructions

1. Clean both bowls thoroughly; paint each with two or three coats white glass paint. Let dry.

2. Coat bowls with two coats sparkle varnish; let dry.

3. Smaller bowl is head; turn upside down and dot two black eyes onto bowl with paintbrush handle midway down bowl.

4. Cut two 3" x 13" strips from end of fleecy fabric; glue together to make one long scarf. Cut 2" fringe in ends.

5. Fold remaining fleece in half wrong sides facing to measure 6" x 13". Using ruler, mark line from outside bottom edge to center fold at top to create folded triangle; cut along line and glue long edges together; turn right side out.

6. Turn brim up ½", then roll again 2"; glue pompom to point of hat.

7. Place hat over head bowl, pulling it snugly in place.

8. Set head bowl in neck of larger body bowl. Tie scarf around neck of larger bowl; glue three buttons down center of body and remaining buttons across center front of hat brim. ✂

Standing Room Only

Some people prefer to stand while arranging florals, painting large surfaces or pouring candles. If you elect to stand while crafting, make sure the work area or table is no lower than hip level.

Be aware of your posture. Avoid hunching over your work. Have a high stool or director's chair handy so you can sit or lean if your legs get tired.

Take breaks and remove area rugs to avoid tripping and slipping. **$**

It's Free!

Good public relations is the best kind of advertising—it's free! It is worth the investment of your time.

• Visit a scout group and teach a craft. Plenty of parents are involved who are potential customers. Many other organizations also would enjoy learning a new craft.

• Offer to set up a display at a local school's teachers' lounge. Teachers have little time to shop the craft shows and malls. Bring your crafts to them. Small items are best for this group.

• When exciting events happen in your business, write up a press release for the newspaper. Examples: You get a new wholesale account, you win a ribbon at a show, you've added a new craft mall or you donate to a fund-raiser.

• Contact a local TV station and volunteer to go on air and talk about crafting. You might demonstrate a simple craft or show samples of your work.

• Join local guilds, crafting groups and art associations. Network and be an active member to learn about opportunities. Join national guilds, societies and associations. Keep on top of the trends, events and activities.

• If you are involved in a charitable activity involving crafting or if you make a unique item, contact a craft magazine. Many have regular columns featuring crafters. Many also "spotlight" individual artists. Write up your story and send it in. Many cover pieces are from individual artists/craftspeople. Include a clear photo or slide of your work. **$**

Gingerbread Heart Wall Hanging

Continued from page 157

write "Hoping your Christmas is Sweet" on heart as shown. Using white marker, add blanket-stitch border around edge of heart.

9. Glue stars and candy canes to gingerbread men's hands as shown; glue gingerbread men to heart.

10. Tie each piece of ribbon in a bow; glue to gingerbread men.

11. *Hanger:* Coil wire around pencil; slide off and expand coils. Thread wire through heart from front to back; twist ends to secure and shape coiled wire into hanger. ✂

Everything In Its Place … Even the Trash

All work areas should contain a waste can. It doesn't matter if yours is a brown paper grocery bag or a heavy-duty garbage can on wheels. Having a place to put waste keeps the work area clean and clutter free.

Vivian Summers, a quilter, shares this tip: "I tape a small paper bag to the side of my sewing machine table and I also have one taped to my cutting table. With little effort I simply toss threads and fabric scraps too small to save in the trash, and when full, I easily toss the bags into my garbage can." **$**

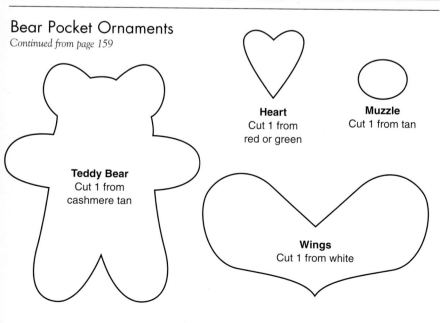

Bear Pocket Ornaments

Continued from page 159

Heart
Cut 1 from red or green

Muzzle
Cut 1 from tan

Teddy Bear
Cut 1 from cashmere tan

Wings
Cut 1 from white

Gingerbread Friend Ornaments

Hang this charming duo up at your booth and let them sell themselves. You can be sure you'll sell many of these adorable, quick projects!

Design by Karen de la Durantaye

Materials

For the Pair

- Fabric: 4 (8" x 7") pieces tan (bodies), ¼ yard plaid (dress, collar and vest), 4 (3" x 2") pieces dark green with gold pin dots (hair bow and bow tie)
- 2 (8" x 7") pieces 16-ounce polyester batting (or double layer 8-ounce batting)
- Pinking shears
- Dimensional paint: black, white
- 4 (⅜") natural or bone buttons
- Heavy white crochet thread or string
- Pink powdered cosmetic blusher
- Coordinating sewing threads
- Sewing machine
- Hand-sewing needle
- 2 (6") pieces jute twine
- Hot-glue gun

Ginger

1. Trace one gingerbread friend on right side of one piece tan fabric. Sandwich one piece batting between fabric with right sides of fabric facing out (batting layer should be 1"–1½" thick; use a double layer of lighter batting, if desired). Pin layers at corners.

2. Machine-sew along traced lines. Trim with pinking shears within ¼" of stitching. Turn over (side on which pattern is traced is the backside).

3. Add white paint "icing" across head, arms and legs; dot on eyes with black. Let dry overnight.

4. Blush cheeks with cosmetic blush.

5. *Skirt:* Cut 5" x 6" piece plaid fabric. Fold edges under ¼" along both 5" sides; press, then fold in half lengthwise. Press again. Sew gathering stitch along raw edges and pull to gather fabric to 1½" wide; knot.

6. *Collar:* From remaining plaid fabric cut two pieces 4½" x 3¼". Lay pieces together, right sides facing; trace collar on one side. Sew through both layers along traced lines. Using scissors, cut out collar within ⅛" of stitching. Carefully slit *one layer of fabric* for turning. Turn right side out; press.

7. *Hair bow:* Lay two green fabric pieces together, right sides facing; trace hair bow on one side. Sew, trim

Continued on page 174

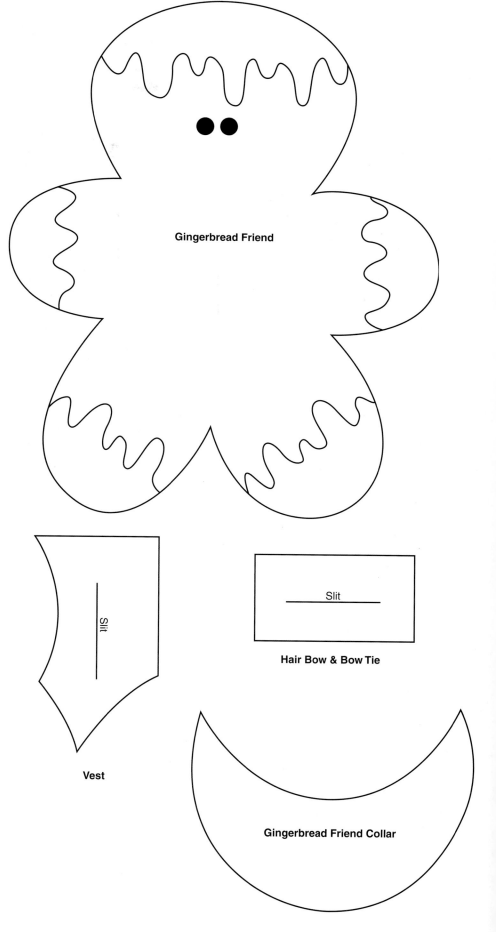

Gingerbread Friend

Slit

Vest

Slit

Hair Bow & Bow Tie

Gingerbread Friend Collar

Clay Pot Gingerbread

Garnished with cinnamon and potpourri, this is a darling holiday decoration. Display this project with your other seasonal items.

Design by Mary Ayres

Materials

- 2½" clay flowerpot
- 10" wooden spoon
- 2 wooden craft spoons
- 2" round fabric and Battenburg lace doily*
- Red satin ribbon: ½ yard ⅛"-wide; ¼ yard ¼"-wide
- 5" x 7" rectangle red print, check or plaid fabric with pinked edges
- Large pieces of cinnamon-scented potpourri
- 2"–3" cinnamon stick
- Jute twine
- 1¼" x 12" torn strip fabric
- Acrylic craft paints*: country red, honey brown, light cinnamon
- #5 and #8 natural bristle paintbrushes
- Black twin-tip permanent marker*
- Extra-fine-tip opaque white permanent writer*
- Craft glue
- Fine sandpaper
- Transfer or graphite paper
- Stylus

Doily from Wimpole Street Creations; Americana paints from DecoArt; ZIG Memory System marker and writer from EK Success Ltd.

Instructions

1. Lightly sand large spoon as needed; wipe off dust. Paint all three spoons brown; let dry.

2. Referring to directions for dry-brushing under "Painting Techniques" (General Instructions, page 190), dry-brush edges of all spoons with cinnamon; let dry.

3. *Face:* Referring to instructions for "Using Transfer & Graphite Paper" in the General Instructions, transfer face to convex surface of spoon. Paint cheeks red; let dry. Using side of marker's bullet tip, add eyes and nose; using fine tip, draw mouth and outline cheeks. Using white writer throughout, add highlight dots to cheeks, nose and eyes; add zigzag outline around face and craft spoons.

4. *Dress:* Overlap short ends of fabric rectangle ¼"; glue to form tube. Put dress on large spoon; gather fabric under mouth and glue so top of dress is ½" below mouth. Wrap ⅛" ribbon around dress ¼" from top and tie in bow at center front; trim bow ends even.

5. *Arms:* Glue narrow ends of craft spoons to back of dress.

6. *Collar:* Trim fabric center from doily; glue Battenburg lace around neck under bow.

7. *Hair bow:* Tie ⅛" ribbon into small bow; trim ends and glue bow to top left of head.

8. Coat bottom 3" of spoon handle and inside of pot with glue; stick handle into pot and fill pot with potpourri. Wrap jute around bottom of pot rim and tie knot on front slightly off to right. Trim jute ends to 1½" and unravel.

9. Wrap ¼"-wide ribbon around cinnamon stick; tie in bow and trim ends even. Glue colorful pieces from potpourri in center of bow. Glue cinnamon stick on top of jute knot at an angle. ✂

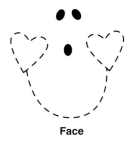

Face

Snowmen Pins

Spend afternoons before a big craft show making dozens of this quick and easy project. Your customers will love these pins, and you'll have high sales to show for it!

Design by Ann Butler

Materials

- 2½" x 3½" ribbing fabric
- 1" x 4½" torn strip coordinating flannel
- Coordinating sewing thread
- Hand-sewing needle
- Face button
- Thick tacky glue
- Shiny bright orange dimensional paint*
- 1" pin back
- Decorative snow paste (optional)

Scribbles paint from Plaid.

Instructions

1. *Hat:* Fold ribbing in half, wrong sides facing and matching 3½" edges; sew together along 3½" side. Turn right side out. For brim, fold up one edge ¼" twice; secure with glue. Close top of hat by wrapping with thread ¼" from top. Glue hat over top edge of face.

2. *Scarf:* Fold flannel strip in half; glue fold to back of face button.

3. *Nose:* Slowly squeeze orange paint onto face, lifting applicator tip to form nose. Let dry.

4. If desired, apply a little snow paste to hat. Let dry, then glue pin back to back of face button. ✂

Getting Organized

The best way to handle an overwhelming job like organization is to break it down into smaller tasks.

The first step is to become a list maker. Memory is an interesting and mysterious concept for most creative individuals. Don't rely on your memory to get organized. Grab a notebook or journal and make it the permanent location for all your lists.

As you become more organized, this notebook will take form with categories and subcategories. But if you are a beginner, take it slow and be content with finding a place for your list notebook. Commit that place to memory!

Getting Started

Your first list should be a list of questions that will help you get organized.

- What you need more time to do?

- What do you feel needs organizing within your business?
- What items/tasks would help you accomplish, schedule and coordinate, rather than confuse your business?
- What activities frustrate you most?

Key to Success

The real key to organization is to know what you want to organize. Breaking down what you want to accomplish will allow you to focus on your goals.

Putting your thoughts into writing is simply a way to organize the thoughts. Seeing it in black and white makes it all just a little less overwhelming—unless, of course, your list gets lengthy!

If the list is giving you heart palpitations, break the list up into smaller lists. This is actually a good thing. Dividing a list means you have just taken a giant step toward organizing the chaos! $

Snowman Birdhouse

Try a variation on color when making a supply of these to sell. This project can add beauty to your home throughout the winter months!

Design by June Fiechter

Materials

- Empty cardboard roll from bathroom tissue
- Muslin fabric to wrap around cardboard roll
- 4½" square wooden clock face (without clock movement)*
- 3 (1") wooden stars
- 8" (¼"-diameter) wooden dowel
- Approximately 38 (⅞"-long) wooden teardrop shapes
- Sealer
- Acrylic craft paints*: light chocolate, dark brown, navy blue, tompte red, white
- Brown antiquing gel*
- Crackle medium*
- White transfer paper
- 16-gauge hardware wire
- Hot-glue gun
- Craft drill and small bit
- 4" square card stock
- Floral foam
- Small nail
- Dried Spanish moss
- Black fine-line permanent marker
- Small paintbrushes
- Craft glue

Clock #53207 from Walnut Hollow; Ceramcoat, paints, antiquing gel and crackle medium, all from Delta.

Instructions

1. Glue a smooth, even layer of muslin over cardboard tube. Push tube down over floral foam; break away excess foam outside tube so foam remains inside tube in a tight-fitting plug.

2. Paint exterior of tube navy blue; let dry.

3. From card stock cut a circle slightly

larger than the opening in end of tube. Cut a straight slit from one edge to center; fold into cone shape to fit on top of tube. Hot-glue cone to maintain its shape, then hot-glue cone to one end (top) of tube.

4. *Shingles:* Glue teardrops around cone-shaped roof in three overlapping layers.

5. Paint roof, wooden base (square clock) and dowel light chocolate; let dry. Referring to manufacturer's instructions, apply crackle medium to roof and base as directed. Before crackle medium dries completely, paint roof and base white. Using red, line upper edge and stripe lower edge of square base. Let dry.

6. Referring to directions for "Using Transfer & Graphite Paper" (General Instructions, page 190), trace snowman onto tube slightly left of center front (center back is seam of muslin covering).

7. Paint snowman and snow at base white; shade with a pale blue made by mixing a tiny amount of navy with white. Referring to photo, paint mittens and every other section on vest and hatband red, then paint cuffs of mittens and remaining sections of vest and hatband white. Paint hat and

trim on vest chocolate; paint underside of hat and twig arms brown.

8. Using fine-line marker, add outlines and detailing; add eyes, nose and buttons.

9. Apply antiquing gel to roof and base as directed by manufacturer.

10. Drill small hole in base beside original hole; drill another hole into side of tube about ½" to right of hat's crown.

11. Hot-glue dowel into larger hole in base; push remaining end of dowel up into foam in base of birdhouse; hot-glue to secure.

12. *Perch:* Push small nail into side of birdhouse about ½" below small hole drilled in step 10.

13. Drill small hole through each wooden star; paint each red.

14. Hot-glue one end of wire into smaller hole in wooden base; wrap around birdhouse, threading painted stars onto wire and kinking wire to hold them in place as you go. Hot-glue end of wire under base of roof.

15. Hot-glue Spanish moss around base of dowel and to cover foam in bottom of birdhouse. Glue a few strands into hole drilled in side of birdhouse. ✄

Snowman Birdhouse

Is That a Left-Brain Task?

There must be an unwritten rule that clearly states that creativity and organization are not compatible traits in one human being—especially if that human is a crafter.

The toughest battle for many crafters involves the ongoing confrontation with the endless list of paperwork—customer orders, orders for supplies, invoices, phone and utility bills, state sales tax, show applications, correspondence, etc.

Tame That Paper!

The rule: Touch the paperwork *once.* Don't let receipts, orders and applications stack up. The higher the pile, the more likely you will ignore it because it has become overwhelming.

Set aside an hour each workday or a day each week to handle paperwork. Learn to place/file it or pitch it!

Let a Pro Deal With It!

If possible, hire an accountant. This is not financially feasible for most businesses in the start-up stage, but it is recommended that you have at least one meeting with an accountant or CPA to review your accounting options.

You can use a simple journal record with two main headings: Income and Expenses. Keep a record of all income and all expenses. The goal is to make sure your income covers all your expenses.

Once your income becomes larger than your expenses, you are making a profit on paper. **$**

Large Snowman Candleholder

Place and light scented candles inside this friendly snowman for a bazaar hit! You can usually charge more for hand-painted projects like this.

Design by Shelia Sommers

Materials

- Porcelain snowman candleholder*
- Acrylic craft paints*: autumn brown, black, chocolate cherry, dark chocolate, dark jungle green, empire gold, leprechaun, Lisa pink, periwinkle blue, poppy orange, pumpkin, purple smoke, tomato spice, white
- Acrylic sparkle glaze*
- Paintbrushes: ½" and 1" flats, ¼" and ½" angular, 10/0 liner, #4 and #6 filberts
- Glossy-finish spray varnish
- Old toothbrush

Snowman Candle Holder #81-6960 from Creative Xpress; Ceramcoat paints and Sparkle Glaze from Delta.

Surface Preparation

Apply two coats of spray varnish to outside of each piece. Porcelain is a slick surface, and varnish will provide sufficient "tooth" for paints to grab onto as you apply colors.

Painting

1. Paint face and body under coat white.

2. Paint eyes black, adding tiny white highlight to each. **Note:** *Using the tip of a pencil to dot on the highlight will make a perfectly round circle.*

3. Thin Lisa pink with water to produce a very transparent shade; paint cheeks.

4. Paint nose pumpkin; referring to instructions for shading under "Painting Techniques" (General

Continued on page 174

Christmas Gift Box

Display this beautiful box filled with wonderful holiday treats. Quick and easy to make, this exquisite box looks like it took hours to complete.

Design by Marlene Watson

It's a Classic!

The following list includes some of the most enduring and popular motifs, colors and themes in crafting. They draw a positive response no matter what the season. Classics like these are dear to consumers, and make year-round hot sellers!

- Angels, Santa
- Hearts, roses, daisies
- White, blue, red, gold, gingham, plaids
- Stars, quilt patterns
- Farm animals, especially pigs and cows
- Cats, dogs and teddy bears

While not as venerable as some of the aforementioned themes, motifs and colors, the following also have been popular sellers in recent years:

- Birds in general, and cardinals and robins in particular
- Poppies, mums, ivy and ferns
- Birdhouses, watering cans, water fountains and stepping stones
- Bumblebees, butterflies and dragonflies
- Frogs and turtles
- Ocean fish, plus trout and bass, flies and lures
- Sea horses, starfish and sand dollars
- Sailboats
- The colors teal and rose
- Teapots and teacups
- Aromatherapy
- Candles
- Wind chimes
- Handmade paper

Materials

- Silver rub-on transfers*: snowflake, sleigh ride, holly vines
- Wooden gift box with lid*
- Royal purple acrylic craft paint
- Glorious gold metallic acrylic craft paint*
- Glossy-finish spray sealer/finisher
- Foam brush

Chartpak Rub-On Transfers; box from Wayne's Woodenware; Americana Dazzling Metallics paints from DecoArt.

Instructions

1. Paint outside of box and lid with two coats purple paint, allowing paint to dry between coats. Paint inside of box and lid gold.

2. Leaving backing tissue in place, cut label off bottom of sleigh ride and holly vine transfers.

3. Remove backing tissue from holly vine and center transfer on lid. Lift one corner of transfer slightly and begin rubbing toward your finger across transfer with craft stick, pulling cover sheet free as you rub. When cover sheet is released, wipe across transfer with backing sheet to be sure it is perfectly smooth.

4. In same manner, apply sleigh ride transfer to front of box.

5. Cut snowflake images apart; in same manner, apply snowflakes one at a time to sides of lid and ends of box.

6. Apply a coat of sealer/finisher to box and lid. ✂

Painted Polar Bear Tray

Serve up freshly baked holiday cookies on this festive polar bear tray. This piece will delight your guests throughout the winter and holiday months.

Design by Mary Ayres

Lights, Glue Gun, Crafting!

Good lighting is essential to successful craft projects. Every technique and medium uses color. Poor lighting often leads to errors in color judgment.

Work near a window during the day for natural lighting or make sure your area lighting is full spectrum. Details are clearer in full-spectrum light and you avoid eyestrain.

Design Options

When designing a work area, consider fluorescent bulbs and tubes. Home improvement centers offer full-spectrum lamps. This type of lighting is generally more expensive than regular light systems.

An inexpensive way to get full-spectrum lighting is to use different-color light bulbs or tubes in the same fixture.

Fluorescent lighting offers the full spectrum. Soft white lights are easier on the eyes; harsh, bright lights tend to add glare.

Light Where You Need It

Lighting should be overhead or off to the side. Take a minute to check that your lighting reaches the entire work area.

Many crafters have selected halogen lights, but this strong, bright light tends to heat up the work area. **$**

Materials

- 9³⁄₁₆" x 12½" wooden tray*
- Acrylic craft paints*: baby blue, bright green, lamp black, sapphire, slate grey, true red, white wash
- Paintbrushes: #5 and #8 natural hair bristle, #6 round
- Fine-tip black permanent marker
- Transfer or graphite paper
- Stylus
- Fine sandpaper
- Tack cloth

Tray from Nicole Industries; Americana paints from DecoArt.

Instructions

1. Sand tray lightly; wipe with tack cloth.

2. Using photocopier with enlarging capabilities, enlarge pattern to 133 percent. Referring to instructions for "Using Transfer & Graphite Paper" (General Instructions, page 190), transfer bear outline and scarf details onto tray, aligning bottom of bear with tray edge.

3. Paint background baby blue; let dry. Referring to instructions for dry-brushing under "Painting Techniques" in the General Instructions, dry-brush diagonal strokes of white and sapphire across sky until desired look is achieved; let dry.

4. Paint bear white. Let dry, then dry-brush inner ears, around outside of muzzle and random patches on body and head with slate grey. Dry-brush cheeks with red.

5. Add eyes and nose with black. When dry, add white highlight to nose; using end of paint-brush handle

Painted Polar Bear Tray
Enlarge 133% before transferring

dipped in white, add highlight dots to cheeks and smaller highlights to eyes.

6. Using bright green, paint areas of scarf marked with diagonal lines; paint remaining areas red. Paint top edge of tray red; paint remaining unpainted areas of tray bright green. Let dry.

7. Using black marker throughout, add dashed lines down muzzle and between scarf sections; outline bear and muzzle with short lines as shown, and draw "buttonhole stitch" around edges of scarf and along both edges of tray's red top edge. ✂

Pain in the Neck?

To prevent an aching back or stiff neck, stand and stretch your muscles every 30 minutes.

Be on the lookout for repetitive motions. Don't cut fabric for 15 minutes straight. Don't base-coat with back-and-forth strokes repeatedly for hours. Don't make 100 floral picks in one afternoon.

Repetitive motions lead to fatigue and overstressed muscles that can result in long-term problems like carpal tunnel syndrome. **$**

Avoid Carpal Tunnel Syndrome

Carpal tunnel syndrome was first recognized in the computer industry among data-entry personnel. The continuous, repetitive action of their hands as they typed led to chronic fatigue, numbness and pain.

This damage can be permanent so take your health seriously. Be aware of your body and the messages it might be sending you. If you experience pain or numbness, re-evaluate your work area. **$**

Gingerbread Friend Ornaments

Continued from page 165

and turn as for collar (step 6). Press.

8. Glue skirt to body; glue on collar, covering skirt's raw edges.

9. Gather hair bow around center with coordinating thread; knot and glue to head.

10. Thread heavy crochet thread through three buttons and knot on front; trim ends. Glue one button to front of hair bow and two to collar.

11. Thread jute twine hanging loop through top of ornament.

Roger

1. Complete steps 1–4 for Ginger.

2. *Vest:* Construct vest in same fashion as Ginger's collar (step 6) using two 4½" x 4" pieces plaid fabric. When slitting fabric for turning, keep in mind that you will need a right and a left vest half; slits should be on back.

3. *Bow tie:* Follow procedure for making Ginger's hair bow (step 7). Gather bow tie and trim with button as described in steps 9 and 10; glue to Roger's neck.

4. Glue vest halves to Roger, folding back lapels as shown and securing with dots of glue.

5. Thread jute twine hanging loop through top of ornament. ✂

Large Snowman Candleholder

Continued from page 170

Instructions, page 190) throughout, shade with poppy.

5. Shade snowman next to scarf and under coat with autumn brown; shade smile with a wash of autumn brown.

6. Apply two coats sparkle glaze to face and body.

7. Paint hat black; paint hatband tomato.

8. Using blunt end of pencil, add large white dots to raised areas of hat. Add several large dots to brim.

9. Paint scarf tomato; shade with chocolate cherry.

10. Paint coat leprechaun; shade with dark jungle green; using jungle green, paint raised stitch marks around edges of coat and cuffs.

11. Paint mittens dark jungle green.

12. Paint coat buttons and bag autumn brown; shade area inside buttons next to thread and under bag next to draw-string on bag with dark chocolate.

13. Paint thread in buttons dark jungle green.

14. Thin white slightly with water. Using a good liner brush, paint lettering on bag.

15. Thin periwinkle with water to a very transparent shade; paint snowflakes in bag. Add a light wash of white. Let dry, then, using liner and white, add lines and dots to each snowflake.

16. Thin periwinkle with water to a very transparent shade; add a wash of color to inside of lantern in back of candle.

17. Paint candle white; shade with autumn brown. Paint wick autumn brown.

18. Paint flame gold; shade bottom of flame with pumpkin, bringing color halfway up flame. Let dry, then softly shade with opaque red only one-quarter up flame from bottom.

19. Paint outside of lantern black; add white highlights to edges.

Finishing

1. Load old toothbrush with white; speckle or spatter outside of pieces. Let dry completely.

2. To keep paints from rubbing off, spray with two or three coats varnish, allowing varnish to dry between coats. ✂

Fire Starters Gift Set

Make several of these in red and several in green to set a festive mood at your booth. This is a perfect gift item for those hard-to-shop-for family members!!

Design by Barbara Woolley

Materials

Fire Starters

- 7 (4-ounce) waxed-paper cups
- 1 pound paraffin
- At least 4 big handfuls dryer lint
- 7 small pinecones
- Candle scent of your choice
- Double boiler for melting paraffin
- Spoon or stick
- Stove or hotplate
- 3 sheets soft handmade paper*
- 2 yards coordinating 1"-wide fabric ribbon
- 2 yards coordinating braid trim
- Adhesive application system and adhesive sheets*

- Gift tag
- Narrow satin ribbon

Gift Box

- 8" x 3" papier-mâché box
- 4 (2") wooden ball knobs
- Soft handmade paper*: 3 sheets in dark color and 3 sheets in lighter coordinating color
- 2 yards coordinating 1"-wide ribbon
- Coordinating craft paint
- Paintbrush
- Craft glue
- Adhesive application system and adhesive sheets*
- Small pinecone
- 2 (3") sprigs pine greenery

Paper Reflections paper from DMD Industries; XYRON 850 Adhesive Application and Laminating System and XYRON 150 Create-A-Sticker adhesive sheet from XYRON Inc.

Fire Starters

1. Referring to manufacturer's instructions, carefully melt paraffin in top of double boiler.

2. Tear lint into tiny pieces; blend carefully into melted paraffin along with scent.

3. Fill cups ¾ full with paraffin mixture; set pinecone into wax in each cup and set aside to harden.

4. Using adhesive system, apply adhesive to back of paper; apply sticker adhesive to back of ribbon and trim.

Continued on page 185

Snow Friends Welcome Sign

This beautiful piece can greet visitors to your home all winter. Its muted hues offer a pleasant change from the traditional colors of winter.

Design by Vicki Schreiner

Materials

- 18" x 9" wooden garden arch sign*
- 12 (¾" x 1½") primitive-style wooden hearts*
- Acrylic craft paints*: butter cream, black, black cherry, brown velvet, dark foliage green, dusty mauve, eucalyptus, Georgia clay, village green, Wedgewood blue, white
- Clear glaze base*
- "Aging" varnish*
- Satin-finish interior spray varnish
- Paintbrushes: ½" and #4 flat, #3 and #6 rounds, #1 liner
- Craft adhesive
- Applicator sponge
- Removable tape
- Black graphite paper
- Ballpoint pen
- Old paintbrush handle
- Toothpick
- 2 (1") sawtooth hangers for wood
- Fine sandpaper

Sign #11-0432 from Provo Craft; hearts from Crafts Etc!; Ceramcoat acrylic paints, clear glaze base and Instant Age Varnish, all from Delta.

Preparation

1. Smooth rough spots on sign, sanding in direction of grain; wipe off dust.

2. Referring to instructions for base-coating in "Painting Techniques" (General Instructions, page 190) and letting paints dry between coats throughout, base-coat sign back and outer beveled edge, and fronts and sides of hearts with two coats butter cream; base-coat front of sign with two coats village green.

3. Using photocopier, enlarge sign pattern to 200 percent. Referring to directions for "Using Transfer & Graphite Paper" in the General Instructions, transfer pattern outlines onto sign, tracing over lines with ballpoint pen and holding pattern in place with removable tape. Do not transfer stippling dots; these are for reference in shading.

Painting Sign

1. Tape off border stripe with removable tape along all inner and outer straight edges; do not tape off curve.

2. *Painting tip:* An easy way to prevent paint from seeping under taped-off areas is to always apply one coat of original base-coat color, let dry, and then paint with color indicated. Using applicator sponge throughout, apply one coat village green to taped-off areas; let dry. Apply two coats butter cream.

3. Remove tape. Using #4 flat brush, paint curved area of stripe with two coats butter cream.

4. Using #3 or #6 round as needed, base-coat areas: *eucalyptus*—all lettering; *black*—hat; *dusty mauve*—hatband and scarf; *white*—face.

5. Transfer details of design to painted areas. Base-coat nose with Georgia clay and eyes with black.

6. *Plaid pattern:* Use liner to add Wedgewood blue crosshatching; add a dark green line to the right side of every other blue line and a white line to the right side of remaining blue lines.

7. *For shading, mix equal parts glaze base with each color, then shade, working on a small area at a time.* Load brush with small amount of paint mixture, apply to area to be shaded, then quickly dry brush on paper towel and pat applied paint with dry brush to blend and soften. Let dry completely, then repeat to darken. Shade hatband and scarf first with black cherry; let dry completely, then shade again with brown velvet. Shade face and nose with brown velvet and all lettering with dark green.

8. *For highlighting, mix equal parts glaze base with each color.* Load brush with small amount of paint mixture and stroke onto paper towel until dry; pounce brush on area to be highlighted. Let dry completely, then repeat to brighten. Highlight as follows: *white*—center of hat, across center of brim and down center of nose; *dusty mauve*—cheeks.

9. Using liner and black, add eyebrows, mouth and crease lines across nose.

10. Using toothpick dipped in white, add two tiny highlight dots to each eye.

11. *Hearts:* Referring to Fig. 1, use paintbrush handle and toothpick dipped in village green to decorate hearts. Add larger dots with brush handle, working from top of heart down; redip only when beginning a new heart, so each heart will have

Continued on page 183

Fig. 1

Snow Friends Welcome Sign
Enlarge 200% before transferring

Hearts & Holly Lap Blanket

Once your customers see this beautiful fuzzy blanket, they'll want to take one home. It is perfect for snuggling in on a cold winter night!

Design by Chris Malone

Materials

- 44" square leaf green plush felt*
- 9" x 12" felt sheets: ruby, deep rose, 2 kelly green
- 2 skeins dark green #3 pearl cotton
- #5 pearl cotton: pink, dark red, medium green
- 14 (⅝") round shank buttons (any color)
- Sewing threads to match ruby, rose and kelly green felt
- Hand-sewing needle
- Embroidery needle

Rainbow Plush Felt from Kunin.

Five Ways To Be Organized in Your Studio

1. Schedule six months out. Post all deadlines, due dates, and deliveries.

2. Clear work areas at the end of each day to the best of your ability. Return tools and supplies to the same place each day. This is a great time to clean, oil or maintain tools.

3. Break down a product/design into as many steps as possible. Work each step to the maximum, then move to the next.

4. Keep a current list of supplies or materials that are low or need to be ordered within the next month so you don't run out without notice.

5. Take breaks. Every 30–60 minutes, stand and stretch or take a short walk. Refreshing your body and mind leads to clearer thought and more effective use of time. Use an answering machine when in production; interruptions break the rhythm of production. **$**

Instructions

1. Using 1 strand dark green pearl cotton, blanket-stitch around all edges of plush felt.

2. Cut 10 holly leaves from kelly green felt; one heart and eight 1¼" circles from ruby; and two hearts and six 1¼" circles from rose.

3. Pin ruby heart at center of one side of blanket, positioning tip 2½" from edge. Pin each rose heart 9" from ruby heart. Arrange leaves as shown; pin in place.

4. Blanket-stitch around leaves and hearts with 1 strand pearl cotton, using medium green for leaves, dark red for rose hearts and pink for ruby heart.

5. *Berries:* Using doubled length of matching sewing thread, sew gathering stitch around edges of felt circles; place buttons shank side up in centers of circles and gather felt closed around it; knot and clip thread ends.

6. Using doubled length of green thread, sew berries to tips of leaves, sewing cluster of three at each pair of leaves and a single berry at each single leaf. ✄

Holly Leaf
Cut 10 from kelly green

Heart
Cut 1 from ruby & 2 from deep rose

Angel Kitties Vests
& Jumper

Adorned with stars, these matching vests and jumper are wonderful wearable items for spreading holiday cheer.

Designs by Angie Wilhite

Materials

Jumper

Note: *Amounts given are for adult's jumper; amounts of materials needed for adult's vest and child's vest are given in parentheses.*

- Adult-size jumper of your choice
- ⅙ yard (¼ yard, ⅙ yard) each of complementary fabrics: red plaid, light tan, gold
- 12" x 6" (9" x 18", 12" x 6") blue fabric
- Matching all-purpose sewing threads
- Spools of matching rayon embroidery thread
- 6" (9", 6") square heavy brown paper
- ⅓ (1, ⅓) yard fusible transfer web*
- ⅛ (⅛, ⅛) yard heavy-duty fusible transfer web*
- ⅛ (⅙, ⅛) yard fusible interfacing*
- ½ (1⅓, ½) yard(s) tear-away fabric stabilizer*
- Hand-sewing needle
- 2 (4, 2) black ⅛" buttons
- Permanent fabric adhesive
- Sewing machine with satin stitch
- ⅔ (1⅓, ⅔) yard(s) fine jute twine
- 2 (4, 2) small safety pins
- Fine-point black permanent marker
- Pink powdered cosmetic blusher
- Cotton-tip swab

Additional Materials for Vests

- Adult's or child's denim vest

Wonder-Under and Heavy-Duty Wonder-Under transfer web, Sof-Shape interfacing and Stitch-n-Tear stabilizer, all from Pellon.

Project Note

Double-check the size of patterns against your garment and adjust as desired before cutting fabric.

Jumper

Use photocopier to enlarge Kitty Star pattern 120 percent before cutting; use star pattern as shown.

1. Launder jumper and fabrics without using fabric softener; iron as needed.

2. Following manufacturer's instructions, fuse interfacing to backs of gold and light tan fabrics. Then apply

'Tis the Season to Buy!

The leading holiday for craft buying and sales is Christmas, followed closely by Halloween. However, holidays like St. Patrick's Day, Mother's Day and Valentine's Day are excellent for gift sales, too, including jewelry, home decor and scented crafts.

Check your calendar and keep these dates in mind as you plan your production. Also keep an eye on the dates for holidays like Thanksgiving and Hanukkah, which change from year to year.

Also, promote your crafts as great party favors and as gift ideas for birthdays, weddings and anniversaries. **$**

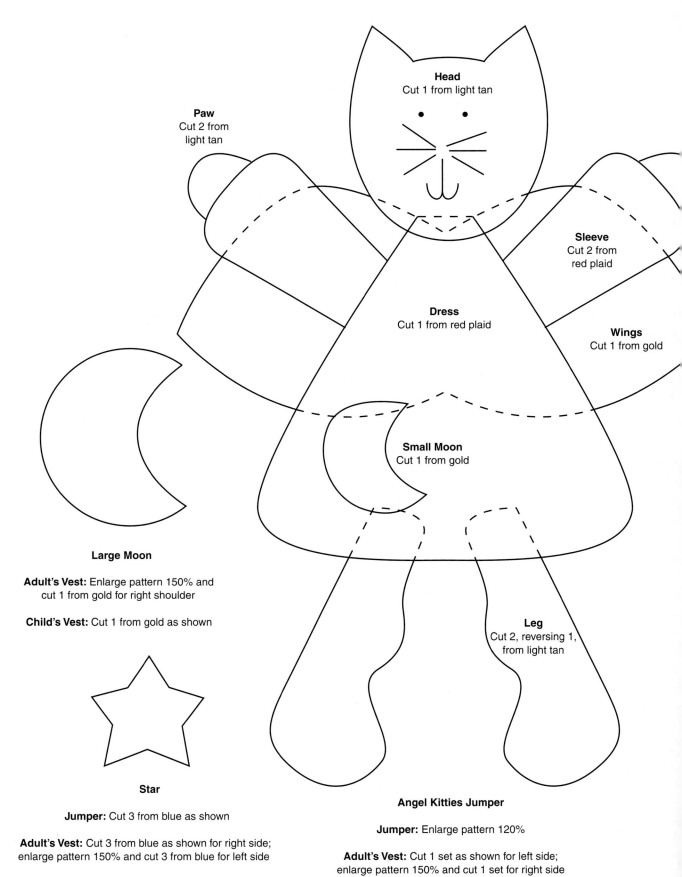

Head
Cut 1 from light tan

Paw
Cut 2 from
light tan

Sleeve
Cut 2 from
red plaid

Dress
Cut 1 from red plaid

Wings
Cut 1 from gold

Small Moon
Cut 1 from gold

Large Moon

Adult's Vest: Enlarge pattern 150% and
cut 1 from gold for right shoulder

Child's Vest: Cut 1 from gold as shown

Leg
Cut 2, reversing 1,
from light tan

Star

Jumper: Cut 3 from blue as shown

Adult's Vest: Cut 3 from blue as shown for right side;
enlarge pattern 150% and cut 3 from blue for left side

Child's Vest: Cut 3 from blue as shown;
enlarge pattern 150% and cut 3 from red plaid for left side

Angel Kitties Jumper

Jumper: Enlarge pattern 120%

Adult's Vest: Cut 1 set as shown for left side;
enlarge pattern 150% and cut 1 set for right side

Child's Vest: Cut 1 set as shown

transfer web to backs of all fabrics—including those backed with interfacing—*except* blue.

3. Trace enlarged patterns onto paper side of fabrics: head, two paws and two legs, reversing one, from light tan; small moon (for dress) and wings from gold; dress and two sleeves from red plaid. (Large moon is not used on jumper.)

4. Peel backing from pattern pieces; fuse to bib of jumper as shown.

5. Cut two 6" squares blue fabric; fuse heavy-duty transfer web onto backs of fabric squares. Remove paper backing; sandwich brown paper square between fused fabrics and fuse layers together. Cut three stars from fused layers.

6. Cut fabric stabilizer to fit behind stitched motif; pin or baste inside jumper.

7. Thread sewing machine bobbin with all-purpose thread and needle with matching rayon thread. Matching thread to fabric color, satin-stitch around design pieces, beginning with those pieces that appear to be at the back of the design and working your way forward. Remove fabric stabilizer; trim threads.

8. Sew buttons to face for eyes. Dot nose with cotton swab and

blusher. Draw whiskers and mouth with fine-point marker.

9. Cut two 7" pieces and one 10" piece twine. Tie each shorter piece in a simple bow. Glue stars evenly spaced along 10" piece; glue bow at each end. Safety-pin ends of star garland in kitty's paws from inside jumper. Remove stars before laundering jumper.

Adult's Vest

Use patterns as shown for kitty and star on left side; use photocopier to enlarge patterns 150 percent for cat, star and moon on right side.

1. Complete steps 1 and 2 as for jumper.

2. On paper side of fabrics, trace patterns using same colors as for jumper (step 3); trace patterns in size given for left side of vest *and* a second, enlarged set including one large gold moon enlarged 150% for right shoulder.

3. Peel backing and fuse pattern pieces to fronts of vest as shown.

4. Fuse 9" squares of blue fabric to 9" paper square with heavy-duty transfer web as for jumper (step 5). Cut three stars and three enlarged stars from fused layers.

5. Repeat steps 6–8 as for jumper.

6. Repeat step 9 as for jumper, gluing large stars along 10" piece twine and small stars along 8" piece. Tie four 6" pieces into bows.

Child's Vest

Use kitty, star and moon patterns as shown for one side; enlarge star pattern 150 percent before cutting red plaid stars for other side.

1. Complete steps 1–3 as for jumper. Cut also one large moon from fused gold; enlarge star pattern and cut three additional stars from fused red plaid.

2. Peel backing from pattern pieces; fuse to vest as shown.

3. Complete steps 5–9 as for jumper. ✂

Meet You At the Library

Check your local library for answers to your questions about crafting and business. Look for reference books under headings like accounting for small businesses and bookkeeping.

And remember: There are no dumb questions, just questions we don't ask!

There to Help You

Several organizations help small-business people. You can adapt small-business practices and policies to your craft business. **$**

Association of Small Business Development Centers
8990 Burke Lake Road
Burke, VA 22015
(703) 764-9850

Service Corps of Retired Executives (SCORE)
c/o Small Business Administration
409 Third St. S.W.
Sixth Floor
Washington, DC 20024
(800) 634-0245

Snow Friends Welcome Sign

Continued from page 177

three larger dots gradually reducing in size. Add tiny dots with toothpick.

Assembly & Finishing

1. Using adhesive, glue hearts together in sets of three, side by side, at corners of sign.

2. Apply one coat aging varnish to entire sign with ½" flat brush.

3. Using liner, line snowflakes onto background, adding dots at ends with brush handle dipped in white. Let dry.

4. Spray entire sign with one coat varnish.

5. Affix hangers to back of sign. ✂

Table of Ergonomics

Your worktable should be sturdy and hold the weight of your supplies and equipment. The height of your worktable should be no lower than your stomach (use your belly button as a placement guide) while you are sitting.

It's important that you not hunch your shoulders or slouch over your work. While it's natural to want to get closer to your materials, excessive slouching strains back and neck muscles. **$**

Holly Day Memo Board

Colorful "holly berry" pushpins will make this memo board an instant best seller. Velvet and cord accents make it a beautiful spot to keep notes and messages.

Design by Sharon Reinhart

Materials

- 6" square cork panel
- 1 yard green-and-gold braided cord
- 1⅜"-wide green velvet craft ribbon: 12" piece and 3 (3½") strips
- Matte-finish "soft" paints*: holiday green, ebony
- Single holly leaf rubber stamp*
- Flat-back thumbtacks
- ⅜" flat-back red round rhinestones (or large enough to cover tacks)
- Jewel glue
- Craft glue
- Gold embroidery thread
- 7 (1") squares adhesive-backed magnet
- Foam paintbrush
- Stapler
- Craft pins

Tulip Ultra Soft Paints from Plaid; and Denami Designs rubber stamp.

Instructions

1. Mix two parts green paint with one part ebony. Apply paint to stamp using foam brush and stamp image randomly over cork square, reapplying paint each time. Clean stamp immediately with wet cloth and set cork aside to dry.

2. Glue rhinestone to head of each tack with jewel glue; let dry.

3. Using craft glue, glue braid around edge of cork square, beginning and ending at center top. Push pins through cord into cork every couple of inches to hold cord in place as it dries.

4. *Bow:* Trim each end of each short ribbon to point. Gather each piece in

center, forming two "mountain" folds, and secure with stapler. Stack three stapled pieces and secure by wrapping gold embroidery thread around them several times; knot. Use craft glue to glue on braid so as to conceal thread; clamp to hold while glue dries.

5. Fold over 1" on end of remaining ribbon to form loop; secure with glue. Notch opposite end of ribbon. Glue

bow over loop; glue ribbon down center back of cork panel.

6. Attach a magnet to back of cork panel in each corner; attach remaining pieces to ribbon with one behind bow and remaining two at top and bottom of cork board.

7. Push in rhinestone pushpins to simulate holly berries. ✄

Fire Starters Gift Set

Continued from page 175

5. Cut paper into seven 3" x 8" strips. Cut trim and ribbon into seven 8" pieces. Peel away backing from paper strip to expose adhesive; wrap around cup. Remove backing from ribbon; wrap around top of cup; remove backing from braid trim; wrap around cup over ribbon. Repeat on remaining cups.

6. Place fire starters in gift box. Type or write label and instructions on a small gift tag: "Fire Starters — Place under kindling and light one side of paper cup." Attach tag to pinecone with a piece of satin ribbon.

Gift Box

1. Paint inside of box, lid and ball knobs.

2. Using adhesive system, apply adhesive to back of paper; apply sticker adhesive to back of 9" piece ribbon.

3. Measure box; cut darker paper to fit. Peel away backing from paper strip to expose adhesive; cover box. In same fashion, cover sides of lid and about ½" fold-over with lighter paper.

4. Glue lid to box bottom. The lid top is now the bottom of the box. It may be painted, covered with a circle of paper, or further decorated as desired.

5. Glue ball knobs to bottom of box for feet.

6. Remove backing from 9" ribbon; wrap around top edge of box. Tie remaining ribbon in bow; glue to box as shown. Arrange pine sprigs and pinecone on bow as desired and glue in place. ✂

Host a Business Party!

Consider inviting a small gathering of your peers to a monthly or quarterly meeting to exchange ideas for displays, marketing, packaging, production and trends.

Most local libraries have meeting rooms. The library is a great place to gather because you can use the magazines and books to spur ideas and spot trends.

You might also ask the library staff if you could set up a table in the fall to sell your network group's crafts. In exchange for the space, offer to donate a small percentage of your sales to the library or offer to teach classes. **$**

Go Clean Your Room!

Any work area should be clean and clutter free. Dust and other impurities from the air can smudge or discolor craft supplies. Wipe down the work area with a household cleaner and paper towel.

Our own hands are often the culprits behind dirt and oil on a craft. Wash your hands before and during a crafting session. **$**

Neatness Counts!

It's always a good idea to cover the work area or worktable with newspapers or an old plastic tablecloth. Most craft supplies clean up with soap, water and a little elbow grease, but why worry about it at all when it can be as easy as tossing the newspaper into the recycle bin?

Always cover a wooden table. Paints, glues, candle wax and other materials can damage the varnish used to seal most wood tables. **$**

Snowflake Bulletin Board

Decorative push-pins with dainty snowflakes make this project complete. Make an ample supply; customers will want one for themselves as well as gifts for others.

Design by Sandra Graham Smith

Materials

- 2 (10½" x 14") pieces flat corrugated cardboard
- 10½" x 14" sheet cork
- Tacky craft glue
- 12" x 18" sheets craft foam: blue, white
- 1" snowflake punch
- ½" snowflake rubber stamp
- Hangers or magnet strip(s)
- Blue stamp pad
- White card stock
- ½" clear glass flat-backed "marbles"
- Slick-surface adhesive*
- 4 clear acrylic pushpins

Aleene's Glass and Bead Glue.

Bulletin Board

1. Using craft glue throughout, glue cardboard together in double layer; glue cork sheet on top. Let dry.

2. Measure and trim blue craft foam to make a rectangle a little larger than 10½" x 14"; cut out center to make a

1"-wide blue foam frame.

3. From remaining blue foam, trim strips to cover all four edges of bulletin board; glue to edges; let dry.

4. Glue blue foam frame to front of bulletin board; let dry.

5. Punch 28 snowflakes from white craft foam; glue evenly spaced around frame; let dry.

6. Attach hangers or large magnet strip to back of bulletin board.

Pushpins

1. For each pushpin, cut a ⁹⁄₁₆"-diameter circle from card stock; stamp blue snowflake in center of each. Let dry.

2. Apply a drop of slick-surface adhesive to flat surface of each marble; press down onto snowflake so stamped image shows through marble; let dry.

3. Apply adhesive to top of each acrylic pushpin; glue to marble. Let dry. ✂

Fabric & Bead Pen

Bring elegance to your booth with this unique pen. Using different fabrics and embellishments will brighten up your display.

Design by Ann Butler

Materials

- Ballpoint stick pen
- 6" x 3" fabric
- Craft glue
- Double-sided sticky tape
- Clear glass microbeads
- 7" coordinating ribbon (optional)
- Foam plate
- Toothpick

Instructions

1. Measure pen; trim fabric and tape to size to neatly cover pen.

2. Using toothpick to spread glue, coat wrong side of fabric with glue; glue onto pen; let dry.

3. Peel backing from one side of tape; slowly roll pen onto tape to cover.

4. Carefully pour beads onto foam plate. Remove remaining backing from tape on pen and roll pen in plate to cover with beads. Apply a drop of glue to end of pen; cover with beads.

5. Tie ribbon bow around pen. ✄

The IRS: Your New Best Friend

Most businesses like yours use a Schedule C to report yearly income and expenses to the federal government.

You may need other forms, such as those for showing depreciation and contributions to your own Social Security, so do your research and understand what the IRS expects from you.

The federal government offers many booklets to help you understand federal paperwork. Use them!

Make use of their toll-free number (check your phone book for a local branch, too) and Web site if you have any questions. **$**

(800) 829-1040
http://www.IRS.gov

Five Ways To Be Organized in the Office

1. Touch mail once. Read mail the same time each day. Then, either act on it, record and file it, or pitch it!

2. Keep one master calendar/schedule. Write everything down on the calendar as it happens. Start your day with a quick look at the current day and the next three days.

3. Use an answering machine. Return calls at a set time each day. Use voice mail and leave messages for clients/suppliers/customers.

4. Don't allow your desk to become crowded or stacked. It is human nature to avoid confusion. Try to clear your desk each time you leave it. Every six months, remove all items, papers, catalogs, magazines, newsletters, etc., that you have not found useful.

5. If possible, computerize your office. This tool is amazing! Today's computer programs take half the work out of organizing billing, invoices, correspondence, and many everyday office tasks. **$**

Put It All Together!

You have more than 100 sure-to-sell craft ideas at your fingertips. You've read tips on starting and maintaining a successful crafting business. What's next? Put it all together and do what you love—crafting while making money! **$**

Index

Projects

Springtime Market

Summer Sales

Fall Festival

Winter Celebration

General Instructions

Materials

In addition to the materials listed for each craft, some of the following supplies may be needed to complete your projects. No doubt most of these are already on hand in your "treasure chest" of crafting aids. Gather them before you begin working so that you'll be able to complete each design quickly and without a hitch!

General Crafts

- Scissors
- Pencil
- Ruler
- Tracing paper
- Craft knife
- Heavy-duty craft cutters or wire nippers
- Plenty of newspapers to protect work surface
- Safety pins

Painted Items

- Paper towels
- Paper or plastic foam plate or tray to use as a disposable paint palette for holding and mixing paints
- Plastic—a garbage bag, grocery sack, etc.—to protect your work surface
- Container of water or other recommended cleaning fluid for rinsing and cleaning brushes

Fabric Projects

- Iron and ironing board
- Pressing cloth
- Basic sewing notions and supplies
- Rotary cutter and self-healing mat
- Air-soluble markers
- Tailor's chalk

Using Transfer & Graphite Paper

Some projects recommend transferring patterns to wood or another material with transfer or graphite paper. Read the manufacturer's instructions before beginning.

Lay tracing paper over the printed pattern and trace it carefully. Then place transfer paper transfer side down on wood or other material to be marked. Lay traced pattern on top. Secure layers with low-tack masking tape or tacks to keep pattern and transfer paper from shifting while you work. Using a stylus, pen or other implement, retrace the pattern lines using smooth, even pressure to transfer the design onto the surface.

Painted Designs

Disposable paper or plastic foam plates, including supermarket meat trays, make good palettes for pouring and mixing paints.

The success of a painted project often depends on the care taken in initial preparations, including sanding, applying primer and/or applying a base coat of color. Follow instructions carefully.

Take special care when painting adjacent sections with different colors; allow the first color to dry so that the second will not run or mix. When adding designs atop a painted base, let the base coat dry thoroughly first.

If you will be mixing media, such as drawing with marking pens on a painted surface, test the process and your materials on scraps to make sure there will be no running or bleeding.

Keep your work surface and your tools clean. Clean brushes promptly in the manner recommended by the paint manufacturer; many acrylics can be cleaned up with soap and water, while other paints may require a solvent. Suspend your paintbrushes by their handles to dry so that the fluid drains out completely and bristles remain straight and undamaged.

Work in a well-ventilated area when using paints, solvents or finishes that emit fumes; read product labels thoroughly to be aware of any potential hazards and precautions.

Painting Techniques

Base-coating: Load paintbrush evenly with color by dabbing it on palette, then coat surfaces with one or two smooth, solid coats of paint, letting paint dry between coats.

Dry-brushing: Dip a dry round-bristle brush in paint; wipe excess paint off onto paper towel until brush is almost dry. Wipe brush across edges for subtle shading.

Floating: Dampen brush with water. Touch one side of brush to paint, then sweep brush back and forth on palette to work paint into the brush. Apply the color around the edges of the area you are working on as directed in painting instructions.

Rouging: Dip dry, round bristle brush in paint and wipe paint off onto paper towel until brush is almost completely dry and leaves no visible brush strokes. Wipe brush across area to be rouged using a circular motion.

Shading: Dip brush in water and blot lightly once on paper towel, leaving some water in brush. Dip point of brush into paint. Stroke onto palette once or twice to blend paint into water on bristles so that stroke has paint on one side gradually blending to no color on the other side. Apply to project as directed.

Side-loading and highlighting: Wet flat brush with water; dry on paper towel. Dip corner of brush into paint and brush back and forth on palette until color goes from dark value to light. Apply to project as directed.

Stenciling with brush: Dip dry stencil brush in paint. Wipe brush on paper towel, removing excess paint to prevent seepage under stencil. Brush cutout areas with a circular motion, holding brush perpendicular to surface. When shading, brush should be almost dry, working only around edges. Use masking tape to hold stencil in place while working.

Stenciling with sponge: Use very little paint on the end of the sponge; too much paint applied at one time will cause the paint to seep under the edges of the stencil. Place a small puddle of paint on the palette, then dab a corner of the sponge into paint; blot off any excess onto palette, blending paint over surface of sponge. Using a light touch, dab sponge over stencil. When changing colors, rinse sponge thoroughly and wring out all traces of moisture. Any water left in sponge can cause paint to become more liquid and increase the possibility of paints seeping under stencil edges. ✄

Buyer's Guide

Projects in this book were made using products provided by the manufacturers listed below. Look for the suggested products in your local craft- and art-supply stores. If unavailable, contact suppliers below. Some may be able to sell products directly to you; others may be able to refer you to retail sources.

Adhesive Technologies Inc.
3 Merrill Industrial Dr.
Hampton, NH 03842-1995
(603) 926-1616
www.adhesivetech.com

Aleene's/Div. of Duncan Enterprises
5673 E. Shields Ave.
Fresno, CA 93727
(800) 438-6226
www.duncancrafts.com

Amaco/American Art Clay Co. Inc.
4717 W. 16th St.
Indianapolis, IN 46222
(317) 244-6871
www.amaco.com

API/The Adhesive Products Inc.
520 Cleveland Ave.
Albany, CA 94710
(510) 526-7616
www.crafterspick.com

Artful Stamper
725 Notre Dame Dr.
London, ON N6J 3V5
Canada
(519) 668-1173
www.artfulstamper.com

Beacon Adhesives/ Signature Marketing
125 MacQuesten Pkwy. S.
Mount Vernon, NY 10550
(914) 699-3400
www.beacon1.com

The Beadery
P.O. Box 178
Hope Valley, RI 02832
(401) 539-2432
www.thebeadery.com

Binney & Smith
1100 Church Ln.
Easton, PA 18044-0431
(800) 272-9652
www.binney-smith.com

Bucilla Corp.
1 Oak Ridge Rd.
Humboldt Industrial Park
Hazleton, PA 18201-9764

Cabin Crafters
P.O. Box 270
1225 W. First St.
Nevada, IA 50201
(800) 669-3920
www.CabinCrafters.com

ChartPak Rub-On Art
1 River Rd.
Leeds, MA 01053
(413) 584-5446
www.chartpak.com

Clearsnap
P.O. Box 98
Anacortes, WA 98221
(888) 448-4862
www.clearsnap.com

C.M. Offray & Son Inc./Lion Ribbon Co. Inc.
Rte. 24, Box 601
Chester, NJ 07930
(800) 551-LION
www.offray.com

Coats & Clark/ J. & P. Coats
Consumer Service
P.O. Box 12229
Greenville, SC
29612-0229
(800) 648-1479
www.coatsandclark.com

CPE Inc.
P.O. Box 649
Union, SC 29379
(800) 327-0059
www.cpe-felt.com

Craft Catalog
P.O. Box 1069
Reynoldsburg, OH 43068
(800) 777-1442
www.craftcatalog.com

Crafter's Pick by API
520 Cleveland Ave.
Albany, CA 94710
(510) 526-7616
www.crafterspick.com

Crafts Etc!
(800) 888-0321
www.craftsetc.com

Creative Beginnings
P.O. Box 1330
Morro Bay, CA 93442
(805) 772-9030
www.creative beginnings.com

Creative Xpress
295 W. Center St.
Provo, UT 84601-4430
(801) 373-6838
www.creativexpress.com

Cridge*Ware
101 Lower Morrisville Rd.
Fallsington, PA 19054
(215) 295-2797
www.cridgeware.com

Darice Inc.
Mail-order source:
Schrock's International
P.O. Box 538
Bolivar, OH 44612
(330) 874-3700

D&CC/Decorator & Craft Corp.
428 Zelta
Wichita, KS 67207
(800) 835-3013

DecoArt
P.O. Box 386
Stanford, KY 40484
(800) 367-3047
www.decoart.com

Delta Technical Coatings
2550 Pellissier Pl.
Whittier, CA 90601-1505
(800) 423-4135
www.deltacrafts.com

Denami Designs Rubber Stamps
P.O. Box 5617
Kent, WA 98064
(253) 437-1626
www.denamidesign.com

Design Works Inc.
170 Wilbur Pl.
Bohemia, NY 11716
(516) 244-5749

DMC Corp.
Hackensack Ave.,
Bldg. 10A
South Kearny, NJ
07032-4688
(800) 275-4117
www.dmc-usa.com

DMD Industries Inc./ Paper Reflections
2300 S. Old Missouri Rd.
Springdale, AR 72764
(479) 750-8929
www.dmdind.com

Dow Flora Craft/ Dow Chemical Co.
P.O. Box 1206
Midland, MI 48674
(800) 441-4369
www.dow.com /craft/
index.htm

Duncan Enterprises
5673 E. Shields Ave.
Fresno, CA 93727
(800) 438-6226
www.duncancrafts.com

DuraClear Eclectic Products Inc.
995 S. "A" St.
Springfield, OR 97477
(800) 693-4667

EK Success Ltd.
125 Entin Rd.
Clifton, NJ 07014
(800) 524-1349
www.eksuccess.com

Fiskars Inc.
7811 W. Stewart Ave.
Wausau, WI 54401
(800) 950-0203, ext. 1277
www.fiskars.com

Forster Craft Division/ Alltrisa Consumer Products
1800 Cloquet Ave.
Cloquet, MN 55720
(800) 777-7942
www.diamondbrands.com/
crafts/index.html

Gourd Central
7264 St. Rte. 314
Mount Gilead, OH 43338
(419) 362-9201
www.gourdcentral.com

The Gourd Factory/ Lindberg Farms
P.O. Box 9
Linden, CA 95236
(209) 887-3694
gourdfac@inreach.com

Harvest Import Inc.
14752 Sinclair Circle
Tustin, CA 92780
(714) 368-9188
www.harvestimport.com

Inkadinkado
61 Holton St.
Woburn, MA 01801
(800) 888-4652
www.inkadinkado.com

Innovo Inc.
1808 Cherry St.
Knoxville, TN 37917
(865) 546-1110

Jacquard Products/ Rupert, Gibbon & Spider Inc.
P.O. Box 425
Healdsburg, CA 95448
(800) 442-0455
www.jacquardproducts.com

K & Company
8500 N.W. River Park Dr.
Pillar 136
Parkville, MO 64152
www.kandcompany.com
(888) 244-2083

Kreinik Mfg. Co. Inc.
3106 Lord Baltimore Dr. #101
Baltimore, MD 21244
(800) 537-2166
www.kreinik.com

Krylon/Sherwin- Williams Co.
Craft Customer Service
101 Prospect Ave. N.W.
Cleveland, OH 44115
(800) 457-9566
www.krylon.com

Kunin Felt Co./ Foss Mfg. Co. Inc.
P.O. Box 5000
Hampton, NH 03843-5000
(603) 929-6100
www.kuninfelt.com

Lara's Crafts
590 N. Beach St.
Fort Worth, TX 76111
(800) 232-5272
www.larascrafts.com

McGill Craftivity
Mail-order source:
Alpine Imports
7106 N. Alpine Rd.
Rockford, IL 61111
(800) 654-6114

**Midwest
Products Co. Inc.**
P.O. Box 564
Hobart, IN 46342
(800) 348-3497

Nicole Industries
P.O. Box 846
Mount Laurel, NJ 08054

**Pellon Consumer
Products**
3440 Industrial Dr.
Durham, NC 27704
(919) 620-7457
www.pellonideas.com

Plaid Enterprises Inc.
3225 Westech Dr.
Norcross, GA 30092
(800) 842-4197
www.plaidonline.com

**Polyform Products
Co./Sculpey**
1901 Estes Ave.
Elk Grove Village, IL 60007
(847) 427-0020
www.sculpey.com

Posh Impressions
22600 A
Lambert St., #706
Lake Forest, CA 92630
(800) 421-7674
www.poshimpressions.com

Provo Craft
Mail-order source:
Creative Express
295 W. Center St.
Provo, UT 84601-4436
(800) 563-8679
www.creativexpress.com

Roylco Ltd.
30 Northland Rd.
Waterloo, ON N2V 1Y1
Canada

Rubber Stampede Inc.
P.O. Box 246
Berkeley, CA 94701
(800) 423-4135
www.rstampede.com

Sakura Hobby Craft
2444 205th St. A-1
Torrance, CA 90501
(310) 212-7878

**ScottiCrafts/DiPalma
Marketing Inc.**
P.O. Box 298
Lovejoy, GA 30250
(800) 850-9901
www.dipalmausa.com

Star Candle Co.
29 Ash St.
Brooklyn, NY 11222
www.starcandle.com

Syndicate Sales Inc.
2025 N. Wabash St.
P.O. Box 756
Kokomo, IN 46903
(765) 457-7277

Toner Plastics
699 Silver St.
Agawam, MA 01001
(413) 789-1300
www.tonerplastics.com

**True Colors
International**
1455 Linda Vista Dr.
San Marcos, CA 92069

**Tulip/Div. of Duncan
Enterprises**
5673 E. Shields Ave.,
Fresno, CA 93727
(800) 438-6226
www.duncancrafts.com

Uchida of America
3535 Del Amo Blvd.
Torrance, CA 90503
(800) 541-5877
www.uchida.com

**Uptown Rubber
Stamps**
1000 Town Center Suite 1
Browns Point, WA 98422
(253) 925-1234
www.uptowndesign.com

VanAken International
9157 Rochester Ct.
P.O. Box 1680
Rancho Cucamonga, CA
91729
www.katopolyclay.com

**Viking Woodcrafts
Inc.**
1317 Eighth St. S.E.
Waseca, MN 56093
(800) 328-0116
www.vikingwoodcrafts.com

**Walnut Hollow
Farms Inc.**
1409 St. Rd. 23
Dodgeville, WI
53533-2112
(800) 950-5101
www.walnuthollow.com

**Warm & Natural/
The Warm Co.**
954 E. Union St.
Seattle, WA 98122
(800) 234-WARM
www.warmcompany.com

Wayne's Woodenware
102-C Fieldcrest Dr.
Neenah, WI 54956
(800) 840-1497
www.wayneswooden
ware.com

**Wimpole Street
Creations**
Mail-order source:
Barrett House
P.O. Box 540585
North Salt Lake,
UT 84054-0585
(800) 432-5776
www.barrett-house.com

Wrights
P.O. Box 398
West Warren, MA 01092
(877) 597-4448
www.wrights.com

Xyron Inc.
15820 N. 84th St.
Scottsdale, AZ 85260
(800) 793-3523
www.xyron.com/
consumer.php

Designer Index